The Book of the Medieval
Knight

Below: The huge castle of Fougères is one of three fortresses on the border between Brittany and the rest of France. Its capture was always of great strategic importance. This gateway is the Porte de Notre Dame, which dates from the fourteenth century.
Previous page: Edward III, from the obverse of his Great Seal.

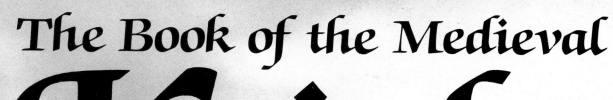

The Book of the Medieval Knight

STEPHEN TURNBULL

CROWN PUBLISHERS, INC., NEW YORK

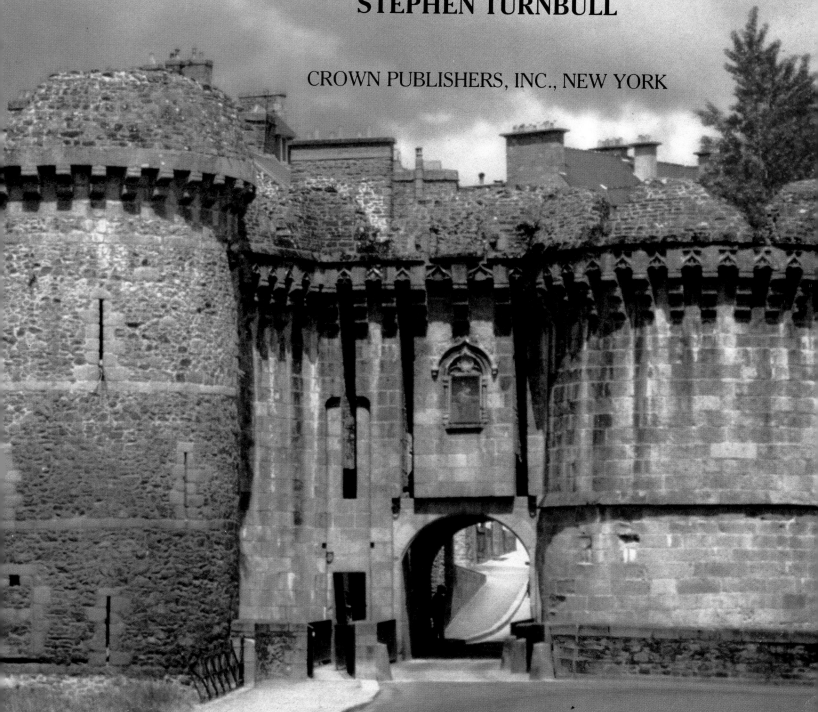

This book is dedicated to my father, William Turnbull,
who first told me about knights

Originally published in Great Britain
by Arms and Armour Press Limited,
2–6 Hampstead High Street, London
NW3 1QQ

Published by Crown Publishers, Inc.,
One Park Avenue, New York, New York 10016

Manufactured in Italy.

CROWN is a trademark of Crown Publishers, Inc.

Library of Congress Cataloging in Publication Data
Turnbull, Stephen R.
The Book of the Medieval Knight
1. Knights and knighthood – – Europe – – History. 2.
Civilization, Medieval. 3. Military History, Medieval. I. Title.
CR4513. T87 1985 940.1 85-11351
ISBN 0-517-55863-7

10 9 8 7 6 5 4 3 2 1

First American Edition

Contents

Introduction

Arms, and the man I sing . . .

ITH THESE WORDS Virgil begins his epic poem 'The Aeneid'. They are as appropriate here, because this book is a celebration of a romantic ideal – the medieval Knight. In my study of the knight's equivalent in Japan – the Samurai – I made the point that the reason for the samurai's survival as a class and as a fighting force lay in their ability to adapt to changing conditions of warfare and of society. The present work has made me realize how much more keenly this conclusion can be drawn for the knights of western Europe. The introduction of new technology, not all of which was unfavourable to knightly warfare, may have provided a challenge, but it also provided a stimulus for change. Those who could change their ideas and techniques survived. Those who could not or would not, fell beneath a hail of English arrows or were impaled upon the tips of Flemish pikes. What sustained the knights through this period of change was their belief that they were members of an international chivalric élite, united by class solidarity, self-regulating and self-supporting through the boredom and horror of war.

I have confined my study to the fourteenth and fifteenth centuries, a narrow period of time usually referred to as the 'High Middle Ages'. The justification for this is threefold. First, its beginning and end mark a neat paradox. At first sight the Battles of Falkirk (1298) and Courtrai (1302), seem to indicate the demise of the mounted knight. He has been defeated, outwitted even, by low-class foot soldiers. Yet it is this very failure that itself provides the spur for a renaissance in knightly life. Our story begins, therefore, with the medieval knight at his lowest ebb, and continues with a reassertion of knightly values, a rediscovery of knightly tradition, and by advances in armour, a reply to the threat from arrows and pikes. Thus it is that, at the end of the period I have chosen, the triumphant Charles VIII of France sets off to war with half his army consisting of mounted heavy knights! One function of this book is to explain that paradox by tracing their military development in detail through the two centuries under discussion. Second, by the beginning of the fourteenth century the traditions, the 'deeds of their ancestors' as the samurai would have viewed it, had already become enshrined into a working

Right: Stokesay Castle in Shropshire is one of the earliest fortified houses, as distinct from pure fortresses, in England, and is unquestionably the best preserved. The Great Hall was built c. 1270–80, and the South tower, seen to the right of the picture, was built no more than twenty years later. The building is a unique example of a knight's domestic architecture, its peaceful nature made even more remarkable by its close proximity to the powerful fortresses of Ludlow and Wigmore.

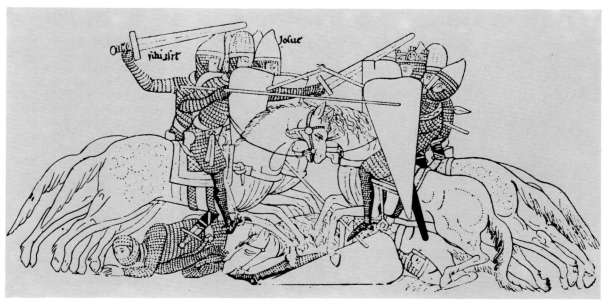

knightly code called 'Chivalry'. It was often more
honoured in the breach than the observance, but it did
exist, and somehow the day to day practice of war fitted in
with it. The High Middle Ages illustrate these points
perfectly. Thirdly, this is a book about people. The same
names crop up again and again. The coats of arms,
handed down from one generation to another, quartered
by marriage and augmented by success on the battlefield,
reflect in history's neatest shorthand the alliances and
relationships that made of these two centuries a continuous civil war. Here they are traced. We note, for
example, that a Henry Percy is mentioned in nearly every
chapter of the book, and each one seems to meet a
violent death. This human factor, of the face behind the
visor, of where these people lived, and who they chose to
marry, is a thread running through the pages. As the
author is an Englishman the book is inevitably written
from an English viewpoint, but I trust it is not written from
the standard English point of view, in other words, that it
avoids the awful chauvinism that attributes all victories to
the archers, and all defeats to either impetuosity or lack of
support from home. The reader will find Crécy in these
pages, but he will also find Cocherel, Formigny,
Tannenberg and Mauron. The international outlook,
which was such a feature of the medieval knight's
character, demands nothing less.

THE KNIGHTLY INHERITANCE
The sources from which the knight of the Middle Ages
derived his style of warfare were also those from which he
gained much of the inspiration that formed the basis of
the code of chivalry. He could trace his origins, with

reasonable accuracy as regards development, to the
heavy cavalry of Byzantium in the sixth and seventh
centuries AD, whose shock of attack countered the
loose mass of the lightly armed Arab horsemen. We
note also the cavalry of Charlemagne, the destruction of
whose rearguard at the Pass of Roncesvalles in 778
provides the most enduring, romantic, knightly legend in
history. Charlemagne's development of cavalry also
tackled the more mundane question of expense.
Throughout knightly history the knight, with his horse and
equipment, was an expensive item compared with the
footsoldier, but the development of feudalism went some
way towards solving the problem. Essentially the lord, the
King or some other great leader, made grants of land and
afforded protection to a 'vassal' in return for military
service. It was a system that encouraged discipline and
cohesion, and laid the foundations for the development
of élite ideals.

The Normans inherited this military tradition, and
during the eleventh and twelfth centuries became
Europe's greatest exponents of two elements of the
developing knightly tradition – the use of heavy cavalry,
and the building of castles. The pattern of government
established in England by the Norman invasion – that of
feudal rule by a military aristocracy based on castles –
would be seen again in the following century in the
attempts by the knights of Europe to rule those lands
which were the territorial prize of the extraordinary
episode known as The Crusades. The backbone of the
Crusading armies was still the mounted knight, whose
chief striking power lay in the coordinated charge. When
discipline was good, and use of the knights was

coordinated with the infantry, they were frequently successful.

The Battle of Hastings had been a classic illustration of the supremacy of heavy cavalry, but even this triumph was mitigated by the fact that a ruse had been necessary to break up the Saxon infantry formation, followed by arrows to 'discomfit' the housecarls sufficiently to allow the knights the freedom to do their work. Nevertheless, the notion that footsoldiers were to be despised was commonly held, even though some skilled footsoldiers existed. Flemish pikemen were used by the French at the Battle of Bouvines (1214) where King John of England was defeated. But for there to be anything like an 'infantry revolution' there had to be a commander able to exploit the arm to the full. One of the first such men was Edward I of England. The famous longbowmen which Edward I and his successors were to use so successfully came originally from South Wales. Little use was made of them in the English army until Edward I's conquest of Wales, where at Orewin Bridge in 1282 the English defeated a Welsh army consisting mostly of north Welsh spearmen, by using large numbers of archers to break up their formation. A similar result occurred near Conwy in 1295.

The other great weapon of the footsoldier was the pike, and in July 1298 Edward I pitted one weapon against the other at the Battle of Falkirk. His adversary, William Wallace, had taken up a strong defensive position on a hilltop, with a wood close behind his army. His pikemen were drawn up in four 'schiltrons', circular formations bristling with points. His knights were held in reserve, a swamp protected the approach, and archers covered the flanks. Edward advanced two of the three divisions of his army, who parted on reaching the swamp, and approached the Scots in flank, where they were able to scatter the Scottish archers. Edward immediately saw that the schiltrons could not be broken by the force of cavalry alone, so the knights prepared for a charge while his archers advanced, shooting into the schiltrons from very close range. The Scottish pikemen did not dare break ranks and attack the archers because of the menacing presence of the knights. When the moment was right Edward launched the knights forward in a charge into the gaps the arrows had made, and a classic victory was gained by combination of arms.

When an army did not have archers to break up a pike formation the result could be very different. At the Battle of Courtrai in 1302 a Flemish army consisting almost entirely of pikemen destroyed an army of French knights. The Flemish position was one of do or die. They had a river at their backs, streams on each side and swampy ground all around; a perfect situation for slowing down the French cavalry, but allowing little possibility of retreat. In the event the French knights charged the Flemish hedgehog, breaking through at some points, but in spite of repeated shock waves the line held. Horses were brought down and men were dispatched by the Flemish knights sheltering within. Eventually the Flemings were able to take the offensive and won the day.

So, as the fourteenth century began, a glorious tradition existed, but it faced a growing threat from commanders able to exploit the new possibilities. It is the way in which the knights reacted to these challenges, and reacted to one another in the closely knit political and military struggles of the High Middle Ages that form the substance of this book. It begins with Edward III of England, as the inheritor of all that was worst of the strange baggage of knightly tradition, as Cervantes puts it: '. . . those happy ages that were strangers to the dreadful fury of these devilish instruments of artillery, whose inventor, I am satisfied is now in Hell, receiving the reward of his cursed invention . . .'

This book could not have been written without the cooperation of many people in England and throughout Europe. Above all I wish to thank my wife Jo and my three children Alex, Richard and Katy, who accompanied me on my travels, climbed castle walls and strode across battlefields, and kept out of my way when I was writing it all down.

Leeds, November 1984   S. R. Turnbull

Below: The 'Tower of League', the south-west tower of the castle of Brougham in Cumbria, built by Robert Clifford at the end of the thirteenth century. Brougham was one of the largest of the castles held by the Clifford family, who played an active part in English military life. Cliffords fought at Bannockburn, Crécy and on campaigns in Germany.

1. A New Arthur

THE KING had fled. His bodyguard had led him away from the battlefield by the side of the small river called Bannockburn. The fight had been well fought. As if it were an omen the Scottish King, the mighty Bruce, had crushed the skull of an impetuous English knight seeking glory while the main armies had yet to assemble. Now the Bruce, with his full forces, had likewise crushed the flower of English chivalry beneath the ponderous advance of his schiltrons. They had kept the knights at bay, to be stung by the arrows of the Scottish archers, and harried in the flank by the light horsemen. The English archers, kept in the rear lest they detract from the glory of the knights, had caused little damage, and when they finally did emerge, to engage the Scots on the flank, they were cut down.

Seeing the Scottish light horse sweeping down upon them, the two knights who had charge of the King's person took hold of his bridle rein, one on each side, and hastened to remove him, making for Stirling Castle. When they seemed to be clear of danger one of the pair, Giles d'Argentan, a distinguished Knight Hospitaller who had recently come to England, took leave of his master. He was not accustomed, he said, to flee from battlefields, and plunged his horse into the nearest schiltron. The King rode on, escorted via Dunbar to the fortress town of Berwick, where he rested within the safety of the walls raised by his illustrious father, the first Edward, 'Hammer of the Scots'.

Thus the second English king to bear the name of Edward ended his major attempt to snuff out the flame of Scottish independence, and laid his country open to a reaction unparalleled for decades. Stirling, to whose relief Edward II had marched, surrendered to the Bruce, joining Perth, Dumfries, Edinburgh and Roxburgh as lost English possessions. During the summer of 1314 Robert the Bruce, his confidence boosted by Bannockburn, launched a series of raids across the border. The impotence of the English monarch allowed the Scots to penetrate more deeply into the kingdom than would have been possible a decade earlier. In August the Scots crossed the Tees and advanced to the gates of the castle of Richmond, in Swaledale. The See of the Bishop of Durham purchased a truce to last until January 1315. Cumberland too paid a ransom for itself, while the valleys of the North Tyne did homage to the King of Scotland.

So the year 1315 opened under circumstances more depressing for England than at any time in the century. The country's rulers, mocked on the battlefield and humiliated by raiding, presented no more impressive sight when out of their armour. When those who ruled attempted to reach agreement on policy, a process from which Edward II, taking his pleasures with Court favourites, usually absented himself, their personal

distastes and rivalry prevented accord. As the English quarrelled the Scots grew bolder, and in 1318 made preparations to claim the prize that was as much symbolic as strategic – the town and castle of Berwick-upon-Tweed. Berwick then was what it had been and was destined to remain for centuries – a hotly disputed fortified town. Guarding the crossing of the Tweed, it was the key to the 'East Marches' of the Anglo-Scottish border. With the help of a little treachery from within the garrison the Scots, under the leadership of Sir James Douglas, scaled the walls of the town in the early hours of the morning of 2 April. Six days later, after some plundering which allowed the defenders to counter-attack quite successfully, the castle also fell. Exultant, the Scots marched south, boldly passing Richmond and burning Northallerton and Boroughbridge. On 1 June the town of Ripon paid 'protection money' of £1,000, and the Scots turned for Knaresborough, then headed off on their deepest ever raid into England – westward up Wharfedale towards Skipton, plundering Otley on the way. Skipton's lord, Robert de Clifford, had paid with his life at Bannockburn. Now the fortress seemed open and undefended. Only the height of the castle, surmounting its vertical rock, ensured that a Scottish army unprepared for siege, would content itself with plunder of the town, and move on.

In July 1319 an English army of 12,000 assembled at Newcastle with the intention of recapturing Berwick. During August the force marched northwards, spurred on by Edward's proclamation of free plunder at the expense of the Scots. Robert the Bruce responded by launching yet another raid deep into England, one so devastating as to oblige Edward to draw off his troops from Berwick and hurry south. John Randolf, Earl of Moray, and Sir James Douglas crossed the border and reached as far as

Boroughbridge without encountering English resistance. As Edward's Queen Isabella was then residing in York a rich royal prize was almost within the Bruce's grasp. Some chroniclers suggest that the Scots had received information as to her whereabouts, but whatever treachery there may have been failed in its purpose, and the Queen was hurriedly evacuated to Nottingham and safety. Resistance to the Scots then fell upon the shoulders of Archbishop Melton of York who, perhaps mindful of the great victory at Northallerton won against the Scots two centuries previously, and known as the 'Battle of the Standard' because of the ecclesiastical banners flown above the English army, set out with a mixed army of clerics, citizens and some men of military experience to withstand this further onslaught. On the afternoon of 20 September the Archbishop found the Scots on Myton-on-Swale near Boroughbridge. Caught between the two schiltrons which the Scots formed like the teeth of a pincer, the citizen army was driven back into the angle where the River Swale joins the Ure, and great was the slaughter. The Mayor of York was killed among countless others, either cut down or drowned as they tried to flee. This little-known battle was almost a second Bannockburn. The Scots withdrew, to discover as they returned home that their raid had had the desired effect – the siege was lifted and a 10-year truce proclaimed. Never had English military prowess sunk so low. During the remainder of Edward's reign the challenges would come from nearer home, and in the north of Britain the Scots were free as at no time in their history.

THE HEIR TO MISFORTUNE
Observing all that went on was a young boy, heir to his unfortunate father, yet sharing none of his characteristics. Edward at the time of Bannockburn had been two years

Left: The keep of Norham Castle. Norham and Berwick were always in the front line of any Scottish advance on England, and Norham was in fact attacked on the very day that Edward III became King of England.
Below left: The unique triangular-plan fortress of Caerlaverock. Most of the structure dates from the thirteenth century, but the castle was largely dismantled early in the fourteenth century in accord with King Robert Bruce's policy of rendering defenceless all military buildings which might prove useful to the English.
Below: Hermitage Castle, grimmest of the Border fortresses, was captured in 1338 by the Knight of Liddesdale, Sir William Douglas, from the English Baron, Sir Ralph Neville, who held it by gift from Edward III. Thereafter it was a Douglas stronghold until the end of the fifteenth century.

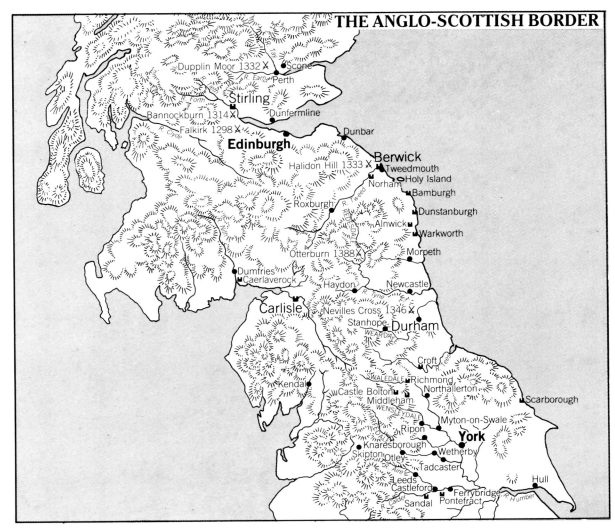

THE ANGLO-SCOTTISH BORDER

old, and grew to manhood as the fierce war with Scotland and jealousy within the court were enacted around him. When the time came for Edward II to go it was in the name of Edward III that pressure was applied, and from a source closer to the King than any before – his wife, Queen Isabella. In early 1325 the Queen was in France on a diplomatic mission to her brother Charles IV. Later in the year, Prince Edward, then nearly thirteen, joined her. At that time Paris was refuge for numbers of discontented exiles, among whom was Roger Mortimer who had escaped from the Tower of London where he had been incarcerated by Edward II following an abortive rising. The Queen provided a natural focus for the development of a movement against her husband; she publicized her estrangement from him by taking Mortimer as her lover. On 23 September she and Mortimer sailed for England at the head of a band of mercenaries and landed in Suffolk. She had foreseen the effect well. The country rose in support and Edward fled to the west. Of his cruel end little need be said. After the accession of his son had been secured there was no place for a deposed monarch, and he was murdered in Berkeley Castle.

The young Edward III was crowned at Westminster on 1 February 1327. Within hours of the crown being placed on his head the Scots showed their defiance by crossing the Tweed at night, setting up scaling ladders against the walls of Norham, and attempting to overpower the garrison. The surprise attack was unsuccessful but, coming at a time when the last king's truce still had a

notional nine years to run, the message was clear – the Scottish people would defy any attempts at being ruled from England, either by Edward II or by the young son and the rebellious faction who had put him there. This hostility was but one element of Edward's inheritance; in the conduct of knightly warfare there were many others equally unwelcome. The question on every statesman's lips was, would the new King be able to learn from his father's experience? The way in which Edward responded to these challenges in the formative years of what was to be a long and successful military career forms the theme of this chapter.

Before considering the launching of this career it is worth spending a few moments considering what it was that medieval man demanded of a King. It is clear from the brief account above of the latter years of Edward II that, whatever it was, he had been unable to deliver it. The overwhelming conclusion must be that paramount among all the expectations of kingship was prowess in the waging of war. The priest at his prayers, the merchant in his counting-house, the peasant in the fields, all had this in common; they possessed an interest in the pursuit of war; and it was to the King, the warrior chief of the land, that they looked for inspiration.

THE WEARDALE CAMPAIGN

It was unfortunate that Edward III's first military expedition was almost a total disaster. Directed against the Scots, it was marred even before the English army set out.

Right: English and Scottish knights skirmishing on the Tyne, from an illustration to Froissart's *Chronicles*. The incident illustrated is typical of the many encounters between the two nations during the period under discussion.

Queen Isabella had acquired on her son's behalf the services of 500 mercenaries from Hainault. In June they were billeted in York, where quarrels broke out between them and the English archers, allegedly over a game of dice. The quarrelling became a full-scale riot, which was put down in brutal fashion by the Hainaulters, leaving 316 Lincolnshire archers dead in the streets, a very bad way for a campaign to begin. At the opposite end of the scale there arose disagreements among the English commanders as to how the campaign should be planned, which the young King was unable to control. All this gave the Scots ample opportunity to take the initiative. At the end of June they raided across the border and threatened Carlisle, while the slow-moving English army had only just left York. Uncertain as to the Scots' intentions it halted at Durham. Only the smoke of burning villages gave any indication of where the enemy lay. The English army was accordingly deployed for battle, being separated into three divisions of foot, each flanked by mounted knights. The Scots were almost certainly outnumbered, but were highly mobile. Froissart gives a particularly vivid description of Scottish military techniques. They were, he writes, 'all a-horse back', the knights and squires being well horsed, while the lower ranks rode sturdy little nags, whose sole object was to transport their rider to the field of battle, (where he would dismount), or convey him rapidly in a raiding party. Froissart continues:

'They take with them no purveyance of bread nor wine, for . . . they will pass in the journey a great long time with flesh half sodden, without bread, and drink of the river water without wine, and they neither care for pots nor pans, for they seethe beasts in their own skins . . . on their horse between the saddle and the panel they truss a broad plate of metal, and behind the saddle they will have a little sack full of oatmeal . . . they lay this plate on the fire and temper a little of the oatmeal; and when the plate is hot, they cast of the thin paste thereon, and so make a little cake . . . and that they eat to comfort withal their stomachs.'

The idea of mounted infantry had also been introduced into the English army by Sir Andrew Harcla, a veteran of Edward II's Scottish campaigns, and these 'hobelars' made up about a quarter of the English host in 1327, but as most of the army were on foot the Scots evaded them completely, leaving the commanders frustrated. Movement by the Scots, apparently shifting camp, suggested the possibility that they were planning to withdraw, and the English attempted to cut off their retreat. Abandoning the baggage train, the English army marched overnight for the ford at Haydon, a crossing of the South Tyne near Hexham. As they crossed to the northern bank it began to rain and after a few days the ford disappeared, leaving the English on the northern bank, and the Scots nowhere in sight. As days passed, and morale sank lower, it was proclaimed that anyone who could find the Scottish army and lead the English to engage them would receive lands worth £100 a year and a knighthood if he were not already a Knight. Fifteen men took up the challenge, and carefully

Right: A few fragments of wall, and a precipitous flight of steps leading down to the River Tweed, are all that remain today of the once mighty fortifications of medieval Berwick-Upon-Tweed. This garrison and frontier town *'par excellence'* changed hands several times, and was the scene of the first major campaign fought by the young Edward III.

Below left: The arms of the Seton family. The sword was added in recognition of the family's contribution to the war against Edward III. Three Setons were killed prior to 1333, including one son who was hanged in front of Berwick as a warning to the defenders.

Opposite page, top: Sir Archibald Douglas at Halidon Hill, 1333. His coat of arms bears the 'Heart of the Bruce' granted to his half-brother, Sir James, and borne by the Douglases ever since. It commemorates the journey of Sir James to take the heart of the late King on crusade. Archibald was killed at Halidon Hill, Edward III's first major victory, and a crushing blow to Scottish independence. (An original painting for this book by artist, Anthony Beasley)

Below, far right: The battlefield of Halidon Hill, looking across the valley to the Scottish positions on Witches' Knowle. The farm visible in the middle distance is known as 'Bog End', testimony to the swampy nature of the ground that played a decisive part in the battle of 1333.

re-crossed the river, while the main body struck camp and headed upstream to look for a suitable ford. The promised reward was gained by Sir Thomas Rokeby, who tracked the Scots to the vicinity of Stanhope on the Wear, where they had established themselves on the southern bank, in a naturally strong position of rocky outcrops, just beyond bowshot of the northern bank.

Nothing would induce them to fight. An attempt at crossing, to taunt them into giving battle, was summarily dealt with by Sir James Douglas's cavalry. A polite, diplomatic suggestion that the Scots should give battle was flatly rejected. The English troops sat down and waited, disturbed by Scottish warcries, and exploited by the exorbitant prices for supplies brought up on pack-horses by enterprising merchants. A vague hope that the Scots could be starved into submission was dashed when they calmly decamped for stronger positions further upstream. The English followed, and on the first night suffered the indignity of a raid during which Sir James Douglas managed to fight his way as far as the ropes of the King's own tent. For the remainder of their stay the English were kept awake by frequent false alarms. The knights from Hainault had more to worry about. As well as sharing guard duties for the English camp, they had also to guard themselves from the English archers, who hated them more than the Scots, and were thirsting for revenge for the incident at York. Within a few days news was brought to the young King that the Scots had once again slipped away entirely unnoticed. He is said to have wept tears of vexation. There was nothing to do but to head south, and pay off the mercenaries. It was as well that John of Hainault was eager to leave England, for the bill he presented could not be met in one payment, and King

Left: The aftermath of a Scottish raid on an English border town. A woodcut from a printed edition of Holinshed's *Chronicles*.

Edward III had to pawn some of his jewels to meet the first instalment.

Edward's first campaign therefore ended in humiliation. The Scots had taken the offensive, had set the pace, and had led Edward a merry dance. The use of mercenaries had been an expensive mistake, and less advantage had been gained from the venture than in some of the campaigns of his ill-fated father, whose military ineptitude Edward was expected to reverse. It was to the young sovereign's credit that he was to show that he differed from his father in one vital respect – he could learn from his mistakes.

DUPPLIN MOOR

Edward had ample time to absorb the lessons of the Weardale campaign. In 1329 King Robert the Bruce died, emphasizing on his deathbed the policy of defensive warfare and guerrilla attacks which his own career had done so much to establish as a success. (Sir James Douglas, the hero of Weardale, carried out the King's last request by taking his heart to the Holy Land.) King Robert was succeeded by his son David Bruce. Not surprisingly the accession was challenged. Following Bannockburn, King Robert had disinherited from their Scottish lands all those who had failed to support him. His death enabled the disinherited to pursue their claims, chief of which was the throne of Scotland for one of their number, Edward Balliol, son of John Balliol, to whom Edward I had awarded the Scottish crown in 1292. Edward Balliol raised an army and travelled to Scotland by sea, landing on 6 August 1332 in Fife, and advanced via Dunfermline towards Perth. It was the Weardale campaign in reverse, but with a much more serious objective. The English invaders, small in number (1,500 in all is the average estimate), had to be brought to battle. Opposing them was a hastily assembled Scottish army of possibly 40,000 men, untrained for pitched battle, and apparently in two minds about the legitimacy of Edward Balliol's claim to the Scottish throne. This we know from an argument which took place between the Scottish leaders immediately before the Battle of Dupplin Moor began. The dispute was resolved by the rivals' deciding that each would be the first to attack the English position; both contingents lurched off in an uncoordinated advance.

The small English force had taken up a defensive position – they had little choice of any other – with their horses in the rear, and the main defence being provided by archers. Edward Balliol, by the exigencies of his position, therefore anticipated what was to become the English way of fighting for the next century and a half, and demonstrated how such tactics could defeat a numerically larger host. The archers concentrated their heavy fire upon the Scottish flanks, driving them inwards. At this point Scottish reinforcements arrived led by the Earl of Mar. Unfortunately this addition to their strength produced an advantage for the English, who had managed to trap the Scottish army in a glen. Mar charged down the narrow pass behind his comrades, making it impossible for them to move. One chronicler described the ensuing scene as being like a burial heap, into which the English poured flight after flight of arrows. The panic-stricken Scots attempted to escape by climbing over one another, making the press worse, until the Scottish army had turned into a writhing heap nearly fifteen feet high, on which English soldiers stood grotesquely, jabbing with their spears at any sign of life beneath them. Weardale was avenged.

The following few months witnessed a furious spate of activity. Edward Balliol was crowned King of Scots at Scone, but once the English military presence was removed, was soon forced to flee to England. For the Scots it was a fateful victory, for Balliol headed straight for a Parliament at York and sought the help of Edward III.

To support Balliol's cause was the opportunity for which Edward had been waiting. Weardale had shown him the strength of the Scots, but Dupplin Moor had exposed their weaknesses. Balliol led where Edward intended to follow, and in March 1333 the deposed monarch returned to Scotland and laid siege to Berwick-upon-Tweed, which by this year was the only major fortification left in south-east Scotland. Robert the Bruce had slighted all English strongholds as soon as they fell into his hands, so as to deny refuge to any English army that crossed the border. But Berwick was more than a castle. It was a border town of strategic and commercial importance, and when the Scots recaptured it in 1318 they had in fact strengthened its defences. The possession of Berwick was now a point of honour.

THE SIEGE OF BERWICK

Once Berwick was surrounded the Scots tried their old ruse of raiding deep into England to draw the defenders off. But this time it only provoked a counter-raid, and provided Edward with some useful propaganda about Scottish atrocities, material which was well used. The King may have lacked the modern means of propaganda, but he had nothing to learn by way of technique. Public proclamations, petitions to the clergy, all served to emphasize the rightness of retaliation. Not that any Englishman living north of Yorkshire needed reminding of the ferocity of a Scottish incursion.

Against this background of righteous indignation Edward assembled his army, spending some time in the careful planning of finance and victualling. Surviving records show how well Edward had learned the lesson of Weardale. Orders were sent to sheriffs of various midland and southern shires to supply food for men and horses, which began to arrive at Newcastle by land and sea. Perhaps another lesson he had learned was that such supplies could not be totally relied upon, for of fifteen shires responsible for deliveries to Newcastle only ten complied, and they supplied only a fifth of the amount Edward had originally demanded. The quantity however, was found to be sufficient, prompting the suspicion that Edward had deliberately over-estimated. Nor did the great religious houses comply with his additional request for the supply of wagons and draught-horses. So poor was the response that the sheriff of York requisitioned the horses and wagons presently in use for the construction of York Minster. As the Scots had made use in the defences of Berwick of a load of timber destined for the Franciscan friars of Roxburgh, ecclesiastical honours might be considered to have been equal.

By the time Edward and his army arrived at Berwick, Balliol had been conducting his siege with steady progress for two months. Four conduits carrying fresh water to the town had been discovered and smashed. As serious for the defenders was their own failure to adopt the scorched earth policy which Bruce had carried out and advocated to the end. Unhindered by shortages the English raided widely, supplementing their foodstuffs considerably by their efforts. The most valuable asset possessed by the English, however, was the presence in their midst, as chief adviser to siege operations, of the very man who in the siege of 1319 had performed the same function for the defenders. This was John Crabb, a Fleming, who had been captured in 1332 by Sir Walter Manny, then purchased by the English King who took him into his employ. No one knew better than Crabb how to find the weaknesses in Berwick's defences, and enormous siege-engines were directed against these weak points. Records survive of the construction of one of these, probably a trebuchet. Forty oak trees supplied the wood, while thirty-seven stonemasons and six quarrymen prepared hundreds of stone balls for flinging at the walls.

Apart from the trebuchets, it is possible that some primitive cannon may have been used, for the English chronicle *The Brut* mentions 'spitouse comyng out of guns'. This could be a later insertion, but we do know that the following year Edward was supplied by an apothecary with the separate constituents of gunpowder, though whether these were designed to fire projectiles, or to be flung as an explosive bomb, remains open to conjecture.

The bombardment of Berwick continued throughout the month of June, and on the 27th the English launched an assault on the walls by land and sea, which proved quite successful because of the failure of the Scots'

attempts at defence. Faggots soaked in tar had been stacked on the town walls ready to drop on to the English assault ships, but before they could be employed the flames from the burning faggots had blown back into Berwick and set a number of houses alight. A 24-hour truce enabled the Scots to control the fire, but the renewed vigour of the English attack forced them to negotiate a further 15-day truce, guaranteed by giving Edward twelve hostages.

This was to be the first of several truces negotiated during the siege of Berwick, and illustrates an aspect of siege warfare every bit as important as blockading, mining or bombardment; that of surrender on terms. One gets the impression that every medieval siege tended to begin with a period of assessment, of trying the opponents' strength and measuring his capabilities. From these 'experiments' conclusions would be drawn about the likely outcome, which frequently hinged on an estimation of the length of time the garrison could hold out, until the besieging army withdrew or a relieving army appeared. Naturally enough the besieging army would be drawing similar conclusions. Both sides were therefore able to negotiate on the basis of several presumptions,

Right: Bacteriological warfare? A trebuchet is used during a siege to throw severed heads of the enemy back into the castle.
Opposite page: The defence of a gateway. In an attack on a castle the most hotly contested spot would be the gateway, protected by drawbridge and portcullis.

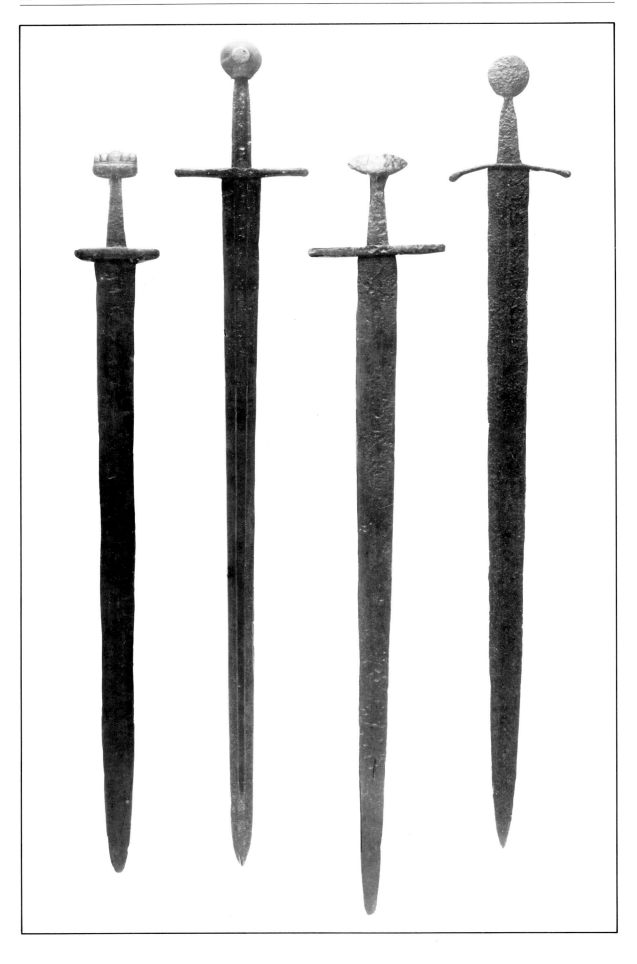

the facts of which were not in dispute. Berwick is a classic example of how such arrangements could be set up in minute detail.

The first such agreement laid down that the garrison would surrender if not relieved by 11 July, fifteen days from the date of signing. Scottish hopes rested on Sir Archibald Douglas (the half-brother of Sir James Douglas, killed in 1330 on Crusade), who was busily, but slowly, assembling a large army. It was unfortunate for Scotland that he had not acted sooner, for his resulting efforts, though dramatic, were not essentially threatening enough for Edward to alter his resolve to maintain the siege unless the very letter of the agreement were followed. Douglas in fact crossed the Tweed above Berwick, and burned Tweedmouth, on the southern bank, while Edward's army watched from the northern bank. During the afternoon of the same day, 11 July, the day mentioned in the agreement, two hundred Scottish knights picked their way over the precarious ruins of the Tweed bridge and flung some supplies into Berwick, and some soldiers actually managed to enter the town. The brave force were attacked by the English as they carried out this limited operation, considered sufficient by Sir Archibald Douglas for him to claim that in terms of the agreement drawn up, Berwick had been relieved by the agreed date, and that the siege must therefore conclude. To drive home the fact that he had force to back his legalistic points, Douglas drew up his army on Sunnyside hill, south of the Tweed, and threatened that unless Edward complied with the agreement the army would move off south and devastate England. His brother, Sir James Douglas, had of course adopted similar threatening postures in the Weardale campaign of 1327. But Edward's circumstances were now much improved. He had been blooded in Weardale. It was perhaps a worrying point that Edward's Queen Philippa was in Bamburgh castle, a comparatively short journey away, but Bamburgh could withstand a siege for far longer than the time during which Berwick might now be expected to hold out. On the point of words, did a handful of soldiers climbing over a broken bridge constitute a relieving force? Edward's catapults were still carrying out their destructive

work, and the northern bank of the Tweed outside the walls had not felt the tread of a Scottish foot since the operation began. Edward decided that the town had not in any sense, technical, legalistic or otherwise, been relieved. He would call Douglas's bluff.

It was now Edward's turn to insist. As the siege had not been broken the town must surrender or the twelve hostages would die. To show he was in earnest Edward erected a high gallows as close to the walls of Berwick as security would allow. The first of the hostages, Thomas Seton, was hanged before his parents' eyes, the third of their children to die in the war against England. Douglas's army stopped dead in its tracks. This was not the hesitant young monarch they had humiliated in Weardale, but a ruthless, calculating military leader, prepared to abide by the conventions of his day and take them to their extremity. Realizing what they were now facing, the Scots returned to the negotiating table.

The resultant agreement was so complicated in its efforts to reach a definition of 'relief' acceptable to both parties and acted upon once it had been carried out, as to make it almost a humorous document, reducing bloody warfare to precise points to be gained or lost. This, however, is to see it from a twentieth-century viewpoint, where warfare is instantly devastating, and the opportunities for havoc elsewhere are so enormously varied. Its only modern parallel must be the patient and precise negotiations that take place when a terrorist faction take hostages and threaten their lives. In terms of numbers involved the siege of Berwick was on this scale. In terms of possible outcome it was on a scale of grand strategy, coldly calculated with an innate grasp of the laws of chance and the notion of risk that is never normally credited to the medieval mind.

The agreement was put in writing and signed on 15 July 1333, proclaiming a truce of the siege until sunrise on 20 July. The town and castle of Berwick would then be regarded as having been relieved if any of the following conditions had been satisfied:

(i) The Scottish army crosses the Tweed by the fishery called Berwick stream to the west of the town at any time before sunrise on 20 July.

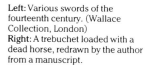

Left: Various swords of the fourteenth century. (Wallace Collection, London)
Right: A trebuchet loaded with a dead horse, redrawn by the author from a manuscript.

(ii) The Scottish army defeats the English army in battle on Scottish ground between the Tweed and the sea by Vespers on 19 July.

(iii) A division of the Scottish army, to include 200 men-at-arms, forces its way through the English lines into Berwick between sunrise and sunset on any of the days, with a loss of not more than thirty men-at-arms. On fulfillment of any of the above conditions Edward would raise the siege and return the remaining hostages at sunrise on 20 July. If none of the conditions had been fulfilled the town and castle of Berwick would surrender to the English at the aforesaid time.

What delicate bargaining, what trading of numbers and locations, one wonders, took place before the above document was produced? It would appear, however, that Sir Archibald Douglas took no part in the arrangements. He had set off on his raid towards Bamburgh and the English Queen, and not even the Scottish commanders had any idea where he had gone, for we know that the day after the agreement was signed three Scottish knights set out under Edward's safe conduct to find him. They tracked him down near Morpeth and persuaded him to return to try his hand at one of the Herculean tasks which the cunning Edward had forced upon Scottish pride.

Despite a considerable numerical superiority (although precise figures for both sides are lacking), it is apparent that the Scottish commanders, in the absence of Douglas, had negotiated themselves into three alternatives which were effectively one: an opposed crossing of the Tweed, where the English had chosen the ground and were obviously prepared to defend with archers – potentially suicidal and was rejected almost immediately as a means of saving Berwick; a pitched battle, the one form of encounter that the great Bruce had insisted against, but which his noble pupil, Sir James Douglas, had successfully achieved in Weardale; the third alternative could only succeed if the 200 Scots were allowed to test their mettle against the siege lines while the majority of the English army were otherwise engaged, and the only way they could be thus engaged would be for the Scottish main body to engage them. Edward had clearly appreciated this from the start, for his dispositions on the return of Douglas illustrate such an expectation. He had three possible threats against which to guard: the main Scottish army, the 200 against his lines, and the likelihood of a sally by the defenders to help either of the other two operations towards a successful conclusion. About 200 men-at-arms were detailed to oppose a minor attack on his lines, 500 were detached to hold back any advance from the town, while the rest of the army were withdrawn two miles north-west of Berwick to the highest, and in the military sense, strongest, ground near to Berwick – Halidon Hill.

THE BATTLE OF HALIDON HILL

Douglas had by now returned to Scotland, and was camped at Duns, some thirteen miles to the west of Berwick. He set out from there on the morning of 19 July, knowing that unless he achieved one of the two remaining tasks Berwick would fall as the sun rose on the following day. From the summit of Halidon Edward could follow his every movement as he approached Berwick along the direct route. Only one direction offered any chance of surprise: to swing to the north behind a hill now called Witches Knowle, which was higher than Halidon. This was the route Douglas chose, his picked force of 200 held in reserve on his left flank. Edward's scouts sighted them at midday. The stage was set for the first battle of

Edward's career. How much of Weardale, of Dupplin Moor, had the young King learned? There was no Bruce, but there could still be another Bannockburn.

Once the Scots had been sighted the English deployed themselves in three divisions, facing across the shallow valley from Halidon Hill towards Witches Knowle and the Scots to the north. The whole area is probably very similar today to the aspect it presented on 19 July 1333. Edward led the centre division, while the victor of Dupplin Moor

and recently deposed King of Scotland, Edward Balliol, took command of the left. His presence was undoubtedly decisive in the dispositions of the English army. The defensive measures he had been forced to adopt at Dupplin Moor had to be shown to be more than merely defensive. Once again an English army had been allowed to seize the initiative. Halidon Hill would prove whether or not such tactics would work against an army unhampered by a restricted front and impetuous support

from the rear. It is not clear how Edward arranged his archers, but it would appear that they formed flanks at an angle to each of the three divisions, the idea probably being to cause in the Scottish army that same constricting, packing movement which had brought about their downfall before. As he was going to fight defensively, letting the Scots come to him, there was little point in the men-at-arms remaining mounted, so the horses were sent to the rear, and kept ready for an eventual pursuit.

After addressing his troops from horseback Edward himself dismounted, a move which was noted by several chroniclers as an innovation and a departure from the traditions of knightly warfare.

The Scots, too, were arranged in three divisions, their men-at-arms also dismounting to support the schiltrons of pikemen with their 12-foot pikes. This decision was no doubt taken in view of the terrain, for not only were the English on a hill, where, as one chronicler relates, 'one man might discomfort three,' but a treacherous bog divided the two armies. If Douglas had had time, these schiltrons could have won Halidon Hill as they had won Bannockburn, but time was not on his side. If Edward was to be defeated it had to be accomplished that very afternoon. Even a delay, with the hope of an eventual victory for the Scottish army, would be immediately nullified by Edward's inevitable reaction of hanging the hostages and recommencing the bombardment of the town. The decline in Scottish morale alone would probably serve to turn a possible victory into defeat.

Immediately prior to the battle proper there occurred one of those incidents that are as much a part of chivalry as gentlemanly agreements to surrender towns when honour has been satisfied – a single combat between champions. The one which had preceded Bannockburn proved a correct augury of that battle, and no doubt the Scots hoped the same for the one which took place before Halidon. Here the author must declare a certain personal interest. The Scottish champion was a knight of the Borders called Turnbull, according to the chronicler Baker, a giant of a man, and identified in Scottish legend as the first to bear the surname, having saved King Robert the Bruce from a charging bull. Whatever Turnbull's previous exploits, we are told that at Halidon he was accompanied by a large black mastiff, and opposed by a Norfolk knight called Robert Benhale. It was perfectly natural for Turnbulls to be present, because their lands were a baronial possession of the House of Douglas, but unfortunately for Douglas the example his champion set was to prove only too accurate a prediction of the outcome of the day. The dog was first to be dispatched, cut clean in two by the Englishman's sword, and was followed shortly after by Turnbull. Accounts vary as to whether he was hacked to death, or run through by Benhale's lance. The outcome was the same: valuable time was lost along with the champion.

To reach the English lines the Scots had to cross the boggy ground mentioned above. Although it has since been drained, the farm presently on the site is called 'Bogend', and the ground is still treacherous after rain. As they struggled through the bog and up the slope, an estimated 500 Scottish soldiers fell as flights of English arrows swept their ranks 'as thick as motes on the sun beam'. Those who got through tackled the divisions of Edward and Balliol, while Edward's right flank had to contend with the strength of Douglas's own division, which included the picked two hundred whose goal was a forced entry into Berwick. They were held on the slopes of Halidon until evening, the men-at-arms balanced in the centre of each division, while the slow advantage passed to the English, the scales being gradually tipped by the volleys of arrows poured into the Scottish rear ranks coming up in support. Soon there were none to support, and the three separate Scottish formations were herded as one, and their rear ranks straggled off down the hill. At this point the English knights mounted and gave chase, scouring the countryside for miles around as the survivors scattered. Casualties were estimated in widely differing figures ranging from 30,000 to 60,000, with negligible losses on the English side. Among the slain were Sir Archibald Douglas and his nephew William. The younger Douglas may not have carried Bruce's heart, but he certainly carried his spirit. At Weardale James had honoured the advice of his late King. If Archibald had had the resources to pursue such a policy to Halidon, with perhaps the moral courage to abandon the now symbolic Berwick, the eventual outcome might have been a certain shame, but no disaster. Instead, in the absence of the able Douglas, the agreement with Edward was seized upon by the defenders as being their best hope. Douglas responded as best he could to a situation that must have appeared to his experienced military mind as always hopeless.

The hanging of Thomas Seton had indicated the kind of man the Scots were up against. Following the battle few Scots escaped, and fewer were offered quarter. I can find no other battle in the whole of the period covered by this book where the defeated troops committed suicide rather than be captured, but this happened at Halidon Hill. No less than four chroniclers indicate that some at least of the Scots flung themselves into the sea in despair. Their expectation of death was fully justified, for a disinterested chronicler confirms that on the morrow of the battle Edward ordered a hundred captives to be beheaded. Berwick, of course, opened its gates as the sun rose, in fulfillment of the agreement. But what a new, ruthless talent had emerged from the ashes of his father's disaster – and this was just the beginning.

Right: Berwick-Upon-Tweed, viewed from the right of the English line on Halidon Hill. In the far distance can be seen Holy Island.

2. King of England– King of France

F EDWARD III had confined his military operations to the Scottish border, the Battle of Halidon Hill would have been relegated to decent obscurity in the textbooks, seen not as a precursor of events to come, but as no more than a rather well-fought battle. But this warrior King of England is not known to posterity for his wars against Scotland. He is remembered because, more than anyone else, he was responsible for starting a conflict that was to divide France and England for more than a century – The Hundred Years War.

I used the word 'divide' advisedly, because essentially the Hundred Years War embodied not a collision of elements that had always been divided, but a split between elements that were, to some extent, united. Nowhere in France was this apparent 'unity' more noticeable than in Gascony, that area of south-west France which a recent historian has called 'England's first colony'. Its southern border was the Pyrenees, its western the Atlantic Ocean. On the other points of the compass its borders varied as Gascony developed to become what India was to a later generation of Imperial administrators and rulers – the jewel in the crown.

HOMAGE FOR GASCONY

Gascony's connection with England dated back to the twelfth century, when its heiress, Eleanor of Aquitaine, one of the richest women in Europe, was divorced from her husband, Louis VII, King of France, and married a certain Henry Plantagenet. From the point of view of the King of France there could have been no worse alliance. This Henry Plantagenet had recently inherited Maine, Touraine and Anjou from his father, and was already both Duke of Normandy and Suzerain of Brittany. With possession of Aquitaine (or Gascony, the names are to all intents and purposes interchangeable) he now controlled more territory in France than the King of France, and in 1154, on the death of King Stephen, Henry became King Henry II of England. The amalgamation of their territories into what was to become the Angevin Empire, the glory of the Plantagenets, would provoke the virtue of internationalism and the vice of conflict, between England and France for the next three centuries.

Queen Eleanor died in 1204, by which time her son John was on the throne of England, and the Angevin Empire was rapidly disintegrating. Only Aquitaine seemed permanent, helped by the loyalty of the Gascon people to their distant Duke. To these inhabitants the King of France was more remote and 'foreign' than the King of England. Richard the Lionheart had reinforced his position by frequent sojourns in Bordeaux and Poitiers. His mother Queen Eleanor preferred to spend as much time as possible there, but the trouble endured by John made him an infrequent visitor, and Henry III waited fourteen years into his reign before visiting the Duchy.

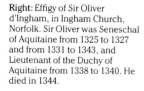

Right: Effigy of Sir Oliver d'Ingham, in Ingham Church, Norfolk. Sir Oliver was Seneschal of Aquitaine from 1325 to 1327 and from 1331 to 1343, and Lieutenant of the Duchy of Aquitaine from 1338 to 1340. He died in 1344.

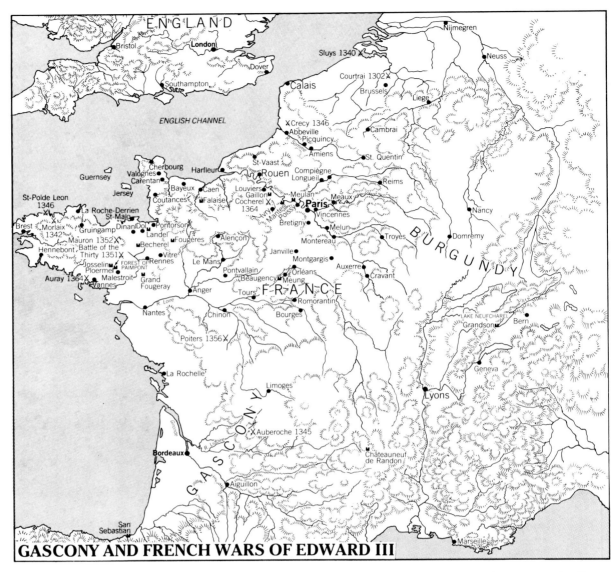

GASCONY AND FRENCH WARS OF EDWARD III

As the personal touch disappeared, government from a distance relied on the maintenance of lines of communication, particularly for the all-important wine trade. The overland route through Calais and Paris to Bordeaux could be travelled at some speed in almost three weeks. But war disrupted overland traffic, leaving the alternative of the possibly shorter, but always hazardous sea journey. With good winds and weather Plymouth to Bordeaux would take two weeks. If there were storms in the Bay of Biscay or marauding pirates it could take a lot longer, and in any event starting dates could not be accurately forecast. In 1355 the Black Prince voyaged to Gascony in eleven days, but he had waited six weeks at Plymouth for a favourable wind. It is not surprising that the King-Duke's administrator in the remote province (who was known as the Seneschal of Gascony) would complain bitterly of the difficulty of his position. Nevertheless, this remnant of the Angevin Empire was always worth retaining. One statistic from later years, the period of this book, will suffice to illustrate the position: that King Edward III obtained more revenue from the wine trade through Bordeaux than he did from the whole of domestic taxation in England. But there was a price to pay. Both diplomatically and militarily the French King was constantly nibbling at the Gascon frontier. It is no wonder that at the time of the accession of Edward III older men looked back to a

golden age when England called the tune over its distant but profitable colony. What irked the English more than anything was the fact that to retain Gascony the King of England had to do homage to the King of France. The rights and wrongs of the arrangement had plagued relations between the countries since the time of John, and much ink had been spilt on the matter. With the coming of the warrior King there was to be a fresh approach.

THE FRENCH SUCCESSION

In 1328 legal disputes about control of the Aquitaine inheritance shrank to insignificance beside the great issue of the day: that of the succession to the throne of France. French law, which had recently declared that a woman could not inherit the throne, was now divided on the issue of whether the crown could pass via a woman to her male heir. What threw the matter into the forefront of international politics was that one of the closest male heirs to the late King was Edward III of England, at that time only fifteen, and firmly under the control of his ambitious mother who had scandalized the French court. As England itself was in a state of political turmoil, the claim that was advanced on his behalf must have seemed a formality, made simply because it was expected of him as a grandson of a French king, a Plantagenet, and, as

Duke of Aquitaine, a Peer of France. Leaving the legal question wide open, the French chose Philip of Valois, cousin of the last three kings, whose father had twice led attacks on Gascony.

With the accession of the new monarch homage from Gascony would be required. To ensure that the young Edward complied with the duty, Philip seized the revenues of Gascony and hinted at a final confiscation, a threat which England was ill-prepared to challenge. Shamed at Weardale by a Scottish army, there was no military force with which Edward could threaten Philip, so on 6 June 1329, at Amiens, he did homage to Philip of Valois. It was an impressive but inconclusive ceremony, both parties maintaining their position as best they could.

Since the beginning of his reign Edward had been reinforcing the English military presence in Gascony, a process that he accelerated once the formal homage had been given. At the same time Philip began to collect forces for its recapture. A document of 1329 contains an estimate of the force required, namely 5,000 men-at-arms and 16,000 foot soldiers. These must have been acquired by May 1337 for on this date Philip ordered the confiscation of the Duchy of Aquitaine. Edward's response was dramatic. Referring to Philip of Valois not as King of France but as 'usurper', he urged his rights in Aquitaine by claiming them through the throne of France, rightly his in terms of the inheritance principle put forward on his behalf ten years previously. To Edward the matter would be simply solved by his being recognized as the rightful King of France.

It is difficult to say how seriously Edward's contemporaries took this claim. What is beyond dispute is that Edward himself took it very seriously indeed, and produced a speedy military response. Paradoxically, however, as Gascony had been the touchstone for the coming conflict, it was to play a minor part in the first few years of the long war. Leaving the defence of the Duchy in the capable hands of his Seneschal, Sir Oliver D'Ingham, Edward began hostilities with a brief and largely inconclusive campaign in Flanders. His strategic problem was this: somehow the war had to be taken to the King of France, Gascony was a huge distance to move an army, and Flanders had been less than successful as a means of challenging the French King. So how was he to obtain a toehold? Where was the door that would let him in? On 30 April 1341 that new door opened.

THE BRITTANY ADVENTURE

That day marked the death of John III, Duke of Brittany. Of all the great French feudatories none had maintained such an independence of mind and action as had the Dukes of Brittany. They were peers of France by virtue of the Duchy, but linked historically with the kings of England, the latter connection dating back to the time of William the Conqueror, who had presented the 'Honour of Richmond' to Alan Rufus of Brittany. The lands of the Honour of Richmond, which included large tracts of North Yorkshire and Richmond Castle, and the title of Earl of Richmond, were thereafter held in the gift of the sovereign of England, and bestowed upon, or withheld from, successive Dukes of Brittany depending upon the allegiance they were currently professing.

The present occasion of a succession dispute for the Duchy, following John III's death, provided Edward III with a valuable opportunity to support one claimant (there was inevitably a pro-French and a pro-English faction) and thereby legitimately carry out operations on the French mainland. The 'English' claimant was John de Montfort, who enjoyed an early success, then crossed to England to seek further support from Edward III, whom he eagerly acknowledged as King of France. Edward, in return, invested him as Earl of Richmond. Meanwhile the French nominee, Charles de Blois, the son-in-law of the King of France, quickly entered the lists, and managed to capture John de Montfort after a siege of Nantes. It appeared that the War of Succession was over almost before it had begun. There remained, however, de Montfort's wife, Joan, Countess of Flanders, whom Charles de Blois had besieged in the town of Hennebont on the west coast of Brittany.

The relief of Hennebont was the ideal expedition for Edward to begin his Brittany adventures. The voyage

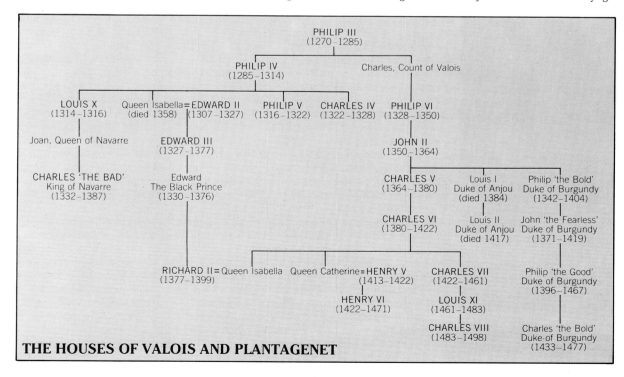

THE HOUSES OF VALOIS AND PLANTAGENET

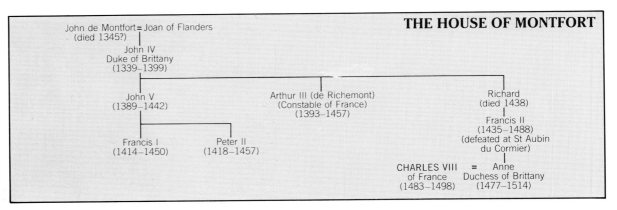

THE HOUSE OF MONTFORT

John de Montfort = Joan of Flanders
(died 1345?)

John IV
Duke of Brittany
(1339–1399)

John V
(1389–1442)

Arthur III (de Richemont)
(Constable of France)
(1393–1457)

Richard
(died 1438)

Francis II
(1435–1488)
(defeated at St Aubin
du Cormier)

Francis I
(1414–1450)

Peter II
(1418–1457)

CHARLES VIII = Anne
of France   Duchess of Brittany
(1483–1498) (1477–1514)

would involve a long sea journey round Cape Finistere, but it was familiar enough sea for those accustomed to the much longer journey to Aquitaine. Nevertheless, with the vagaries of wind and weather the trip took nearly two months, by which time Hennebont had almost surrendered under the pounding of a great catapult. The relieving force was led by a Hainault knight, Sir Walter Manny, whose later exploits fill so many paragraphs of Froissart's heroic chronicles. His ships ran the blockade, and after sharing as generous a banquet as the besieged Countess could provide, added to his reputation by sallying with a detachment of English knights and destroying the catapult.

So a foothold was gained in the name of the de Montfort cause. Now it had to be maintained. The area of the de Montfort support was confined to the south-west of the peninsular, attainable only by sea, while the French could rapidly reinforce an army by land from the east. The difficulty was illustrated in the following year, when the Earl of Northampton landed an army at Brest and began to lay siege to the French-held town of Morlaix. Immediately Charles de Blois set out to challenge him from his base at Guingamp to the east. His army was large, evidence of the control his faction exerted over most of the peninsular,

and Northampton was outnumbered by a probable factor of four to one. Abandoning the siege he advanced to meet the French threat.

THE FIRST BATTLE

The Battle of Morlaix was fought on 30 September 1342, and is noteworthy, if for no other reason, in that it was the first pitched battle of the Hundred Years War. Although totally overshadowed by Crécy and Poitiers, it involved features common to both those famous encounters: the English army outnumbered, a defensive position, and the devastating use of archers. The first of the three factors has already been noted. The second surely indicates the presence in Edward's army of at least one very senior veteran of Bannockburn, for the English dug trenches, covered with grass and brushwood, as booby traps for the French knights. The third factor, the archers, came into play very early in the action, when Charles de Blois sent on ahead a dismounted attack by locally levied troops. The arrows quickly broke the attack before the line of trenches was reached, leaving the surprise intact for the second attack by the mounted knights. The combination of traps and arrows halted this attack as surely as the first, but Charles de Blois had one division left, considerably

Left: Funerary monument of Duke John III of Brittany. It was the death of this Duke in 1341 which precipitated a succession dispute and the Breton Civil War, used by Edward III of England as a pretext for carrying out military operations on the French mainland.
Right: The fortified gateway of the town of Hennebont in Brittany, scene of one of the earliest engagements of the Hundred Years War. Besieged in Hennebont by Charles de Blois, the Countess of Flanders appealed to Edward III for help, which was rendered in the form of a relieving force under Sir Walter Manny.

larger than the first two, and after two 'showers' of arrows the archers were beginning to run short of ammunition. Taking advantage of a lull between attacks, the Earl of Northampton led his men in an organized withdrawal to the wood immediately to the rear of his positions, where the ground cover would give extra protection. After failing to force their way into the wood the French withdrew, giving Northampton the chance to break out and regain the defensive siege line of Morlaix.

The battle, therefore, was far from being decisive, but it had provided valuable experience for both sides. The English once again were able to appreciate the strength of a sensible combination of archers and dismounted knights, and had confirmation that the tactics forced on them at Dupplin Moor and tested at Halidon Hill, could at the very least nullify the strong French attack, even if it would not guarantee an absolute victory. This is a very important point to note with reference to the more elaborate campaigns of Edward III that were to come. The English tactics were not a guarantee of victory, but were the very best insurance policy against defeat.

Winter, however, was fast approaching. Feeling no immediate need for his presence in the west, Charles de Blois withdrew to winter quarters in Nantes which, with

Rennes and Vannes, was one of the three towns that guarded Brittany's eastern frontier. As the English were at that time confined to movements around the coast of Brittany, Robert d'Artois, a renegade French knight whose presence at Edward's court had been an annoyance to the King of France, decided to sail from Hennebont and besiege Nantes. This was a bold move, and out of keeping with the contemporary view that campaigns were suspended in winter-time. He was, however, forced away from Nantes by the French fleet and instead of returning to Hennebont landed near Vannes, the second city of Brittany, and laid it to siege.

The approach of winter made a quick result desirable. The siege of Vannes therefore became a series of furious assaults against its great wall, much of which stands to this day. D'Artois made good use of his archers, who kept up such a consistent covering fire as to clear the battlements of defenders, while the knights advanced to the assault. The attacks were beaten off, but a stratagem after dark drew the attention of the defenders away from a quiet section of the walls, enabling a detachment to raise scaling ladders and attack from within. The French garrison fled, including the city's governor, Olivier de Clisson, whose future son of the same name was to become prominent during the Wars. The disaster however, woke Charles de Blois to the inadvisability of taking to winter quarters while a hostile army was still at large. He thereupon reinforced de Clisson's army, who returned to the fray and managed to dislodge d'Artois from his new conquest. When Edward III landed at Brest in October 1342 it was to hear that d'Artois was dead.

Nevertheless, the confidence which Edward's previous victories and those of this commanders had given him was such that on his arrival he determined to attack all three of the major Breton cities simultaneously. Rennes, Vannes and Nantes were the targets, and it is worth noting that on the approach to them Edward forbade all burning and pillaging, in marked contrast to the later style of warfare that he was to develop. As an attempt to win support from the populace it is to be admired, and one must assume that feeding arrangements had been taken care of. The very boldness of the attempt, for it was now mid-November, was enough to make Charles withdraw from Nantes and appeal for help from the French King. Philip responded, and commanded the army in person.

If Edward's companions had been expecting an early confrontation between the two monarchs they were to be disappointed. Edward was besieging Vannes, again confined to the west coast, and threatened from the north by the combined armies of the King of France and Charles de Blois. Not yet ready to take on such a host, Edward sent urgent requests to England for reinforcements, and prepared to turn his siege lines into defensive ones facing in the opposite direction. Then fate took a hand. The French king's nerve must have failed him. Perhaps Charles de Blois had reminded him of what had happened at Morlaix. Anyhow a truce, the Truce of Malestroit, was drawn up stating simply that each side should keep what it had except for Vannes, which would be neutral. So the two parties withdrew for home. The first Brittany campaign was over. On the face of it little seemed to have been achieved, but the young Edward had been able to test himself and his armies on the mainland of Europe, and as a 'pilot project' the results were encouraging. It had all been a very gentlemanly affair, compared with what was to follow.

Right: Effigy of Sir John de Hardreshull, who held the office of Lieutenant of Brittany from 1343 to 1344, in the church at Ashton, Nottinghamshire.
Centre: Charles de Blois was the French-supported claimant to the Dukedom of Brittany during the Civil War which marked the entry of England into the Hundred Years War. He was captured by the English at the siege of la Roche-Derrien in 1347, and killed at the Battle of Auray in 1364.
Far right: Two civilians, c. 1380, depicted on brasses at King's Somborne in Hampshire. The life of the non-knightly classes formed the background against which knightly exploits were carried out.

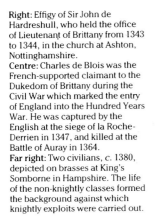
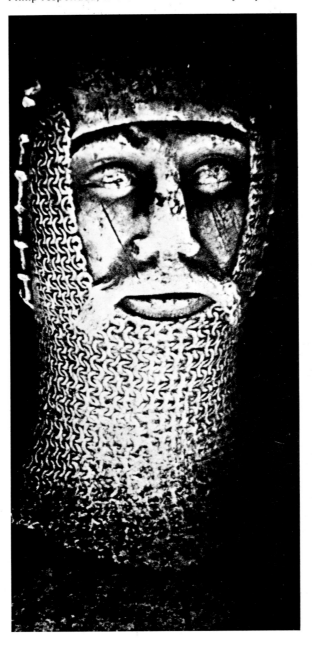

3. The Practice of War

MILITARY HISTORY that concentrated on the art while ignoring the practice of war would be doing less than justice to its subject. To the knights who fought in the Hundred Years War the 'Art of War' was concerned with fighting battles against other knights, of doing brave deeds and seeing them recorded by the chroniclers, many of whom were present at battles like a squad of fourteenth-century war correspondents. Their role, however, was not to produce candid, eye-witness accounts of their observations, the better to inform the public, but to select and produce that which the knightly classes wished to hear.

The picture that has come down to us from the pages of Froissart, with its brave challenges, its combat and its courtesy to captured nobles, therefore represents a very minor part of the activity that went on under the name of war. Battles, for that is basically what Froissart is concerned with, lasted a few hours. War lasted weeks or months. Battles involved knights as fighters and leaders. War involved them as commanders, disciplinarians and, very frequently, self-seeking parasites as bad as the once pardoned felons they led. Battles were fought by soldiers. War was fought by nations in arms, and included priests, civilians, women and children, as fighters and victims. Above all, in the 1340s and 1350s, when the names of Crécy and Poitiers pass into history, battles such as these provided welcome relief from the day to day practice of war.

THE RAISING OF ARMIES

It would be appropriate at this stage to look at the means whereby these armies were recruited. The days of feudal service, mentioned briefly at the beginning of the book, were drawing rapidly to a close, and paid service was beginning to take the place of service by right or obligation.

Edward III of England had to raise an army consisting of much more than noble knights. Beside the indispensable archers were labourers, servants and sailors, all to be accommodated because of the particular talents they had to offer. Miners were much in demand when siege operations were contemplated. The ancient manner of recruiting men of lower rank was by 'Commission of Array'. The commissioners appointed by the King would confine themselves to their particular county and were required to raise troops. The process began with the choosing, testing and arraying of the available levies; clothing, equipping and paying them. The orders for an Array naturally specified that the Commissioners choose the best men available, but this was not always done. A levy of archers arrayed in 1341 were noted as being 'feeble'.

The second method of raising troops, and the one which Edward III was to refine to an efficient operation, was the raising of armies by Contract. A number of knights would act as recruiting agents, and would draw up a Contract with the King for the number and type of soldiers they would provide. These Contract Captains would then sub-contract with the soldiers they acquired.

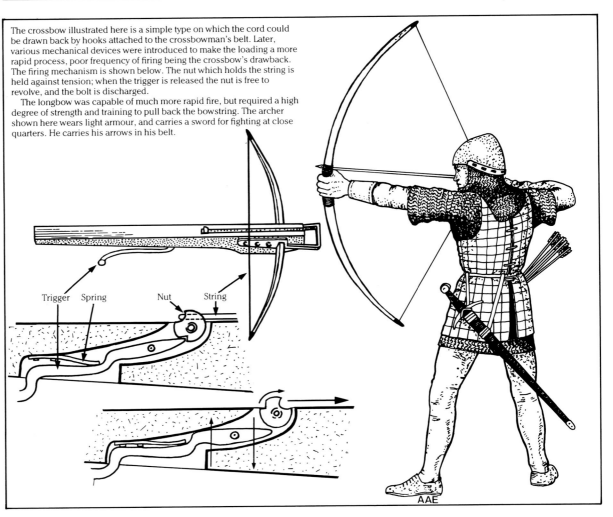

The crossbow illustrated here is a simple type on which the cord could be drawn back by hooks attached to the crossbowman's belt. Later, various mechanical devices were introduced to make the loading a more rapid process, poor frequency of firing being the crossbow's drawback. The firing mechanism is shown below. The nut which holds the string is held against tension; when the trigger is released the nut is free to revolve, and the bolt is discharged.

The longbow was capable of much more rapid fire, but required a high degree of strength and training to pull back the bowstring. The archer shown here wears light armour, and carries a sword for fighting at close quarters. He carries his arrows in his belt.

Trigger   Spring   Nut   String

The details drawn up would include the number of men, their ranks, their rates of pay and period of service. The latter item was usually fixed as forty days initially, with extensions at given rates. The daily rates of pay from early in Edward III's reign were: earl 6s 8d; banneret 4s 0d; knight 2s; man-at-arms 1s; mounted archer 6d; foot archer 3d; Welsh spearman 2d. In 1341 the Earl of Warwick supplied under contract 3 bannerets; 26 knights, 71 men-at-arms; 40 'armed men' and 100 archers.

The third manner of recruiting an army was by volunteers. Under certain circumstances, criminals could gain a pardon for service and as many as one in ten of Edward's army may have been ex-outlaws. But from 1346 onwards it was not only criminals that were tempted to volunteer. Early successes brought back tales of plunder to be had, and certain commanders soon acquired a reputation for generosity with their troops. A leader skilled in war would have no trouble in recruiting, and Sir John Chandos, who began his career with very meagre lands, could by 1359 collect an army of willing followers which surpassed in size and quality that of any of the nobility. The overall needs of Edward III for large numbers of troops at short notice for possibly long campaigns encouraged a change from levies such as those described above to paid service, although the knightly 'feudatories' formed an initial nucleus.

THE ROAD TO TOTAL WAR

On 12 July 1346, Edward III landed at Saint-Vaast, at the tip of the Cotentin peninsular, to begin what has become known as the Crécy campaign. Edward had landed in France with the intention of making war upon the French king, in a larger and more thorough operation than either the Flanders or Brittany expeditions. The fighting of a battle, let alone a decisive battle involving a major clash of arms, must have been regarded at best as an optional extra if conditions were right, and, at worst an event to be scrupulously avoided at all costs. How then could Edward be contemplating war without actively courting battle?

The answer to this apparent paradox lies in the nature of fourteenth-century warfare and of the attitudes of the knights towards it. It is very clear that the knights who fought for Edward III were under no illusions about the nature of the tasks they were required to undertake, tasks which took them very far from their purely military use as heavy cavalry, and even farther from their ideals of chivalrous conduct.

The first characteristic of fourteenth-century warfare was that so far as existing communications would allow, it was total war. The Hundred Years War was a conflict between two nations, and in terms of taxation and loans to finance it, the whole population was involved in paying. So, whether they marched with the armies or not, those who had financed it expected results, as shown by numerous parliaments that were decidedly cool about making further finance available. As a result it is hardly surprising to see great development in the use of propaganda, designed largely to arouse consciousness in the involvement against the enemy. The use of such methods against the Scots was noted briefly in the account of the siege of Berwick. Through letters and dispatches, through pulpit and market-place, those concerned with the preparations for war, the transport of troops and supplies, the voting of taxes and the prayers for the dead, were all made aware of their part in the great enterprise.

Total war has two sides, however. The foregoing records the need and ability of the population to give. The other side of the coin notes their suffering. If the former were found in both countries during the Hundred Years War, the latter was confined disproportionately to France. Scottish raids across the border (often immaculately timed to coincide with English involvement in France) and a succession of French raids across the Channel (which the naval battle of Sluys halted for twenty years) did little more than add to Edward's propaganda efforts against his enemies. But the bulk of English operations in France, far from being battle-seeking, honour-seeking, marches to knightly glory, consisted of the systematic application of the means of destruction to the civilian population.

The most deadly of these was fire. Destruction of an enemy's property by burning was not new in the practice of war, nor was it confined to the English operations in France, but the course of the movement of English armies was always marked by a wide swathe of burned ground, leaving no habitable building for men or beasts. The French historian, Denifle, wrote that 'fire was the constant ally of the English', and the chronicler Baker, more ready than many of his contemporaries to describe this aspect of warfare, described the scene near Cambrai one dark night in 1339, during one of Edward's first incursions into Europe. From the top of a church tower he could see the countryside lit up for miles in every direction from the fires of the English.

Destruction by fire was only the final stage of the process of devastation carried out during these expeditions, for which the French term 'chevauchée' is commonly employed. The first stage consisted quite simply of obtaining food and drink for the army as it went on its way. Some food was brought from England, and lines of communication were maintained as best they might, but 'living off the land' was imperative if the invading army was to survive. The second stage of the destructive process, plunder, is best illustrated by the first major action fought by Edward III during the Crécy campaign. He had advanced down the Contentin peninsular, and a certain amount of pillaging had taken place to augment supplies, but there were other instances of pillaging that went far beyond the needs of the army. Various historians have suggested these stemmed from lawless elements within the King's army, or revenge by those troops whose south coast towns had had to suffer marauding from the French. Whatever the reason, on approaching the town of Caen the official policy was to be little different.

From the military point of view the capture of Caen is an excellent example of the taking of a town by assault. As a means of conducting warfare such an approach had much to recommend it. It spared both sides from the discomfort of a siege and forced a result comparatively quickly. Assaults were carried out simultaneously on various gates of the town, and Edward's fleet also played an important part. As he had advanced eastwards the ships had followed, conducting a chevauchée of their own along the Normandy coast. Reaching the mouth of the River Orne it had sailed up to Caen about the same time as the army were attacking the town. This was probably more by luck than judgement, as such synchronization of land and sea forces was very difficult to organize. The arrival of the fleet enabled prisoners, wounded and booty to be sent back to England.

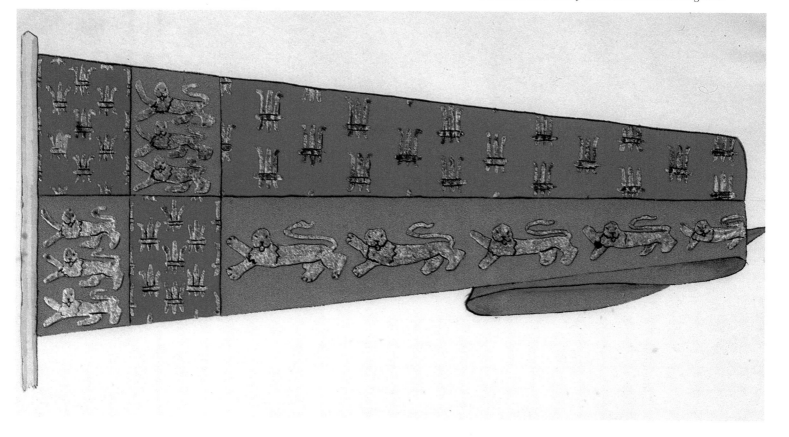

Below: The standard of Edward III, proclaiming on a grand heraldic scale his claim to the French throne.

We are told by one chronicler that Edward had it proclaimed throughout his army that no one should imprison women, children, nuns or monks or harm their churches and houses. His order appears to have been totally ineffectual. According to Froissart, Sir Thomas Holland 'mounted his horse and rode into the streets and saved many lives of ladies, damosels, and cloisterers from defoiling, for the soldiers were without mercy'. Godfrey de Harcourt brought the situation to the King's notice, and then rode from street to street trying to enforce order. Froissart blames the depredations upon the 'bad fellows and evildoers who must inevitably be found in a king's army'.

In fact, the plunderers came from every social rank. One anonymous chronicler records that: 'The English desiring spoils brought back to the ships only jewelled clothing or very valuable ornaments.' The proximity of the fleet made it easier to get the loot home than on most campaigns. Froissart notes that the ships were 'charged with clothes, jewels, vessels of gold and silver . . .' By 1348 much of it had been dispersed throughout England. Walsingham claims that: 'There were few women who did not possess something from Caen, Calais or other overseas towns, such as clothing, furs, cushions. Table-cloths and linen were seen in everybody's houses. Married women were decked in the trimmings of French matrons, and if the latter sorrowed over their loss, the former rejoiced in their gain.'

The strangest item of plunder from the sack of Caen was a single document. It had been written at Vincennes in 1339, and set out in detail the plans of the French King for invading England. It included military arrangements

Below: The Battle of Crécy, 1346, from Froissart's *Chronicles*. Note the English longbowmen in action against the French crossbowmen, one of whom is seen reloading his weapon.

between the King and the Duke of Normandy, sources for finance and the maintenance of sea communications, and even the division of spoils. The document was immediately taken to London by the Earl of Huntingdon, where it was read publicly by the Archbishop of Canterbury at Saint Paul's churchyard. The details may have been several years out of date, but the find contributed greatly to the propaganda side of Edward's war effort.

Such was the chevauchée. But how, it may be asked, did it fit into the practice of war? What was the point? The answer is that for the majority of the campaigns of the Hundred Years War the chevauchée *was* the practice of war. Its ultimate aim was political. France was too large a country for occupation to be considered. Garrisoning even parts of it, such as Brittany and Normandy, were expensive in terms of soldiers' wages and the inevitability of sieges, as we shall see in later studies of Brittany and Henry V's campaigns. The chevauchée did rapidly what occupation took so long to do. It demonstrated the power of the English King and challenged the French King to react either by defence or counter-attack.

In the 1340s and 1350s neither technique had been perfected to such a degree that it could dissuade an enemy from using a chevauchée-style of warfare. If there were no reaction, loyalty to the king was seriously undermined, and it should be remembered that both monarchs were striving to retain the loyalty of their men, and loyalty depended upon success. The other argument for the chevauchée is that in inflicting devastation upon the non-combatant population, political and financial pressure was brought upon the French King. Devastated areas could not pay taxes, and without taxes armies could not be paid. Thus in a non-military way, with every likelihood of success, war was continued steadily, in marked contrast to the ultimate sanction of a pitched battle. We must also remember that at this stage in the war Edward had only limited experience from which to judge how his army might fare against a full French army. In the Brittany campaign the results of Morlaix had been encouraging but inconclusive. A further victory in Gascony in 1345 must have added to his confidence. This was the Battle of Auberoche, fought on 21 October. Little is known of this engagement, which arose from a limited expedition to Gascony under Henry of Lancaster, accompanied by the formidable Sir Walter Manny. A French army was besieging Auberoche castle, which the English had recently taken, and were themselves surprised by another English army, who approached them through woods, the archers and men-at-arms advancing by different routes – a potentially hazardous operation.

Successful though both these campaigns were, they were not enough to provoke the French King into committing his entire army to battle. Not that this would be entirely necessary to Edward's plans. The French King was being hounded enough without that particular gamble.

BATTLE OF CRECY

Whatever the aim of the current campaign, whether it was just another chevauchée or whether Edward did have some other objective in mind, we shall never know, for he had kept even the destination of their landing secret from his men until they had set sail, and had let it be known that his mighty army was intended for the relief of Gascony. Regardless of the initial aim, it was a campaign that ended in a battle, a battle so overwhelming in the victory gained that it was to become the best-known engagement of the entire Hundred Years War – the Battle of Crécy.

Crécy was fought because Edward III was trying to avoid the army of the King of France until he could join forces with a Flemish army which had invaded France at the same time. Once Philip got on Edward's tail all notions of a chevauchée were abandoned in favour of a rapid march north to link up with his allies. The operation (which would be repeated in the following century by Henry V and, again, would lead to a crushing victory) reflected great credit on both sides – until the fighting began.

The Flemish army, accompanied by a small English contingent, set out at the beginning of August. At that time they were about 200 miles away, separated from Edward by two formidable rivers, the Seine and the Somme. Philip was at Rouen, forcing Edward to find a crossing farther upstream in the direction of Paris. For the next ten days the rival armies shadowed each other on opposite banks of the Seine. Louviers was sacked, and the castle of Gaillon captured, but not until Poissy was a bridge found. This was only partly destroyed and was weakly guarded. As Philip appeared to be continuing upstream Edward took his chance. Sending his son, the Black Prince, on towards Paris as a diversion to keep Philip guessing, the bridge was repaired and the army crossed on 16 August. Edward headed due north, aiming for a point on the Somme about midway between Abbeville and Amiens, where he might expect to encounter the Flemings in about a week's time.

Having so successfully given Philip the slip, it must have been with some astonishment that Edward arrived on the Somme on 21 August to learn from his scouts that Philip's army had already crossed at Amiens and were ahead of him on the opposite bank. It may not have been his entire army, for they would have had to cover 24 miles a day to make up Edward's lead, but the fact remained that Philip had triumphed in the pursuit. Four miles lay between him and Edward. Fifty-five miles lay between Edward and the Flemings, and a reconnaissance force under the Earl of Warwick reported that all known crossings were impregnable.

The solution was provided by one Gobin Agache, a French prisoner. In return for the offer of a handsome reward, Agache disclosed the existence of a ford at Blanchetaque, where a man could cross at low tide in water at knee height. The army moved off before dawn to cover the six miles to Blanchetaque, and waited for the tide to fall as the army closed up behind its advance guard. Philip had anticipated the move and had guarded Blanchetaque with a force of 500 knights and 3,000 infantry, including Genoese crossbowmen. The crossing was led by Hugh Despenser, and was uneventful until they came within range of the crossbows, but the English archers managed to scatter them and the crossing proceeded. This itself was quite an achievement and no doubt the surprise element contributed a great deal; but the duel between longbow and crossbow was a foretaste of what was to come.

Edward had thus successfully surmounted the second of the two major physical obstacles in his path. All the omens were favourable; his army was in good shape, they had acquitted themselves well and morale was high. It was at this point that Edward made his fateful and historic decision not to wait for the Flemish army but to give battle, on ground of his choosing, to the French army that had pursued him. The ground he chose was on a ridge immediately to the north-east of the village of Crécy. The ridge is formed by a small valley, the Vallée des Clercs, the eastern end of which merges into a plateau immediately before the village of Wadicourt. On the highest point of the ridge stood a windmill, an ideal command post, while on the right flank attack was discouraged by the village of Crécy and the river which runs through it. The English numbered between 12,000 and 13,000. Their right wing was commanded by young Prince Edward, then only sixteen years old, with Godfrey Harcourt to assist him. The left wing was occupied by the Earl of Northampton, whose action at Morlaix had been carried out under similar circumstances. The lines of battle stretched between them, the archers deployed in wedge-shaped formations to enable them to provide fire that would force the French cavalry to concentrate in towards the part of the line held by the dismounted English knights. All afternoon they waited. A brief storm forced the archers to disconnect their precious bowstrings, which they placed in their caps to keep dry.

The French army was composed of a number of different contingents. The 'regular' troops consisted of the King's personal retinue of household troops, and the Genoese mercenaries, who always fought as one body under their own commander. Next came the foreign armies: the blind King of Bohemia with his son Charles, King of the Romans; John of Hainault, who was brother-in-law of Edward III's Queen Philippa; the Duke of Savoy, and James I, King of Majorca. There were also considerable numbers of levied French troops, indicating that the English were outnumbered, though by much inferior soldiers.

The French advanced late in the afternoon of 26 August 1346, their unwieldy and uncoordinated movement being noted by the English on the ridge, and in particular the English King high in the windmill. The Genoese crossbowmen led the way, to be met at a range of 150 yards by a tremendous volley of longbow arrows. They also had the doubtful distinction of being the first soldiers in European warfare to be subjected to cannon fire in open battle. The

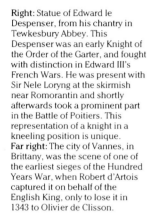

Right: Statue of Edward le Despenser, from his chantry in Tewkesbury Abbey. This Despenser was an early Knight of the Order of the Garter, and fought with distinction in Edward III's French Wars. He was present with Sir Nele Loryng at the skirmish near Romorantin and shortly afterwards took a prominent part in the Battle of Poitiers. This representation of a knight in a kneeling position is unique.
Far right: The city of Vannes, in Brittany, was the scene of one of the earliest sieges of the Hundred Years War, when Robert d'Artois captured it on behalf of the English King, only to lose it in 1343 to Olivier de Clisson.

Right: The windmill at Crécy as it was before its demolition by a patriotic Frenchman in 1898. Edward III used it as his command post during the battle.

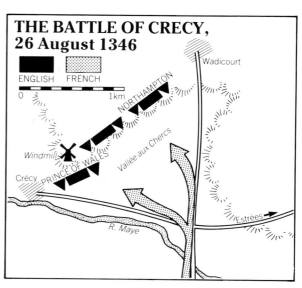

THE BATTLE OF CRECY, 26 August 1346

ENGLISH   FRENCH

0   1km

Wadicourt

NORTHAMPTON

Windmill

PRINCE OF WALES

Vallée aux Chercs

Crécy

Estrées

R. Maye

combined effect was too much for them. The Genoese broke and fled, but coming up behind was the division of the Duke of Alençon. Accusing the Genoese of treachery, his knights rode them down and pressed on to engage the Prince of Wales's division. Soon the whole line was fighting, the French casualties to the hail of arrows being quickly replaced from the rear.

It was at this point that the well-known incident concerning the Black Prince, recounted by Froissart, occurred. Fearing for the safety of his young charge, Godfrey Harcourt requested the Earl of Arundel to launch a flank attack to relieve the pressure on the Prince, and at the same time asked the King for reinforcements. By the time the messenger reached Edward in the windmill, the King could see that the flank attack had already taken place, so there was no need to risk his precious reserve. 'Let the boy win his spurs,' was his alleged comment. Baker says that, in fact, a small force of knights, probably under the command of the Bishop of Durham, were sent, and found the Prince in good heart and with more than a thousand French dead before his troops. The Battle of Crécy continued until after dark, leaving dead on the field among others, King John of Bohemia and the elder brother of Charles de Blois. Monks from the nearby abbey listed the dead. The total of French lords and knights numbered 1,542, and of the lower ranks there were many more.

What were the reasons for the victory? Clearly, Crécy was the culmination of the process which had triumphed at Morlaix, Dupplin Moor and Halidon Hill. The knights dismounted, and the two arms of archers and men-at-arms supported each other in a disciplined coordination of effort. The French, on the other hand, were an army of mixed nationalities, with vague leadership and no cooperation. Their missile troops – the Genoese – were concentrated in one body, and directed against one portion of the line largely because they were mercenaries and would only fight that way.

Crécy was the remarkable end to a remarkable campaign. The chevauchées would continue, but never again

would Edward III be wary of engaging a French army on his own terms. It was not only the Black Prince who had won his spurs that day.

THE YEAR OF VICTORIES

As the terrible chevauchée has been our theme in this chapter, it is worth continuing with a brief account of another battle that resulted from a chevauchée operation, but one this time directed against England – Neville's Cross.

In his distress at the defeat of Crécy, Philip begged King David II of Scotland to invade England. This David seems to have been willing enough to do for he crossed the border with quite a large army and advanced towards Durham, laying waste many places *en route*, including the abbey of Lanercost. A commission set up later to look into the losses suffered by one landowner from this raid, Robert Herle of Northumberland, reported that on 15 October, a Sunday, five villages were laid waste; the houses and crops were burned, and the tenants plundered of 70 oxen, 83 cows, 142 bullocks, 32 heifers, 316 sheep, and other goods. What, the tenants might have asked, was a King of England going to do about it? The point has been made earlier about the response to raiding on any scale, that of defence and retribution. The former had already been carried out, and the latter was soon to follow. Before leaving for France Edward had guarded against the possibility of Scottish attack by deliberately excluding from recruitment any men from north of the Humber. As the Bishop of Durham was fighting beside the King in France, the task of organizing defensive measures fell upon the Archbishop of York. Assisted by the northern lords, notably Sir Ralph Neville and Sir Henry Percy, and probably the ex-King of Scotland, Edward Balliol, he assembled an army of comparable size to the Scots, whom he found encamped near Durham.

It must have pleased the English commander, Sir Ralph Neville, to discover that the place at which they decided to make a stand against the Scots bore his name – Neville's Cross. It lies on a ridge of hilly ground to the west

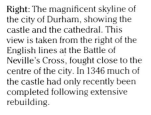

Right: The magnificent skyline of the city of Durham, showing the castle and the cathedral. This view is taken from the right of the English lines at the Battle of Neville's Cross, fought close to the centre of the city. In 1346 much of the castle had only recently been completed following extensive rebuilding.

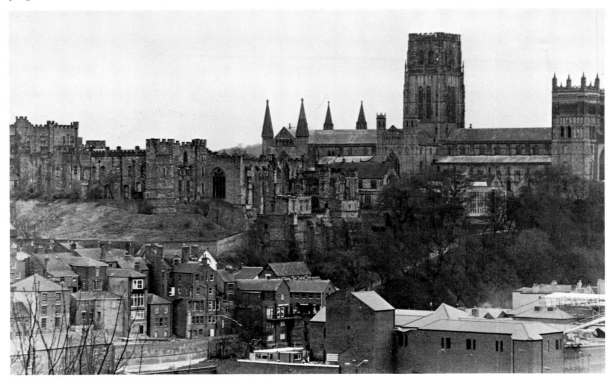

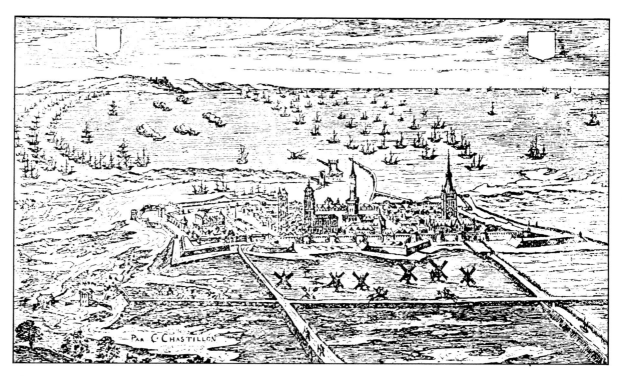

Right: The defence and supply of the town of Calais was always given top priority in any English strategic plan. For fourteen years, following its capture in 1347, it was supplied totally from England.
Below: The site of the Battle of Neville's Cross (1346), looking north towards the valley which divided the Scottish line in two. As they advanced across this broken ground the terrain naturally turned the wings in on each other, adding considerably to the effect of the English archery, which produced another notable victory in the year of Crécy.
Overleaf: A mêlée at a tournament, miniature from a manuscript entitled: 'Traité de la forme at devis comme on fait les tournois' by Rene of Anjou.

of Durham, a site comparable to that of Crécy, and Neville probably adopted dispositions similar to those of Crécy. The presence of the Archbishop of York, and the threat to the holy relics of St Cuthbert preserved in Durham cathedral, made the affair into something of a crusade. Perhaps remembering the stories they had been told about the Battle of the Standard in 1138, a group of monks left the city and proceeded, bearing the banner of St Cuthbert, into the area between the armies, where they knelt in prayer.

The two elements of the Scottish right wing came down the hills in schiltron formation, but became entangled with each other in a ravine, whereupon the English archers poured in their deadly fire on the disordered Scots. The English knights then swept down in as neat a combination of arms as would have distinguished the King of England himself. David of Scotland was captured, and languished in the Tower for some years.

While his countrymen were fighting the Scots, Edward was settling in to a year-long operation to capture the port of Calais. The town was well defended, so blockading and slow starvation were the only weapons suitable. The siege lasted until August 1347, by which time a relieving force under King Philip had arrived before the gates, only to withdraw shortly afterwards – perhaps the memory of Crécy was too fresh. The well-known story of how the

surrender was accepted from six burgesses of Calais, bare-headed and with halters round their necks, was the dramatic and humiliating climax. The embellishment that Edward wished to have them executed, but was dissuaded by his Queen is probably apocryphal. His intention was to make Calais an English town, and he had no reason to alienate the population, though such an act was entirely in character, and we have seen similar behaviour on his part at Berwick.

THE POWER OF THE BOW

King David soon had company in the Tower. Another English army had been active in Brittany under Sir Thomas Dagworth, keeping up the nominal cause of the house of de Montfort for the Dukedom, even though the heir to the title was still a prisoner of his rival, Charles de Blois. On 9 June 1346, two months before Crécy, Sir Thomas Dagworth's army was attacked by a much larger force under Charles de Blois at Saint-Pol-de-Léon, in the north-west of Brittany. Although repulsing the first assault a second wave of cavalry charges followed, so that Dagworth's little force had to face attacks from three sides as the French army enveloped them. Once again an English army took a stand and poured in such a vicious flight of arrows that a virtual massacre ensued. Thus three times in one year three separate armies, fighting in widely different places, used broadly similar tactics to achieve notable victories.

Charles de Blois raised a fresh army in 1347 and laid siege to the English-held town of la Roche-Derrien. Sir Thomas Dagworth at the head of a relieving force led a surprise night attack on the French camp. Resistance was stiff, inspired by Charles de Blois who emerged from his tent with no armour, and plunged gallantly into the fray, until he was captured. It was he who came to join the King of Scotland in his lonely sojourn, ending another phase in the long story of the 'sideshow' of the Breton Civil War. So the year that had begun as a ride of havoc ended as a procession of triumph. The combination of knights and archers, on and off the battlefield, had resulted in a year of victories.

KNIGHTS IN ARMOUR

It is appropriate to pause at this stage and look at the means of defence currently being employed by the knights, which seemed to be proving so ineffectual against the use of mass archery.

During the fourteenth century the overall trend was the gradual transition from mail to plate armour. When the century began mail was worn everywhere on the body,

Right: One of the grave pits excavated at Wisby in Sweden, where a Danish army defeated a levied army of Swedes in 1361. Many of the bodies bear evidence of fatal head wounds caused by arrows piercing their mail hoods. Helmets of plate, the best defence against arrows, were still owned only by the better-off sections of society.

Opposite page, left: Brass of Thomas Cheyne, Esq., from Drayton Beauchamp, Buckinghamshire. Note the close-fitting 'gipon' worn over the armour, and the sword belt slung around the hips. His helmet, a 'bascinet' bears an 'aventail' of mail. At this time, the mid-fourteenth century, plate armour was far from complete, and the leg defences are of brigadine.

Opposite page, right: Sir John de Cobham wears a suit of armour that would have been common on the battlefields of Crécy or Poitiers. This style of bascinet has cheek-pieces to protect the face, and there is greater use of plate to protect the body.

except for a helmet and perhaps plate defences for the knees. Extra plates were added every few years, until by the end of the century their descendants rode into battle completely encased in plate.

The great lesson of the longbow was: the extreme vulnerability of mail to a swift, sharp arrow. Crossbow missiles had a similar effect, but it was the sheer quantity of longbow arrows fired that made their deadliness so noticeable. The crossbow, however, was responsible for the most dramatic surviving evidence of the vulnerability of mail. In 1361 a Danish royal army slaughtered a levied army of Swedish peasants and townsmen at Wisby. The sole protection for the Swedes was mail, and after the battle their bodies were heaped into a mass grave. Excavations of the grave during the 1930s revealed that at least 125 men had suffered fatal headwounds from arrows and crossbow bolts which had struck their mail hoods. In many cases the arrowheads were found inside the skulls.

Mail afforded better protection against a swordstroke where there was no direct piercing action, but here again the results could be serious, for a strongly driven cutting stroke, though not parting the mail, could drive the links down into the flesh and produce a very nasty wound.

The first plate additions took the form of roundels to protect the elbow joints and armpits, linked by plates along the outside of the arm called rerebraces for the upper arm and vambraces for the lower. Metal shinguards called schynbalds and plate shoes called sabatons provided defence for the leg. A knight who fought at Bannockburn would probably have worn this form of armour. By the time of Halidon Hill, in 1333, plate gauntlets were available instead of mail mittens, and an additional plate headpiece, attached to the mail hood, might be worn under the helmet.

The development of armour to protect the torso is more difficult to elucidate, largely because most monumental effigies of the period show a surcoat which almost completely covers what lies beneath. It seems clear, however, that as the long surcoats became shorter, some form of body armour was developed, either as a single breastplate, to which the sword, helmet or dagger could be attached by chains, or a series of plates, which we know eventually extended round the wearer's back as well.

The picture of Crécy which comes down to us, therefore, is one of tremendous development taking place in defensive armour, but perhaps not rapidly enough to cope with the development of archery. Full plate armour was on its way, but for the present it looked as though the knight had met his match.

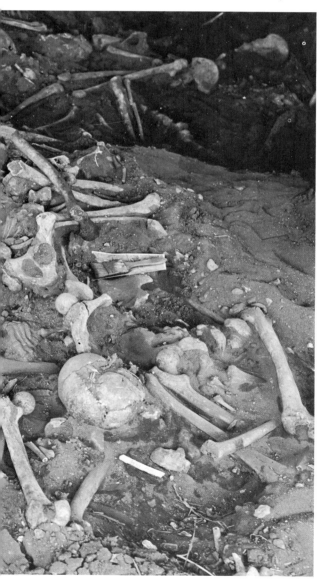

Right: Tomb of Hugh Despenser and his wife, Elizabeth Montacute. Sir Hugh's effigy, dated about 1349, illustrates the style of armour which is probably typical of the time of the Crécy campaign.

Right: The magnificent skyline of the town and fortress of Carcassonne, burned by the army of the Black Prince in 1355, as part of his far-reaching chevauchée designed to defend the frontiers of English Gascony.

4. A King's Ransom

N THE LAST chapter it was argued that the practice of chevauchée raiding, which appears at first sight to be a regrettable and cruel addition to the practice of war, in fact formed a vital part of it, and that battles and combat between knights were the exception to this general pattern. It now remains to ask how the chevauchée idea fitted in with the *art* of war, in other words with the knightly code of behaviour – the art of chivalry. Were such activities as burning, looting and ransom not contrary to the tenets of chivalry? If they were, and continued to be practised on such a large scale, was chivalry itself of any worth, or was it merely a cloak for disguising martial excesses, a veneer of gentility spread over the rough, brutal reality of knightly life?

These are difficult questions to answer, and made more difficult by the tendency of many students of the subject to ignore the dynamic nature of the chivalric concept. Throughout the history of knighthood the notion of chivalric behaviour changed as much as did the military role of the knight as a heavy cavalryman, with which it is closely linked. As new technology produced change in knightly behaviour, so these altered circumstances produced changes in knightly belief and self image. It is not enough to take a static view of chivalry as a concept unaltered from the time of Charlemagne, via the Crusades, to the romance of the Court of Burgundy, quoting examples from each while ignoring their historical and social context. The nature of chivalry is extraordinarily complex, involving a multitude of dimensions.

THE KNIGHT AND DISCIPLINE

I have made one assumption which requires justification: that the knightly class were to some extent responsible for the devastation caused, even though much of it must have been actually carried out by foot soldiers. To what extent was this a failure of discipline, a turning of a blind eye, or active encouragement under orders? In the years following the capture of la Roche-Derrien Sir Walter Bentley, the King's Lieutenant in Brittany, was to express deep concern about the conduct of certain English soldiers, who he said emphatically were not knights but 'men of low degree'. These men had been so ruthless in their determination to extort money from the Bretons for their own enrichment that they were afraid to apply for official leave to go home to England, but instead bought themselves safe conduct through France, thereby to dispose of their ill-gotten gains. The comments in the previous chapter concerning the sack of Caen make similar points, when we read of knights curbing the excesses of their troops. No chronicler of the period explicitly links the evil deeds of war with the knightly classes – this would be too much to expect, but it is no excuse to claim a lack of discipline. Discipline was the weakest point of any medieval army, but within the English army it must have been better than most, for without discipline none of the great English victories could have taken place. The breakdown of discipline comes under exceptional, and largely non-military circumstances – the boredom of garrison life in Brittany or the excitement of a town fallen releasing months of pent-up energy. But it is hard to escape the conclusion that the point at which discipline was enforced was the point at which the knightly class had had their share of the loot, and their troops had also had what their leaders regarded as sufficient. After all, it was the prospect of loot,

and the desire to fight for a successful and open-handed commander, that led many to join up in the first place. The knightly class, as the leaders of men, must bear their share of the responsibility for the excesses they created and the results from which they profited. Quite clearly, the discipline exerted by the knights had a strong element of self interest.

If the knights were partly to blame how could contemporary writers react to it? Froissart, as we have seen, ignored it. But one writer tackled the subject head on. He was Honoré Bonet, who wrote *The Tree of Battles*, a study of war illustrated by numerous incidents drawn from the struggle that was happening at the time. He deplores plunder and pillage, but in these words:
'The way of warfare does not follow the ordinances of worthy chivalry or of the ancient custom of noble warriors who upheld justice, the widow, the orphan, and the poor. And nowadays it is the opposite that they do everywhere, and the man who does not know how to set a place on fire, to rob churches and to usurp the rights and to imprison the priests, is not fit to carry on war. And for these reasons, *the knights of today have not the glory and praise of the old champions of former times.*'

This tendency to contrast unfavourably the knights' comportment with that of their illustrious forebears is a common theme in the literature of the time. It is an easy statement to make, but it is perhaps significant that it is made at a time when the knight's prowess in the battlefield was also coming under some scrutiny. Here too, owing to the use of foot soldiers, the prowess of the knight was not 'what it had been'. It would therefore be easier to argue that there had been a knightly decline, particularly if the knights most seen to be in a military decline were one's enemies, rather than to embarrass one's patrons by admitting an improvement in technology and use of the despised foot soldier.

Left: A nineteenth-century engraving depicting a mêlée. In this form of tournament the knightly activity most resembled a mock battle. The knights wear heavy tilting helms on top of which are ornamental crests. In the right foreground a squire tends to a fallen knight.
Below left: Knights at a Tourney, from a fifteenth-century manuscript illustrating the life of Sir James Astley.
Right: The defence of a fortified town. Based on a miniature in Froissart's *Chronicles*, the defenders appear to be throwing everything at the attackers! Note the gateway hinged at the top, designed to be closed quickly in an emergency.
Far right: Brass of Sir Edward Dalyngrigge, the builder of Bodiam Castle, with his wife.

Which brings us to the second question. If the evils of war were part of the art of war, what purpose did chivalry serve? Had its ideals become so divorced from the harsh realities of medieval warfare that it was no more than a charade, an empty spectacle, a romantic excess, more honoured in the breach than the observance? To answer this question we must examine it in the context of the times. The mid-fourteenth century may have witnessed war on a larger scale, but it was also the time when the concept of chivalry received its greatest impetus for many years in the founding of a number of Orders of Chivalry, among which the most notable was the Order of the Garter. It is impossible to avoid the conclusion that the two were in some way connected. Chivalry in the fourteenth century was the code of behaviour of a military élite. Some of its values had changed and would change. Others remained immutable. We will examine what these values were later, and I shall argue that chivalry, and in particular the fourteenth-century developments of it, came about not as a means of rejecting the reality of war, but rather as a way of accepting it. The concept of chivalry was not an artificial creation, but an expression of caste solidarity among the knightly class, without which they could not survive.

Let us consider what influences were being brought to bear upon the fourteenth-century knight. If he were French he had to suffer the horror of seeing his comrades killed around him in large numbers. If he were English he had to swallow his aristocratic pride and fight beside the archers. On campaign he had to overcome any feeling of revulsion at the work he was required to do. What more natural reaction could there be than for knights to seek solace among their companions, inspired by the heroic tales of their ancestors, so that when courage was needed it could be found within the group. Chivalry was the glue which bound this society together. To express this in the

form of an institution of knighthood for a 'super-élite', such as the Order of the Garter, was a masterpiece of psychology, an achievement by Edward III that must rank beside his use of fighting men from the lower end of the social scale. At once it gave chivalry a new meaning. It inherited from the religious orders of knighthood their notion of brotherhood, and provided support to the knights in the context of serving the King.

THE TENETS OF CHIVALRY

Two ideas were central to the notion of chivalry, both of which may be examined in social terms. The first regarded warfare as a positive experience, ennobling in itself. In the same way that the king was expected to be a leader in war, so were his knights expected to follow, and to lead in their turn. The knight was first and foremost a fighting man, and war was the natural state of his life.

If war were ennobling, the implication was also there that it was only the knightly classes who were ennobled by it. The belief among knights that they were as much a military as a social élite comes over very strongly in the passages quoted in the last chapter dealing with the attribution of atrocities to the lower classes of soldier. Real fighting was for knights. When the Gascon Jean de Grailly, Captal de Buch (the first foreign knight to be chosen for the Order of The Garter) was captured he demanded to know of his captor whether or not he was a man of gentle birth, 'for he would sooner die than surrender to one who was not'. During a skirmish at Longueil a group of English knights were cut to pieces by a force of peasants, and were mourned by their comrades because they had been killed by such ignoble hands.

Another important characteristic of knighthood was its international outlook. The knights of rival countries were united by a caste solidarity that went far beyond seeking out from one another a suitable opponent for combat.

Left: Caesar's Tower, Warwick Castle, as seen from across the River Avon. It is a purely fourteenth-century work, finished early enough to house prisoners taken in 1356 at the Battle of Poitiers. The great tower, which rises 147 feet above its base, is built on solid rock and has never been mined.
Right: A fine example of a tilting helm. This form of helmet, produced for extra protection when taking part in tournaments, was very heavy and would not be used in battle. (Wallace Collection, London)

Their mental world was that of an international chivalric class, equally at home on the mainland of Europe as in England. Sir Walter Manny, a Hainaulter, and the above-mentioned Jean de Grailly, Captal de Buch, are excellent examples, but the royal families produced the most striking illustrations. Edward may have been after the throne of France, but his claim was that it was his by right of inheritance, as part of that great Anglo-French tradition of monarchy which from his point of view made the Hundred Years War effectively a civil war, fought between rival houses, where the national boundaries counted for little, and language was already in common. When the old, blind King of Bohemia was killed at Crécy both King Edward and his son were deeply grieved.

This international brotherhood was put on display at the numerous tournaments held during Edward's reign. During one set of jousts held at Windsor in 1358 safe conduct was granted for foreign knights to attend, and captive French knights then in England also took part. Worthy knights, whatever their origin, were genuinely honoured and admired for their own sake, irrespective of their allegiance. So the Marshal D'Audrehem might be praised by his enemies after Poitiers for being 'ever at all times right greatly to be esteemed, for he was a very goodly knight'.

The most sublime expression of this international brotherhood was found in the Crusade, where knights from different countries combined their forces in a common effort. This will be discussed in detail in a later chapter. For now it is pertinent to ask, if chivalry can be understood in social terms, can we find similar concepts existing in different societies under similar conditions of warfare? What evidence is there? One parallel can be found in Japan. There are obvious wide cultural differences, but sufficient common elements, with regard to the code of warrior behaviour, to indicate an underlying social reason common to both. The clearest parallel is that both the European knight and the contemporary samurai based their activities on an unwritten code that greatly idealized their behaviour. The samurai regarded warfare as a natural state. They despised the lower classes, and took both comfort and inspiration from the tales of the deeds of their ancestors. Japanese war chronicles such as the *Taiheiki*, which describe events in the 1330s and 1340s, read in translation like the pages of Froissart. Central to both is the notion of honour. The pride of family, of accomplishments, all are deeply tied in with the concept of personal honour. But what is to be done if one's honour has been besmirched? Here the two cultures differ widely. The samurai held the belief that disgrace could be removed by the act of suicide. Nothing like this notion appears in European chivalry, and nothing would have been farther from the thoughts of the King of France at Crécy. Nor need it be entertained as an alternative to being captured, certainly not among knights, but we noted previously in the discussion of Edward's horrible pursuit after Halidon Hill that many, apparently lower-class, Scots flung themselves into the sea in their despair. For a knight of goodly family capture was not a thing to be feared, because ransom would speedily follow.

The business of ransom, and it was big business, is a fascinating study. Nothing like it exists in the samurai culture. What it has in common with the samurai is that both knightly societies officially despised the mercenary aspect of life, but accepted it fully in practical terms. The samurai received a reward from his lord on presenting the severed head of his enemy. The European knight, mercifully, tended to present the whole knight in good condition, and received his reward by means of the captive's family, tenants or lord paying for his release. Religious notions of chivalry may have condemned the pursuit of gain in battle, but to the knights themselves it had much to commend it, and Bonet, after a lengthy discussion, decides in favour of it. 'All that a man can win from his enemy in lawful war he may of good right retain . . . good custom and usage are approved, and among Christians great and small there exists the custom of commonly taking ransom one from another.' Bonet, however, does insist that only a 'reasonable and knightly ransom should be demanded'. His criticism of the knights of his day, from which we quoted above, includes comments on ransom, saying that 'they cause them to pay great and excessive payments and ransoms without pity or mercy'.

There is no space here to attempt a proper comparative 'study of the European knight and the samurai. Let it suffice for now that in a distant country at the same time as Crécy and Poitiers, another military élite was expressing broadly similar feelings, and enjoying a similarly idealistic view of its place in the world.

AN IDEAL WORLD
Many of the points discussed above are illustrated in their European context in the events of the years that followed 'The Year of Victories'. Idealization of behaviour, ransom, pride and honour, are all there, notwithstanding the fact that the years following Crécy were marked by numerous very unchivalric deaths from the Black Death, which is believed to have carried off one of every three persons in Europe. The exact nature of the Black Death is still something of a mystery. It was probably bubonic plague, though anthrax has also been suggested. Its greatest devastation occurred among the common people, and only slightly affected the knightly classes.

Right: This column, between the towns of Ploërmel and Josselin, commemorates the Battle of the Thirty in 1351, between two picked forces of knights from the French and English garrisons.
Far right: Josselin Castle. From its courtyard, Josselin now bears the appearance of a decorative 'château', but a view such as this, from the river, retains its medieval flavour. Josselin was the major French stronghold in Central Brittany during the earlier part of the Hundred Years War, and it was the garrison of Josselin which took part in the famous Battle of the Thirty in 1351.

When war began again it was Brittany that felt its effects. Sir Thomas Dagworth, the victor of la Roche-Derrien, was killed in an ambush and was replaced as King's Lieutenant by Sir William Bentley, who proved to be a wise administrator and a strict disciplinarian of his garrison troops. Resentment against the English presence was growing high in Brittany by the 1350s, because while John de Montfort and Charles de Blois were absent Brittany became a battleground for rivalries. In 1351 this culminated in one of the strangest battles of the Hundred Years War. Its circumstances were so bizarre that the 'Battle of the Thirty' has often been confused with a tournament. Certainly Froissart's language is picturesque enough, but this encounter was in deadly earnest.

In the centre of Brittany were two strong castles: Josselin, commanded by Jean de Beaumanoir, for the pro-Blois party and, seven miles away, Ploërmel, under the English knight, Richard Bembro (Bamburgh?). For some time the two garrisons had skirmished as they ravaged the countryside on raids or foraging expeditions. In March 1351 the two leaders arranged an armed encounter between thirty knights from each side, to be fought at a spot midway between the two fortresses. The battle took place on 27 March 1351. From Josselin were thirty Breton knights under Jean de Beaumanoir facing an international brigade of twenty English, six Germans, and four Bretons. The battle became a series of duels to the death, which lasted for several hours, interrupted by a break for rest. At the end of the day the French were victorious. The English commander was killed, together with eight of his men, and the rest were taken prisoner, including two who were to become very famous knights, Sir Hugh Calveley and Sir Robert Knowles. Much courage was shown, as the chroniclers proudly tell us, of which one example will suffice. During the struggle de Beaumanoir, badly wounded, asked for a drink. 'Drink your blood, Beaumanoir,' replied his companion, 'your thirst will pass.'

So much for romance, but what a picture the Battle of the Thirty conjures up if we look beyond the immediate situation! Here we have two garrisons of proud, ruthless, highly trained knights, eager to make a name for themselves yet frustrated by the inactivity of garrison life. Raids and foraging, and the occasional encounter with their rivals, serve to break the monotony of their existence, as well as giving the opportunity to ride about the countryside in full armour. Then the opportunity arises of engaging their rivals in a genuine knightly battle, exactly like the scenes they have always cherished from the romances – a battle just like the 'good old days', without the presence of foot soldiers. The battle is fought and won in a limbo of knightly virtue. Its effect on the

overall conduct of the war in Brittany and beyond is insignificant, but, win or lose, at the level of knightly conduct it is the creation of a legend. There is no better illustration than this of the constant paradox of chivalric life – the idealization of behaviour being given its impetus by the unpleasant reality of the warfare they were required to carry out. In chivalry the two extremes come together. Several years later, as the English knights were due to set out with the Black Prince on his Spanish expedition, the chronicler refers to their eagerness for 'chivalric encounters without foot soldiers and bourgeois'.

There can be no greater contrast with the Battle of the Thirty than the encounter which took place the following year only a few miles distant – the Battle of Mauron. Mauron was the result of a French attempt to reconquer Brittany and oust the English garrisons once and for all, and as such was fought with the weapons of reality. France now had a new King. Philip VI had died in August 1350, to be succeeded by his son John (Jean le Bon). The appellation 'the Good' indicated no particular moral stance, but rather should be taken as 'John Goodfellow', a lover of mirth and display. Like his rival, King Edward of England, John the Good revelled in tournaments and the gaudy trappings of chivalry. One of his first acts on becoming king was to found a French order of knighthood, the Order of the Star, to rival and, he hoped, eclipse Edward's Garter. On the wider scale, by August he had assembled sufficient knights and foot soldiers to move on Brittany. He sent an army to besiege the fortress of Fougères which, strategically, held the key to the Breton/Norman frontier. The attack was beaten off by Sir William Bentley, who promptly put in order the defences of the rest of the Duchy.

King John set a French knight, Guy de Nesle, in charge of his army with the title of 'Governor-General of Brittany'. Early in August, de Nesle led his army over the border and marched on Rennes, intending ultimately to cross Brittany to Brest. Leaving Fougères wide on his right flank,

de Nesle easily took Rennes, as Bentley was wisely concentrating his forces near Ploërmel, south-west of Rennes. He had two alternatives: to fall back towards Brest; or to advance north, cut off the route west to Brest, and give battle to the French army. Bentley decided upon the latter course – and all the recent military history suggested a good chance of victory. Thus it was that on 14 August 1352, the rival armies were approaching each other near the town of Mauron.

Bentley had an army of about 3,000, and wisely chose to remain on the defensive. He drew up his forces, dismounted in a single line with no reserve, the knights in the centre, the archers on the flanks. The French army, according to Baker's Chronicle:

'under the Marshal's leadership, of set purpose set up their position with a steep mountain slope behind them, so that they could not fly; their purpose was to increase their zeal for fighting by knowledge of the impossibility of flight, as is usual with courageous men. There were also present many of the Order of the Knights of the Star, who in their profession had sworn never in fear to turn their backs on their foes . . .'

Guy de Nesle had dismounted his soldiers, except for a single body of 700 knights whom he deployed on his left flank. These were the first into action, and charged the English archers on Bentley's right flank. It was the same situation as at Crécy, but here the results were very different. The archers gave way, and about thirty of them fled to the rear. The immediate result was that the knights on the archers' left could receive no covering fire, and they too were forced back by the French cavalry. Fortunately for the English, their left flank stood firm against the dismounted attack and this allowed the knights in the centre to gain the cover of a wood. The English archers on the left not only slowed the French dismounted attack, but also led a counter-offensive. Encouraged, the English knights followed suit and soon the French army was broken, and victory plucked from the jaws of defeat.

The Battle of Mauron brought a temporary halt to the Breton Civil War. The French had been so crushed that they were not to interfere until 1364, when Edward III would be calling the tune. It also made a sad end to King John's new Order of the Star. No less than 89 of its new members fell at Mauron. The little-known battle was an English victory, but it had nearly been a defeat. The temporary embarrassment of the archers on the right flank, scattered by a well-timed cavalry charge, serves to illustrate the fact that archers were not invincible. The point we have made throughout, of the need for a combination of arms, is well shown by what had happened subsequently: the archers and knights supported one another in the counter-attack, which the French had failed to do in the initial stages.

It was a lesson which was to be reinforced four years later, in a battle which eclipsed Crécy in its scale and in the enormity of the results it produced – the Black Prince's great victory of Poitiers. Poitiers, the pivotal battle of the Hundred Years War, has never quite entered into popular history as have Crécy and Agincourt, but it marked a turning-point in the fortunes of war, and also shows in its execution nearly all the features of the chivalric life which we have been discussing in this chapter.

THE RELIEF OF AQUITAINE

Possession of the Duchy of Aquitaine – Gascony, or Guyenne as it was known to the chroniclers of the time – had been a major factor in Edward's original claim to the throne of France, but since 1341 Aquitaine had become a secondary theatre of military operations. Compared to the turmoil of Brittany, and the chevauchées of northern France and Normandy, Gascony had witnessed border skirmishing and little more. As French influence waned in the more northerly territories, pressure increased on Gascony, leading to a group of pro-English Gascon nobles, including the Knight of the Garter, Jean de Grailly,

Captal de Buch, to call on the King of England for help to withstand new French aggression. In July 1355, Edward responded by appointing his eldest son, Edward Prince of Wales, as King's Lieutenant in Gascony. It was the beginning of an extraordinarily successful association between the Black Prince and the Duchy.

The nobility of chivalry, that honour which finds its highest expression in its recognition by an enemy, came to be personified in this young man during his reign in Aquitaine. Many chroniclers praise his military skill, the splendour of his court, and his generosity. Superlatives pour from their pens in describing the Prince's accomplishments. He was indeed a noble knight, and like most others began military operations to defend Gascony by the now familiar unglamorous and brutal chevauchée.

He was accompanied by about 2,600 men, who had been brought across from England in July 1355, including a large number of experienced military leaders, many of whom had fought with him at Crécy: the Earls of Warwick, Oxford, Suffolk and Salisbury, and knights such as Sir John Chandos and Sir James Audley. The almost classic chevauchée was launched in October, the initial objective being the lands of the Count of Armagnac. Much booty was taken, and great devastation was wrought. The important towns of Carcassonne and Narbonne were burned, although their inner castles withstood attack. In effect, the Black Prince demonstrated the extent of his powers by burning his way to the Mediterranean coast and back, avoiding pitched battles and all but minor skirmishes with French troops. The Gascons were delighted, especially those whose lands had been similarly ravaged by the Armagnac troops, and Bordeaux enjoyed the presence of a successful military leader in its midst.

After further limited operations the Black Prince set out on another major chevauchée in August 1356. The spring had seen a great build-up of supplies, horses and weapons destined for Gascony, and such was the

Below left: The site of the Battle of Mauron in 1352. This little-known battle destroyed the newly founded Order of the Star, despite a temporary reverse of the English archers at the hands of the French knights.
Below left and right: The ideal and the reality: the delicate features of the funerary effigy of Duke John II of Brittany contrast with the skull excavated from the grave pits of Wisby which still bears the remains of a mail hood similar to that depicted on the Duke's peaceful head.

demand that at one stage even arrows were in short supply. Edward had sent an agent to England to obtain 1,000 bows, 400 gross of bowstrings and 2,000 sheaves of arrows, but because the King had so many armies active (the Earl of Lancaster had carried out a chevauchée in Normandy that summer, coming to within 75 miles of Paris) no arrows could be obtained, and the Prince had to order his agent to Cheshire to seize all available arrows from the fletchers. Once sufficient supplies had been procured the chevauchée went ahead, north through the Perigord towards Bourges. There was a skirmish at Romorantin, and from there the march led to the Loire near Tours, which he could not cross because all the bridges had been broken. Frustrated in his hope of linking up with Lancaster's army, the Prince turned south and headed homeward, until his way was blocked by a large French army at Poitiers.

BATTLE OF POITIERS

The Prince's army was about 6,000 strong, and the French numbered more than 20,000. Prince Edward drew up his men behind a hedge which ran perpendicular to the road out of Poitiers just beyond a fork. The Earl of Salisbury commanded the right wing, the Earl of Warwick the left, while the Black Prince headed the reserve in the rear. The French army was deployed in four divisions. Only the vanguard, under Marshal d'Audrehem and Marshal Clermont, were mounted. Next came the Duke of Normandy, then the Duke of Orléans, and finally King John. For convenience on the march from Poitiers, where they had left their horses, they had discarded their spurs and had shortened the length of their lances to five feet.

By the morning of Monday 19 September the French had shown no signs of attacking, and the Black Prince was thinking of moving off again towards home and safety. As a first step he began to move the supply wagons back, and this caused the French vanguard to think that the army was retreating. They therefore advanced to the attack in two columns, following the two roads through the hedge. Many broke through, protected from the fire of the archers by their breastplates, a new advance in military technology that looked towards the complete plate armour which would be seen later. The Earl of Oxford took charge of the archers, however, and ordered them to move sideways into the neighbouring marsh, which protected them from the over-zealous knights and allowed them to fire more obliquely at the unprotected horses rather than at the heavily armoured riders.

The second French column now arrived on foot. The hedge, which had offered some cover, was probably trampled flat, the masses of men-at-arms collided, and a huge mêlée ensued. Having exhausted the English troops, the French withdrew in good order, to leave room for a further assault by their comrades, but the following column, under the Duke of Orléans, had already fled the field without engaging. All that remained was the column of the King of France, still wending its way from Poitiers.

This was a mighty force, however, and the English chroniclers are surprisingly frank about the effect its appearance had on the weary English. Baker tells us bluntly that 'The great number of the enemy frightened our men.' There may have been some desertions at this point, perhaps in the guise of escorting wounded to the rear, and there was certainly some grumbling about the number of men they had left behind to defend Gascony.

The Black Prince was faced with probably the most difficult decision of his career, but the result of his decision made him a hero. He could not have known about the disappearance of the Duke of Orléans' division, and must have thought that he was facing almost the entire French army, whose small vanguard had done so much to worst him. His army had been battered, but had maintained that defensive posture which had been the

Right: The Battle of Poitiers 1356, from Froissart's *Chronicles*. Once again, the English longbow was to be used to devastating effect. A stylized view of the castle of Poitiers, like Caerlaverock triangular in plan, is seen at the rear.

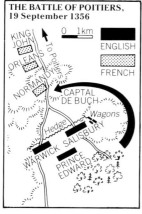

THE BATTLE OF POITIERS, 19 September 1356

Far left: Sir Nele Loryng, one of the original Knights of the Garter, and a companion of the Black Prince during the Hundred Years War. This illustration, redrawn from a manuscript, shows him in a robe ornamented by garters.
Left: John the Good, King of France, who was defeated at the Battle of Poitiers in 1356 and died in captivity in 1364.

hallmark of the English since the beginning of the Hundred Years War. The French were in the open, deficient in archers. It would be in the English tradition to let them come on. But Edward decided otherwise. With the decisiveness he had inherited from his father, the Black Prince of Wales ordered the English army to attack.

The knights mounted up and spurred their horses forward in a classic chivalric heavy cavalry charge. Two charges in fact took place – one frontally under Sir James Audley, the other, led by the Captal de Buch, into the French right flank. Following the mounted knights, the archers joined in. The great French column, assailed furiously on two sides, crumbled and broke. Geoffrey de Chargny, bearer of the sacred 'Oriflamme' of France, was cut down and killed, and in the confusion a great prize came to hand. To capture a King? – what honour, what glory awaited the man who could claim to have captured the King of France! And taken he was, by so many people that he was nearly crushed to death in the tumultuous fighting over his person. That night, among the field of the slain, the King sat down to supper with his captor – the Prince of Wales.

Poitiers was a major turning-point in the Hundred Years War. The King of France, the King of Scotland, and the Duke of Brittany were now all prisoners in England. It should have established Edward III as unquestioned conqueror of France. We will see in the next chapter why it did not quite do that, but Poitiers remains, tactically, one of the most perfect of medieval battles. It made the

name of the Black Prince, and confirmed the ascendancy of English arms in the conventional warfare of the great pitched battle. During the next twenty years the French had to learn other ways of countering this tremendous challenge.

We noted above the efficacy of plate armour at Poitiers, which caused the English archers some hesitation. This incident is the clearest indication we have that the 'plate revolution' was getting well under way by 1356. Mail was already becoming a second line of defence, filling the gaps where, at this stage, the plates did not quite overlap. Defensive plates could now be provided for the inside of the arms as well as the outer surfaces, and for the rear of the legs. The aventail, which hung round the neck, was now the only mail part which showed, and in time this too would disappear from view.

Poitiers is also the classic illustration of the combination of dismounted and mounted troops. It began as a repetition of Crécy, with the damage being done by the humble archers. It ended with as fine a cavalry action as any chivalric knight could have hoped for. If the knights had been bored by garrison work, disgusted by the chevauchée, and shamed by the archers, Poitiers was the perfect antidote to all these feelings which were so much a part of the cult of chivalry. Here a knight had commanded, and knights had led. As leaders of men and an élite in their own right, Poitiers was a triumph of the knightly class. The Garter had gone to war, and returned victorious from a knights' battle.

5. The Lion and the Eagle

I F THE ENGLISH are traditionally supposed to remember better their defeats than their victories, the same cannot be said of those on whom the defeats have been inflicted. Joan of Arc is probably the one French name to be well-known in England from the Hundred Years War, yet in this chapter we shall examine how France performed a similar miracle of recovery in the third quarter of the fourteenth century. This recovery stemmed from a number of factors, not the least of which were the service of loyalty to the French King, and inspiration to the French armies, rendered by a Breton knight called Bertrand du Guesclin. Unlike the Maid of Orléans, he is practically unknown outside his own country, yet it was he whose initially unconventional style of warfare produced the counter to the terrible chevauchée, and although of lowly birth he rose to the highest office that France could bestow, honoured by the young monarch whose humiliation he had redressed.

The reason why du Guesclin's career is so little known outside of France lies to some extent in the timing of his

Left: Edward the Black Prince of Wales, as he would have appeared at the Battles of Crécy and Poitiers, represented in the magnificent equestrian statue of him at Leeds.
Right: The coat of arms of Bertrand du Guesclin, the 'Eagle' of this Chapter, as opposed to the 'Lion' of the Black Prince, is depicted here in stone relief work above the doorway of a house associated with du Guesclin in Dinan. The eagle is black, on a white field, with a red bend.

appearance on the military scene. While he was winning modest victories for France, his nobler, but less adaptable, contemporaries were busy suffering catastrophic defeats, and the popular English chauvinism which tends to close the history books at Poitiers and re-open them at Agincourt dwells little on the years between. This chapter, which deals with his life as seen against the background of the French recovery against the English practice of war, will perhaps make amends.

If du Guesclin's reputation in England has suffered by neglect, neither has it quite recovered from the body-blow dealt by one of his own countrymen. Professor Perroy's well-known dismissal of him as '. . . this mediocre captain, incapable of winning a battle or being successful in a siege of any scope . . .' has influenced a generation of military historians, who have delighted in quoting the number of times du Guesclin was captured, and have noted without question his supposed ugliness, the latter being rather unfair unless his tomb effigy in Saint-Denis is more flattering than nature justified. Perroy does later give grudging praise of his 'iron authority and strict discipline', and concludes that he '. . . became the man who, with slender means, wiped out the shame. . . . His glory eclipsed that of all other captains. . . .' Nevertheless, Perroy's implied dismissal of his achievements has led to some lack of appreciation which is difficult to overcome.

DU GUESCLIN'S EARLY LIFE

It is the 'slender means' to which Perroy refers that give the clue to the difficulty in assessing du Guesclin's military achievements. Lack of resources of one kind or another were the hallmark of much of his life. He was born in about the year 1320 near Dinan in Brittany. He was the eldest of ten children and apparently, a bit of a handful, being boisterous to the point of brutality, his heavy features and incredible strength terrifying his younger brothers and sisters. Only the intervention of a nun, who foretold his future greatness, prevented his distraught parents from disowning him.

His adolescent years were spent, we are told, organizing the local children in gangs to fight one another, the young Bertrand always playing the part of commander. In 1337, at the age of seventeen, he went to Rennes where a tournament was being held to honour the marriage of Charles de Blois with Jeanne de Penthièvre. He rode a carthorse belonging to his father, and was met by jeers from the well-to-do young knights assembled for the joust. His father, apparently, was there in an official capacity, which begs the question of why an impoverished Breton family had been invited to a tournament. In fact the whole incident is apocryphal, and comes from the pen of du Guesclin's first biographer, Cuvelier. His *Chronique de Bertrand du Guesclin* is a heroic poem composed shortly after du Guesclin's death in 1380, by which time he had already become a legend in his own lifetime. Cuvelier's work is one of the last flourishes of the 'chanson de geste', written by a man who was effectively one of the last minstrels, an admirer both of the knight who formed his subject, and the tradition of the heroic poets of the eleventh century. The *Chronique* is, therefore, a dramatic hagiography, embellished by some imagination, but based, according to Cuvelier, on eyewitness accounts by du Guesclin's contemporaries. There is evidence that Cuvelier had access to reliable written sources, but the tournament story cannot be included among them. It finishes in suitable style. After his haughty dismissal we find our hero borrowing a horse and armour from one of his cousins who is just leaving, and with a closed visor concealing his identity (of course!) this unknown knight enters the lists. He is challenged, and proceeds to win every joust set against him. After a dozen combatants are unhorsed his own father presents a challenge. To the amazement of the crowd, Bertrand declines, but continues to joust with others, until a Norman knight opens his helmet with the point of his lance, displaying the stranger's identity to the admiring crowd and a delighted father.

Little is known of his movements during the first years of the Breton Civil War, except that he is mentioned as a man-at-arms in the Blois forces, and may have been present at the brief siege of Rennes by the Earl of Northampton in 1342. Such 'regular' activities were, however, the exception. While English armies came and went du Guesclin began the form of warfare at which he was to make his name. For fifteen years he led a vigorous guerrilla campaign from the safety of the great, and to the Breton mind enchanted, forest of Paimpont, pouncing on isolated columns of English or Montfort troops. He raided their castles and towns, and harassed their communications. One of the earliest recorded exploits of du Guesclin, and one of his most dramatic, was the taking of the castle of Grand Fougeray. This incident probably happened late in 1350, if his nineteenth-century biographer, Luce, is to be believed in his statement that the Captain of Grand Fougeray was Robert Bembro, who was to meet his death at the Battle of the Thirty in May 1351.

Whoever the commander was, he was absent from the fortress when a band of woodcutters arrived at the gate bearing firewood. We may presume that du Guesclin's guerrilla operations had made the neighbouring forests hazardous for the English garrison, so the woodcutters with their faggots were welcomed into the castle. As the gate was opened the woodcutters revealed their true colours, flinging down the bundles of wood to prevent the gate from being closed, whereupon their companions joined them in the courtyard and attacked the garrison.

THE KNIGHTHOOD OF DU GUESCLIN

Glorious though such exploits were, du Guesclin was still little more than a self-employed brigand of lowly birth. His unconventional way of fighting may have earned him the praise of the more far-sighted of his contemporaries, but guerrilla fighting was unglamorous work that found a place only in the practice of warfare and not in its code of conduct. Like chevauchées, partisan raiding was not a chivalric exercise. As a result du Guesclin had not received the recognition he deserved, nor had he been admitted to the honours of knighthood. All this was to change within a very few years, by a simple but brilliant feat of arms rendered in person to a very senior French knight, the Marshal d'Audrehem.

In March 1345 d'Audrehem had taken the castle of Landal in north-east Brittany, a useful strategic move as Landal was close to the major French coastal base of Pontorson. Encouraged by his success, d'Audrehem turned his attention towards one of the major English possessions in Brittany – the fortress of Bécherel, midway between Rennes and Dinan. Scarcely six miles from Bécherel lay Montmuran, a strong, French-held castle, where lived the widow of Jean de Tinteniac, who had fallen at the Battle of Mauron. It being Holy Week she invited the Marshal and his reconnaissance party, which included du Guesclin, to join her in Montmuran on Maundy Thursday, 10 April 1354. It is difficult to guess the social stance adopted by the guerrilla on this occasion, but his military mind was as active as usual, and whatever part he took in the festivities must have been a very brief one. The commander of Bécherel was Sir Hugh Calveley, a Cheshire knight of renown, whose reputation for surprise and ambuscade must have been near to that of du Guesclin's, for the latter warned d'Audrehem that it would be perfectly within the pattern of Calveley's operations for him to try a raid on Montmuran to seize the Marshal. (The humble du Guesclin would probably not have commanded a price.) To guard against a surprise attack du Guesclin concealed thirty archers along the road from Bécherel with orders to prevent any approach by Calveley and to warn the garrison of Montmuran. His assumption proved correct, and on hearing the archers engaging with Calveley's troops both du Guesclin and d'Audrehem hurried to the scene of action and a fierce skirmish ensued. Sir Hugh Calveley, flung to the ground from his horse by a violent charge from a certain Enguerrand d'Hesdin, was himself captured as a prize. It was at this point, having fought fiercely and well, leaving few fugitive English to regain Bécherel and tell the tale, that du Guesclin was taken to one side by a knight of Caux called Eslatre des Mares, Captain of the castle of Caen, and knighted on the field of battle, des Mares girding him with his own sword.

According to a strong local tradition, the ceremony of knighthood was formally completed in the small chapel of Montmuran. Here du Guesclin received the white robe of knighthood, and from this time adopted his famous warcry 'Notre-Dame Guesclin!' which was soon to be heard on a wider stage.

Du Guesclin's knighthood was a major turning-point in his life. Handicapped by his origins, and his very uncharacteristic willingness to lead a band of simple peasants in war, a prejudice had built up against him that only the good sense of someone like d'Audrehem could overcome. Once accepted, however, his unquestioned knightly virtues, in particular his ability actually to win battles, all fell neatly into place. How unfortunate for France that the impetus given by his elevation could not have been properly exploited, that his ideas and style of warfare, so suited to the circumstances of the day, could not have been immediately adopted to counter the dreaded chevauchée. Instead, within two years France was to suffer the disaster of Poitiers, and from 1356 onwards was to reel like a ship without a helmsman under the pressure of English attacks.

While negotiations for King John's ransom continued, the 'sideshow' of the Breton Civil War came more into prominence. One month after Poitiers, England's other notable prisoner was released. Upon payment of the bulk of his ransom, and following entreaties by Pope Innocent VI, Charles de Blois was given his liberty after nine long years. With what cynicism, one wonders, did Edward III

Right: The Porte Saint-Pierre at Dinan, little changed from the time of the siege of Dinan by the Earl of Lancaster in 1357. The siege was an attempt to increase pressure on the already heavily invested city of Rennes, but guerrilla activity by du Guesclin, and the resolution of the defenders led to its being abandoned.

agree to the deal? France lay prostrate at his feet, with only one outstanding matter to be settled – the question of Brittany. What better than to send back the cause of the trouble, who would inevitably cause more disasters for France? Militarily, Charles de Blois was now completely impotent. He had agreed to undertake no action until the balance of his ransom was paid, and as a further precaution Edward had also sent to France Charles's rival, John de Montfort. This, incidentally was the son of the former John de Montfort, who had escaped from French custody in 1345 and died shortly afterwards. The young John was brought up in England. His valiant and strong-minded mother, Joan, Countess of Flanders, whose exploits fill so many pages of the beginning of the War, was now a virtual prisoner in Tickhill Castle, a royal fortress near Doncaster, where she had been confined on the grounds of suspected madness since coming to England.

THE SIEGE OF RENNES

In charge of the young de Montfort was Edward's trusted Lieutenant, Henry of Lancaster, now given an official commission as Lieutenant of Brittany. Lancaster arrived in Brittany in August 1356, almost at the same time as Charles de Blois. He quickly assessed the military situation, and on 2 October, in the name of John de Montfort, Duke of Brittany, began a siege of Rennes, which had remained stubbornly pro-Blois. It was likely to prove a difficult task for the small Anglo-Breton army. The line of the walls was long, and Lancaster had very little in the way of siege engines. On the other hand, the layout of the city was familiar from the brief attempt at siege in 1342, and the success at Calais had shown that almost anything was possible given time. The French attempts to assemble a relieving force from among the post-Poitiers débris of their army were sincere, but limited in scope. The Lord of Rochefort was appointed Captain, and established his headquarters at Vitré, nearly twenty miles due east, with 1,000 men-at-arms and 500 archers. It looked like being a time-consuming, but ultimately successful operation for Lancaster – until Bretrand du Guesclin came on the scene and transformed a routine operation into a romantic drama.

Du Guesclin was not within Rennes when the siege began. Born locally, and utterly familiar with the countryside, Lancaster's patient blockade was the perfect target for his guerrilla operations. Avoiding pitched battle at all costs, du Guesclin led the French troops in raids on Lancaster's supply trains, night attacks and general harassment. This continued into the depths of winter, which was a particularly harsh one, suffered all the more uncomfortably by Lancaster's troops lying out in the open.

As the winter progressed du Guesclin's attacks became fiercer, the heavily wooded countryside providing an ideal terrain for this type of warfare. After each sortie du Guesclin would retire to the comfort of Dinan, Fougères or Pontorson, living the life of a knight, and fighting like a bandit. Never had the combination been so happily realized. So firm was his grip on the English troops that in January 1357 the Dauphin Charles, Regent of France during his father's captivity, was able to bring a relieving army as close as Dinan, where he established his headquarters. The presence of this more conventional army forced Lancaster to take upon himself the additional task of besieging Dinan, which would be difficult to accomplish if he were not to loosen his grip upon Rennes.

Although it is du Guesclin's name that has passed most prominently into history concerning the defence of Rennes, we must record the ingenuity of his companions within the city, under the command of Bertrand de Saint-Pern, Captain of the city, and the Lord of Penhoet, Keeper of the castle. Lancaster attempted to mine the walls, but by excellent organization of the populace, who were set to watch and listen for any signs of underground disturbance, the mine was discovered and skillfully countermined.

Lancaster thereupon tried a little psychological warfare. Knowing that the inhabitants were running short of food, and perhaps hoping to demonstrate that du Guesclin's raids were not a total success, the English drove a herd of 4,000 pigs before the walls of hungry Rennes. Naturally enough there was considerable pressure on Penhoet to make a sally and capture the pigs, but he was too astute to fall for such a trick. Instead, he ordered that the gate nearest the herd be opened, and suspended a piglet by its hind legs above the drawbridge. Its squeals soon drew the attention of the herd, which rapidly headed for the gate. The drawbridge was lowered, the piglet was released and as it scutttled back in, still squealing loudly, the herd obligingly followed, pursued by the angry English.

Despite the hardships suffered by both sides, time seems to have been found for the chivalric niceties of war. Lancaster's operations against Dinan appear to have been quite successful, for a 40-day truce was negotiated, the garrison promising to surrender if they had not been relieved at the end of that period. As one of the supposedly relieving armies was presently shut up in Dinan, Lancaster must have thought the risk to be a reasonable one. Among the garrison in Dinan was one of du Guesclin's younger brothers, Olivier, then serving as a horse archer in the company of Jean Raguenel. One morning the young man took it into his head to go riding outside the walls. Even this was a violation of the truce conditions, and it was with great embarrassment that Bertrand du Guesclin heard that his brother had been captured in the environs of Dinan, and was being held by

an English knight with an eye to business. Ransom was always worth a try, and it must have been with some glee that the Englishman discovered that his prisoner was the brother of one of the leading French commanders, which probably accounted for the price of 1,000 florins that he demanded. Du Guesclin, according to Cuvelier, turned red with rage, and challenged the knight to single combat. The challenge was accepted, and the resulting duel took place in the centre of Dinan.

The Englishman's name is something of a mystery. He is referred to as 'Thomas of Canterbury', and du Guesclin's biographer adds the tantalising information that he was the brother of the then Archbishop of Canterbury, which would make his name, Thomas de Islep. However, having briefly entered history this Thomas was soon abruptly to leave it. In the presence of the Duke of Lancaster, who had been permitted to enter the city as witness with twenty knights as escort, the two adversaries charged at each other with such force that both lances shattered on the other's shield. After a long spell of fighting with swords, Thomas struck downwards at du Guesclin's head. He missed and his sword skidded out of his hand. Du Guesclin got down from his horse, retrieved the sword and flung it across the square. Armed only with his dagger, the Englishman refused to continue on foot as du Guesclin invited him repeatedly to do. Instead he reared his horse at his dismounted rival, trying to trample du Guesclin beneath its feet. But du Guesclin had swiftly removed his leg armour and was able to dodge to one side. Forcing his sword upwards he struck deeply into the flanks of the horse. The animal reared out of control, depositing Thomas of Canterbury on the ground. Du Guesclin flung himself on his adversary 'like a lion', dragged off his helmet and punched him in the face with his gauntletted fist. Blinded by his own blood Thomas surrendered. The ransom was liquidated with no charge, Olivier was set free, and the impetuous Thomas of Canterbury was dismissed from the English army.

Incidents such as this did far more than relieve the boredom of a siege operation. They provided the opportunity, under carefully controlled conditions of truce

Opposite page, left: Pedro the Cruel, King of Castile, whose alliance with England led to the Black Prince's involvement in Spain and his victory over du Guesclin at the Battle of Najera in 1367.

Opposite page, right: Philip the Bold, the first Valois Duke of Burgundy, who fought by the side of his father, King John, at Poitiers in 1356, while still a boy of fourteen. His skill and energy enabled him to hand over a powerful political state to his son, John the Fearless.

Right: King Charles V of France, who with his protégé, Bertrand du Guesclin, set in motion a series of military reforms that took advantage of the growing weakness of the English and led to the end of the first phase of the Hundred Years War.

Far right: Edward the Black Prince, from his seal. He is shown wearing his large tilting helm. The arms of England are differenced by a white label for the eldest son.

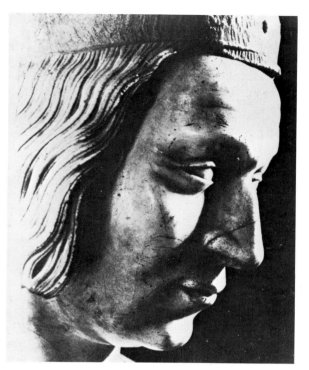

and safe conduct, which were universally respected, for 'sample warfare' to be carried out. To a successful side it meant an increase in morale and the death or disgrace of a vital member of the opposing side. To the loser it meant a loss in confidence without the total defeat of a failed assault.

Rennes was shortly to receive a further fillip to its morale. Tiring of his hit and run raids, du Guesclin was chafing to take a more active part in the defence of the city. His chance came when Penhoet decided to get a message out to Charles de Blois. One of the garrison passed through the lines and gave himself up as a deserter. Admitted into Lancaster's presence, he stated that a relieving army was expected to arrive from the east the following night. His story was believed, and with the 'deserter' acting as a guide, a large detachment of English set out to intercept it. In the darkness the deserter slipped away to join du Guesclin, who immediately launched a raid on the lightly defended English camp, setting fire to the tents and looting such provisions as his army could carry. Laden with useful spoil, du Guesclin led a triumphant entry into the city.

The siege continued lethargically, but on 23 March 1357 a treaty was signed at Bordeaux between England and France, and one of its clauses called for the immediate raising of the siege of Rennes. Despite orders from Edward III, Lancaster refused to comply until early July. His honour was at stake. He had with him in camp the young Montfort, Duke of Brittany, in whose name the business had dragged on for nine long months, and Lancaster had sworn at the outset not to leave Rennes before he had placed his flag on the battlements. By late spring 1357 the city was suffering greatly from hunger, which not even the indomitable spirit of du Guesclin could do much about, and consented to be relieved of siege for payment of 100,000 crowns. At last Lancaster was satisfied. He entered Rennes ceremoniously and with much ostentation placed his banner on the wall. Du Guesclin came forward and offered him wine. The Duke drank it and left the town. As soon as he had gone the banner was torn down and flung into the ditch.

Naturally enough, both sides claimed the Siege of Rennes as a victory. To the French it was to become much more. As Orléans was to be fifty years later, the raising of the siege of Rennes, and its association with a charismatic hero figure, became a symbol of hope for France. Within a year of the shame of Poitiers, Rennes had provided an example of what could be achieved. Its significance therefore developed far beyond its modest military accomplishment.

THE ABSENCE OF PEACE

There was no doubt in royal minds as to who should receive the greatest credit. The Regent of France, Dauphin Charles, in the wording of a grant of a pension to Bertrand du Guesclin speaks of his great 'perseverance, judgement and loyalty by which the city was saved'. Not to be outdone, Charles de Blois granted du Guesclin the town and castle of la Roche-Derrien. Such royal favour meant that du Guesclin had 'arrived'. His tactics had been shown to be effective in French eyes, and there may be some echo of this in the subsequent request by the Duke of Lancaster to be allowed to return to England. To this the King consented, but only after the Duke had carried out a thorough review of the financial and administrative arrangements of the Duchy of Brittany. Finance presented the greatest problem. It was comparatively simple to raise money for short-term expeditionary forces and chevauchées; once the troops had returned home victorious and laden with booty they were taken off the pay-roll. But garrisoning was different. Edward III had already had trouble in Brittany in 1343, when the financial resources of Joan of Flanders came to his aid. As the Countess was now languishing in Tickhill Castle other means had to be found for the upkeep of the garrisons. Local taxes were difficult to gather, and had the added disadvantage of alienating pro-Montfort Bretons, many of whom changed sides during the 1350s. Large garrisons with time on their hands, suffering irregular payment of wages, made matters much worse by what is politely known as 'irregular foraging', the situation that had led to the Battle of the Thirty. Such points were recorded in a memorandum by Sir William Bentley, who served as Lieutenant of Brittany in 1350–53, and he was given extensive powers of inspection and supervision. Discipline within the Anglo-Breton army was to be tightened. Wages were to be paid according to orders. Soldiers were to be ready for action when required, and would not be allowed to leave Brittany without Sir William Bentley's permission.

Against this background of rebellious subjects, weak loyalties towards the English nominee, and the presence of large numbers of under-employed English soldiers irregularly paid, du Guesclin continued his tireless work of wearing down English resistance. Between the years 1358 and 1363 he was twice captured, and subsequently ransomed.

Officially, of course, the country was at peace. The Truce of Bordeaux lasted for two years, and was then extended in the confusion of negotiation over the payment of the French King's ransom. But somehow the talks never reached a satisfactory conclusion, and somehow the English demands continued to rise. Their garrisons were now well-established in Brittany, Anjou, Maine, Touraine and Burgundy. Foreign armies crossed France with impunity, and lawless bands of unemployed, former mercenaries carried out their own private raids and feuds. On the grand scale of things, Edward was preparing the *coup de grâce*, a triumphal march across France with a huge army, the culmination being a coronation ceremony for himself at Reims. The result was not quite so spectacular, but ended in the Treaty of Bretigny, sealed by both monarchs in 1360, which guaranteed the English possession of Gascony. It also bought France a breathing-space, though King John had not long to live. He died on 8 April 1364, and his body was conveyed from its exile in England with great pomp and solemnity, to be received with sadness by the new monarch, Charles V.

So far as the reconstruction of France's military power was concerned, the breathing-space was real enough, and in three particular instances the new king, and his trusted champion, Bertrand du Guesclin, began to rebuild a force and a reputation.

COCHEREL

The first concerned the inheritance of Charles V's younger brother, Philip. The dukedom of Burgundy became vacant in 1361, and the late King had promised it to his young son, who, at the age of fourteen, had fought valiantly beside his father at Poitiers. But there was one other claimant, by an argument every bit as complicated as the Breton succession, on behalf of Charles 'the Bad', King of Navarre. The military threat from Charles the Bad was a very real one, because such was the state of France that a few determined mercenaries could easily besiege Paris. Furthermore, Charles the Bad had extensive possessions in Normandy, including the castles of Meulan and Mantes. The new King, whose coronation had not yet taken place, entrusted the handling of events to du Guesclin, who took the role of 'regular soldier' to present the King, by way of a gift on his accession, with a brilliant victory in the pitched battle of Cocherel, on 16 May 1364.

At Cocherel, which is in Normandy, the forces of the King of Navarre were augmented by a large Anglo-Gascon contingent, the whole being under the command of Jean de Grailly, Captal de Buch, the same renowned Knight of the Garter who had fought at Poitiers. His army took up a defensive position on the small hill of Cocherel, planting their banner in the centre as a rallying-point. The Captal,

in the English tradition, gave orders that the army was to maintain height and let the French come to them. At the request of the Count of Auxerre, the senior French knight present, du Guesclin took command of the French forces and detached thirty brave knights for an assault on the Captal's command post. This provoked little response so, holding most of his troops in reserve, du Guesclin launched a larger frontal attack followed by a feigned retreat. Such manoeuvres are always difficult to execute effectively, but du Guesclin seems to have got it right, for some at least of the Captal's army followed in pursuit. The Captal had little alternative but to follow, at which point du Guesclin delivered a flank attack from his reserve which assured a French victory.

Cocherel brought du Guesclin great credit. He had shown his new monarch that he was able to win conventional battles as well as raids and skirmishes. Admittedly Cocherel was not fought against a full English army, but it augured well for the new partnership that was being formed between the King and his Lieutenant.

BATTLE OF AURAY

The second great problem of Charles V's reign was also solved with the assistance of du Guesclin, but with less happy results. In 1362 Edward III had again played the Breton card, once more returning John de Montfort, now grown to manhood, to his troubled Duchy. For the English garrisons in Brittany the proposed renewal of the conflict was welcome relief from the boredom of occupation, but the French resources to oppose them were stretched to the limit. Bertrand du Guesclin could not be in two places at once, and the campaign against Charles the Bad kept him from taking a full part in Brittany until 1363, when he conducted a siege against the English hornet's nest of Bécherel. The castle held out (it was to provide a challenge for many years to come), so du Guesclin rejoined the army of Charles de Blois for a march to relieve the castle of Auray.

Auray is a picturesque town situated on the southern coast of Brittany, some ten miles from Vannes. It is built on the bank of the River Loch, crossed at the town by a beautifully preserved medieval bridge. In 1364 its castle, of which nothing now remains, was under siege from the de Montfort party and their English allies. The defenders of Auray had made the usual 'deal' with the besiegers that they would surrender if they were not relieved by a certain day. By the evening of the day before the expiry date, a relieving army was encamped across the river, waiting the chance to settle the issue.

John de Montfort wished to attack the French, but was dissuaded by two of his captains, Sir Robert Knowles and Olivier de Clisson, du Guesclin's great Breton rival, who pointed out that the river was deep and the ground marshy, as it is to this day, and the French camp was well defended by a palisade. An attempt at settlement was summarily rejected by Charles de Blois, so John de Montfort passed complete control of his army into the capable hands of Sir John Chandos, who posted scouts along the river to watch for French movement, and forbade any nocturnal raiding.

On St Michael's Day, 29 September 1364, the Franco-Breton army, led by du Guesclin, began to cross the River Loch, to line up north of the Anglo-Breton positions. Today there is a small bridge where the river narrows at the north of the Kerzo marsh, which may well mark the actual crossing point. The crossing was without incident, for an afternoon's truce had been arranged by Jean de Beaumanoir, fighting on the Blois side. It seems incred-

ible that such gentlemanly negotiations could take place, allowing the French to form order of battle unmolested, but from Chandos's point of view it was a sensible decision; it fulfilled the requirements of the deal made about the siege. It drew the French out of their fortified camp and the protection of the marsh, and above all it made a decisive battle that much more likely. The Breton Civil War had dragged on for twenty-five years. It had been a major pretext for which the English had started what was to become the Hundred Years War, and now the two claimants were present with every hope of a conclusive result. Let them cross in peace, reasoned Chandos, and settle the matter by battle. Chilling confirmation of this is indicated by the similar orders from the commanders of both sides before the battle began: no ransom for either de Montfort or de Blois; Auray was to be to the death.

The Franco-Breton army crossed the river in the four 'battles' it would deploy for the ensuing struggle. The first, under du Guesclin, consisted of knights and squires of Brittany. The Earl of Auxerre, who had fought beside him

at Cocherel, took the second, composed mainly of French troops, while Charles de Blois had personal command of the third. The rearguard was under various French knights, including de Raix, de Rieux and du Pont. Each division consisted of about 1,000 men.

The Anglo-Breton army opposed them with a similar disposition. Olivier de Clisson and his pro-Montfort Bretons faced the Count of Auxerre. Sir Robert Knowles, Sir Walter Huet and Sir Richard Burley opposed du Guesclin's division, while John de Montfort faced his rival Charles de Blois. Sir Hugh Calveley, after some protest, took charge of the rearguard. In Froissart's picturesque description of the scene: 'the troops of the Lord Charles were in their best and most handsomest order, and drawn up in the most brilliant manner . . . they marched in such close order that one could not throw a tennis ball among them'.

The battle began with skirmishing between the forward spearmen and an exchange of archery fire, which did little harm because both sides were dismounted. As the archers shouldered their bows and fought hand to hand,

Below: The ruins of Bécherel Castle in Brittany mark the site of a number of fierce and prolonged sieges during the fourteenth century. Bécherel was one of the strongest English bases in the peninsula, and withstood attacks by du Guesclin and de Clisson until it finally fell in 1373.

Charles de Blois launched a vigorous charge against de Montfort which entered deep into the ranks, forcing Sir Hugh Calveley to bring up the rearguard in support. Sir John Chandos fought a commander's battle, moving from one part of the field to another advising and calling up fresh troops. Olivier de Clisson wielded his battleaxe to great effect against Auxerre, until a French battle-axe struck off the visor from his helmet and the point destroyed his eye. The Count of Auxerre was captured, and seizing the advantage, Chandos launched a major advance, supported by Calveley, and headed straight for du Guesclin's division. Some of the French had already begun to retreat. Du Guesclin fought like a desperate man. Having broken all his weapons he was striking out with his iron gauntlets when Chandos pushed through the mêlée and persuaded him to surrender. The words the chronicler puts into Chandos's mouth are so natural they must be near the actual words spoken: 'The day is not yours, Messire Bertrand: you will be luckier another time.'

He was luckier indeed than Charles de Blois. As Froissart reminds us coldly: '. . . if they should gain the battle . . . no ransom should be taken for him, but they should kill him'.

There are two versions of Charles de Blois' death: the inevitable propaganda one of later times, that he was captured and then foully murdered (compare the story of the death of the Prince of Wales at Tewkesbury in 1471), and the more likely version that he died in the thick of the battle, fighting bravely. Elsewhere in the field another vengeance was paid. Olivier de Clisson had been only a boy in 1343 when his father, suspected of treason, had been executed by order of the King of France. No prisoners were taken by his division, leading to the nickname of 'the Butcher', which he was to bear for the rest of his life. The most reliable figures indicate that French casualties at Auray numbered about 1,000 dead and 1,500 prisoners. Charles de Blois was dead, so John de Montfort became indisputably Duke John IV of Brittany. The strange sequel to the story is that for some reason best known to himself he then paid homage to the French King! As du Guesclin was speedily ransomed the Battle of Auray began to look like a French victory.

THE CURSE OF THE FREE COMPANIES

The third problem of Charles V's reign was considerably more difficult. The wars had brought on to the soil of France a swarm of mercenaries, of many nationalities, but united in their desire to fight so long as it brought them profit. They called themselves the 'Free Companies', but the people of France had only one name for these bands of ruthless adventurers: they called them, quite simply, 'The English'.

As a general appellation this was inaccurate and unfair, though it must be admitted that several of the most successful leaders of Free Companies were English knights who have already been mentioned in these pages in considerably more honourable exploits. Honourable, that is, in terms of official sanction and a nominal cause for which they were fighting. Their actual *modus operandi*, of raids on castles and towns, looting villages and despoiling the inhabitants, was not dissimilar from the chevauchée operations they had carried out on behalf of the King of England. The essential differences were their international composition, their utter ruthlessness, and the sheer unpredictability of their movements. The problem had begun with the Battle of Poitiers, was exacerbated by the Treaties of Calais and Bretigny, and rendered acute by the resolution of the Navarre and Breton Wars. It is with a sense of shame that one records the name of Sir Hugh Calveley and Sir Robert Knowles as leaders of these despicable bands. Profit had once been had from the capture and ransoming of the rich. Now it was to be scraped from the bottom of war's empty barrel. But how were they to be controlled? A stable government, such as that exercised by the Black Prince in Aquitaine, could close its own borders to the Companies, but this in turn only put the pressure on to neighbours. As a result the Free Companies flourished where the populace was weakest to withstand them, and where relatively unspoiled lands promised rich pickings. The France of Charles V provided the ideal ground. Each company, numbering no more than a few hundred men, operated independently. All that was necessary was for them to take a few castles and hold a local populace to ransom. On rare occasions they combined forces, as in the 'Great Company' of 1361 – but this was the exception. Otherwise they terrorized at will. Such were the real exploits of the 'soldiers of fortune' romanticized in fiction.

Above: This stained glass window in the chapel at Montmuran Castle represents the surrender of Sir Hugh Calveley to Bertrand du Guesclin after his unsuccessful raid on the castle in April 1354. Calveley's aim had been to capture and hold to ransom the Marshal d'Audrehem, but du Guesclin frustrated his attempt, an achievement which gained him wide recognition.

Right: The main gateway tower of the castle of Vitré. Together with Fougères, Vitré was a major fortress on the borders between Brittany and the rest of France. This tower has been carefully restored and provides a characteristic example of French military architecture of the period.

Far right: The Battle of Auray, 1364. John de Montfort (on right) with his English allies, defeat Charles de Blois in this decisive battle.

Local defence against them was almost non-existent. Towns built as 'bastides' in the previous century had better luck than others. In some places even the churches were fortified, as on the Scottish border. As for getting rid of these brigands there seemed little alternative to paying them to go away and attack someone else – a scarcely satisfactory arrangement, unless the alternative place were a distant country.

Charles V had one great hope. In Bertrand du Guesclin he had a man who understood the psychology of the marauder. Charles persuaded him to try and lead these excommunicated brigands on an audacious campaign across Europe to Hungary in order to stop the progress of the Ottoman Turks. The enterprise would be called a Crusade, and the brigands would gain a heavenly reward. Unfortunately none of them was fooled, but very soon another theatre of war presented itself, and one that was much closer to hand: Spain.

THE SPANISH CAMPAIGNS

The Kingdoms of the Iberian peninsular had so far remained outside the Anglo-French conflict. For the past fifteen years the King of Castile had been Pedro, known to history as Pedro the Cruel. He had married a French wife, but the main victim of his alleged 'cruelty' was his illegitimate half-brother, Henry of Trastamare, who had fled from Castile and taken refuge at the French court. Both England and France had actively courted Castilian support since 1335, motivated entirely by remorseless self-interest, for Castile possessed what neither France nor England had at that time – a well-organized, professional fleet. Their light galleys were fast and manoeuvrable – an enviable prize for a nation whose military success depended on control of the Channel.

Charles V's chance came when Pedro the Cruel began a fierce war with his neighbour, Pedro the Ceremonious, of Aragón. The King of Aragón sought an alliance with France. This was the French King's opportunity to kill two birds with one stone. Henry of Trastamare was brought into the plot, and agreed to all the demands Pedro the Ceremonious was presently making of his half-brother if the Aragón King would help Henry gain the Castilian throne. A sum of 300,000 gold florins was made available to pay the army of the Companies who would carry out the operation. Du Guesclin had no shortage of recruits, numbering among his motley band Sir Hugh Calveley and Matthew Gournay. Calveley's presence is particularly ironical. He and du Guesclin had fought each other for the past twelve years since the affair at Montmuran. In that time each had separately captured the other and held him to ransom! But the whole situation was bizarre. The presence of the mercenary companies disguised the fact that it was an official French campaign, and anyone who asked awkward questions was told they were all going on a Crusade against the Moors of Granada. Thankful to be rid of the Companies, who had threatened his palace at Avignon, the Pope gave the enterprise his blessing, forgave them their sins and contributed a third of their wages.

The campaign proved an easy one. Pedro the Cruel fled and Henry of Trastamare was crowned King of Castile in Burgos Cathedral. Naturally enough Pedro the Cruel invoked the terms of the English alliance which he had signed some years previously. All that remained was for the Black Prince to withdraw the English and Gascon mercenary contingents from Castile, and inform Sir Hugh Calveley and his comrades in arms that henceforth they would be fighting on the other side. It is perhaps worth

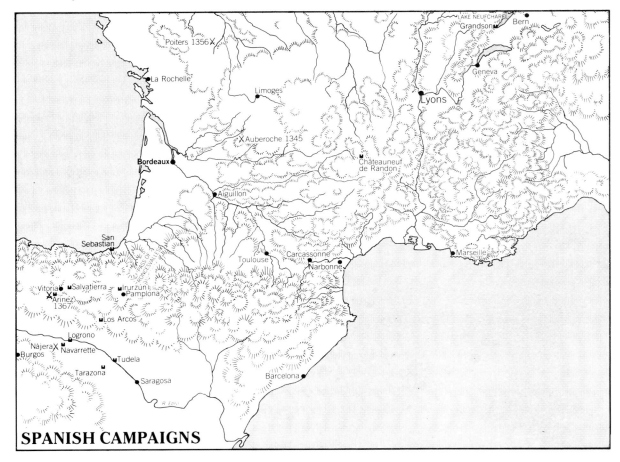

SPANISH CAMPAIGNS

pausing at this point to consider this strange aspect of knightly life. Essentially what was happening was that knights of a lower rank, such as Calveley, were in their own way copying the behaviour of those nobler than themselves. In their rough and ready, often brutal style they were forming a sort of second class of international chivalric élite. The Black Prince had his Order of the Garter. The Companies had their own unwritten code, their fierce loyalty to one another, and their common soldierly spirit which transcended national boundaries as much as did the chivalric and kinship ties of their betters. Du Guesclin and Calveley had this in common. What du Guesclin had, which none of the others could match, was a loyalty to his sovereign and to his sovereign's cause which shone like a beacon through all the duplicity and self-interest disguised as chivalry. Throughout his campaigns du Guesclin remains constant and consistent. Never a soldier of fortune, he was as loyal to his sovereign as the noble Black Prince was loyal to his. This paragon of loyalty was soon to face his severest test on the field of battle, for the expedition to regain the throne for Pedro the Cruel was to be led not by a mercenary, or even a commander like Chandos, but by the mighty Black Prince himself. The Lion and the Eagle were coming to blows.

Recruitment for the English army began in 1366. Approximately half the expeditionary force were English troops and soldiers from the Gascony garrisons. The rest were made up from English Free Companies withdrawn from Spain, Pedro the Cruel's own soldiers, and an international 'Great Company' recruited by Sir Robert Knowles. In all, the force totalled about 10,000 men. They began to cross the Pyrenees in mid-February 1367, ascending through deep snow the Pass of Roncesvalles, the same ground that had felt the tread of Charlemagne, a

chivalric link that was not lost upon the Black Prince. Henry of Trastamare was surprised by the scale of the reaction to his coup, and sent urgent messages to du Guesclin to return to his aid.

Upon reaching the neighbourhood of Pamplona the Black Prince took a strange decision. Instead of making straight for Burgos, Henry's capital, he turned west into the mountains. If he had hoped to gain the advantage of surprise it was probably negated by the difficulty of movement, and the near impossibility of providing for 10,000 men in the high mountains. It also gave du Guesclin ample time to rejoin Henry of Trastamare, to whom he advocated extreme caution. In the Prince's army were many knights against whom du Guesclin had fought with varying results: Chandos and de Clisson from Auray; the Captal de Buch from Cocherel, and his recent comrade, Hugh Calveley. Over all was the mighty Prince of Wales, whose destruction of France du Guesclin had done so much to mitigate. The Marshal d'Audrehem supported du Guesclin's suggestion that their best tactics would be to avoid a pitched battle at all costs, and bottle up the English in the northern mountains where they had providentially strayed. It would be all in a day's work for du Guesclin. But Henry of Trastamare wanted to fight for his throne, and was determined on it, despite a letter from Charles V of France urging him to follow the recommendations of his best generals. Accordingly he led the army to Zaldiaran, blocking the road which the Prince would have to take to reach Burgos. The latter continued his march as far as Vitoria, but Henry was content to remain on the defensive as long as the English stayed where they were. The Spanish skirmishers, however, were very active, and the Castilian light cavalry, called 'jinetes', made life very uncomfortable.

Great strides were made in the use and manufacture of artillery during the High Middle Ages. The illustration below shows an early example. A gun crew of the late fourteenth century are operating their cannon, which is mounted on a sturdy wooden base. Thick ropes hold it in place to ensure lateral alignment.

The primitive handgun gives little indication of the decisive battlefield weapon into which it was to develop. It consists of a tube fixed to a wooden handle, with a touch-hole to which a lighted match could be applied. The hook underneath helps aiming and compensates recoil. The gun was probably used by hooking the weapon on to a wall.

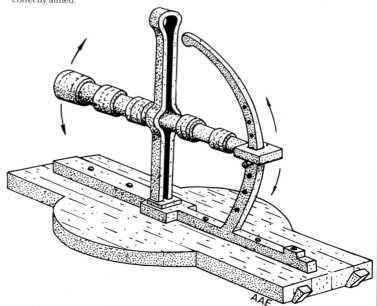

The small, fifteenth-century gun below has a simple ranging mechanism. It is hinged in the middle, and a peg is inserted into the appropriate hole when the gun is correctly aimed.

Far left: The Porte Mordelaise in Rennes, which is all that remains of the medieval walls of the city that withstood a siege from 1356 to 1357. It was probably at the Porte Mordelaise that the incident occurred whereby the garrison acquired a herd of pigs from the English besiegers.

Left: A figure of an archer, carved in wood, on the front of the house in Rennes where Bertrand du Guesclin is said to have stayed during the siege of the city from 1356 to 1357.

Below: The site of the Battle of Auray in 1364, which settled decisively the question of the Breton succession. Charles de Blois was killed at Auray, and Bertrand du Guesclin captured. This photograph is taken from the bridge at the north of the Kerzo marsh, which probably marks the spot where the French army crossed the river prior to engaging the English.

Right: Entrance to the thirteenth-century cathedral of Burgos. On 29 March 1366 Enrique de Trastamare, a puppet monarch of the French, was crowned King of Castile at Burgos. It was the intervention of the Black Prince to aid Enrique's half-brother Pedro 'The Cruel', which led to the Battle of Najera.

Below: The castle town of Vitré, which was of considerable strategic importance in the long-running relationship between France and the Duchy of Brittany. This view is from the north-west, showing the Madeleine Tower on the left, and the Montafilant Tower on the right.

One night Don Tello, Henry's brother, led an attack on the camp of Sir William Felton, who was presently foraging near Vitoria. His first contact was with a separate foraging party under Sir Hugh Calveley, who warned the English vanguard. Felton had little time to prepare for an assault before he was attacked at Arinez by mounted knights, whom the English archers managed to keep at bay until the French dismounted and attacked, supported by light cavalry. After a long resistance on a hill still called the 'Inglesmendi', the English were overwhelmed and Felton was killed. The Black Prince turned his main body to the south-east, coming down from the mountains to the easier terrain. Henry followed a parallel course, and established himself between the Black Prince and Burgos at a little hamlet called Najera, the River Najarilla separating him from the Prince's force.

On Friday, 2 April 1367, the English scouts reported to the Black Prince the astonishing news that Henry had abandoned his position behind the Najarilla and had advanced down the road towards them. His former position would have caused delay to the English advance but, as subsequent events were to show, time was no friend of Henry's either. Morale among his troops was low, and defections had already occurred. In spite of the warnings of du Guesclin and d'Audrehem, he had made a fighting decision. The English army was largely as it had been since leaving Gascony, with the unlamented exception of Charles the Bad, King of Navarre, who had been so demoralized by the defeat of the English van at Arinez that he had arranged his own capture by du Guesclin's cousin, Olivier de Mauny. Of the fighting forces, Sir John Chandos and John of Gaunt led the reconstituted vanguard, with the main body under the command of the Black Prince. The right wing was largely Gascon, the left other Gascons and Free Companies, under the Captal de Buch.

The vanguard of the opposing army was largely composed of French troops under du Guesclin and D'Audrehem, and the élite Castilian knights. They were supported by archers, and some of the dart-throwers, slingers and lancers who made up the Castilian levies. Mindful of the terrible lesson of Crécy and Poitiers, du Guesclin had insisted that the armour worn by the light 'jinetes' be increased. The proud Spanish knights of the élite companies, however, would not hear of dismounting from their splendid chargers. Chivalry demanded a mounted presence.

Henry's army had taken up position behind a small river called the Yalde, swollen by the spring rains and capable of providing as effective a barrier as the Najarilla to their rear. To the north of their position was a high flat ridge, whose southern slope is known as the hill of Cuento. Abandoning the main road, the Prince led his army over this ridge in the dark, to appear due north of the enemy, on their left flank. Du Guesclin calmly re-dressed his troops to meet the unexpected strategy from a direction where the River Yalde was less of a defence. Unfortunately many of his companions did not share his calm. A detachment of 'jinetes' deserted immediately, to be followed by some of the Castilian levies. Needing a swift move, du Guesclin led the van in a charge against their English counterparts. The 'jinetes' were moved up in support from the left, but the English arrows bit deeply and they fell back in confusion. Within a short while du Guesclin's men-at-arms were surrounded. Several times Henry of Trastamare tried to get his main body up in support, but the withering fire of the archers kept him back. With the rout of du Guesclin's division almost

complete, the English army turned its attention to the now unsupported main body of Castilan knights. The chroniclers of Najera are unanimous on two points – its utter confusion, and the totality of the Black Prince's third spectacular victory.

Du Guesclin, captured for the fourth time in his career, was finally ransomed in the following January. He is said to have taunted the Black Prince that he would never dare set him free, and fixed his own price for ransom so as to increase his own importance. In shameless good humour he added that every peasant woman in France would contribute towards the sum. The King of France paid the price. Du Guesclin was literally worth a fortune, and soon had the satisfaction of seeing the result of Najera negated when Henry of Trastamare returned to Castile and contrived to murder Pedro the Cruel with his own hands. There may have been a great English victory – but in the end the French got the Castilian fleet.

THE REVIVAL OF FRANCE

Najera had been a Spanish disaster, not a French one. With du Guesclin safely home, the Navarre and Breton questions settled, the Castilian fleet under French control, and thousands of Free Company soldiers lying dead in Spain, Charles V had the opportunity to take the offensive against England for the first time since Poitiers. Everything was pointing in the right direction. The English knights had always seen their king as a military leader, and throughout his long and brilliant career Edward III had exploited this feeling from Halidon Hill to Crécy, from Sluys to Poitiers, backing it up with the Arthurian mystique and the Order of the Garter. But the King was now a sick man, more inclined to take pleasure in his mistress than to lead an army to battle, or even grapple with the minutiae of preparation. His noble heir, who had served him so well, had never quite recovered from a severe bout of dysentery contracted in Spain, and languished in Bordeaux. By contrast Charles V was the epitome of energy. In 1367 he ordered an inquiry into the number of archers that every town could provide. Regular training was ordered, and in 1369 public sports were forbidden so as to encourage the artisans to practise archery. For France it was a revolution in military thinking. The previous depredations of the Companies also made him look at the state of the nation's castles. Financial help was made available to provide them with troops and artillery, and undertake repairs.

His first moves were political, a little dabbling in the 'internal affairs' of the Duchy of Aquitaine, in complete contravention of the Treaty of Bretigny. When the English response came, it served only to demonstrate what Charles had suspected and hoped for – that the ailing Edward III was no longer capable of original military thought. Once again it was the same pattern of chevauchée raiding. In 1369 John of Gaunt marched from Calais to Harfleur and back without achieving anything. The following year Sir Robert Knowles landed at Calais and marched straight on the Ile de France, burning the Parisian countryside and defying the King in his own capital. It was a daring raid, made more remarkable in that it was led by a knight who was a mere commoner instead of a noble, an almost unique event.

The French King's riposte to a commoner's incursion was to set his own great commoner against him, and du Guesclin was raised to the highest military office that France could bestow – that of Constable, giving him full command of the entire French military effort. It was the summit of du Guesclin's achievement. Perhaps moved

by the promotion of his fellow Breton, Olivier de Clisson, who had fought du Guesclin at Auray and Najera, and then sworn loyalty to the French King that January, joined du Guesclin in a military alliance of tremendous potential.

Charles V knew what his father and grandfather had suffered at the hands of the English chevauchées, but now they could be countered. The French castles were well-stocked and armed. Frustration and pride could alone be their downfall, pride that preferred to risk all against the English archers rather than see their country burn. Charles V had had to suffer this during his regency as Dauphin. It had to be the policy now that he was King, and in his Constable he had the perfect man to do it. Twenty years of experience were now brought to bear against the chevauchée and the English garrisons. Du Guesclin did not despise a war of raids and ambushes, of slowly wearing down an enemy. To complement these operations Charles V entrusted the more aristocratic and more conventional Duke of Anjou with the task of taking the war to the English in Gascony, which he proceeded to do with a subtle combination of siegework and political persuasion.

Meanwhile du Guesclin and 'Butcher' Clisson harried Knowles's columns remorselessly, picking off stragglers, launching night attacks, and reducing the hard commander to a state of indecision. Uneasily he began to retreat towards Brittany, where he hoped to find some refuge among the remaining garrisons with local, pro-English, support. But 'Butcher' had sealed that fate. On 4 December 1370, de Clisson and du Guesclin fell upon Knowles's rearguard at Pontvallain, near Le Mans, and annihilated it. The victory, the nearest thing to a pitched battle the French had dared attempt, became the first French success against an entirely English army since Poitiers. Knowles's remnant struggled home to tell the tale. That is what comes, said his aristocratic superiors, of entrusting the command of an English expeditionary force to a mere commoner. But their criticism was misdirected. Knowles's failure came about because of lack of discipline in an army accustomed to brave adventuring. Frustrated by delay and French attack, his army had fragmented, the rearguard under a Gloucestershire knight called John Minsterworth, choosing to go its own way, and paying the price. None the less, Knowles had to suffer considerable mortification before he was re-admitted to the King's pleasure.

One by one the great English knights were coming to the close of their careers. Late in 1369 Sir John Chandos, gallantly defending Aquitaine, attempted an ambush of a party of French soldiers. The morning was cold, the ground frozen solid. Since losing an eye in a hunting accident five years previously Chandos had never worn a visor. Descending from his horse to assist a fallen esquire who was being attacked by a group of Frenchmen, his foot caught in the long white armour robe that he was wearing against the cold. Slipping on the icy ground, he was recognized and swiftly seized. The point of a spear was thrust into the open helmet, ending the life of the architect of Poitiers and Auray.

The Prince of Wales, his life also rapidly slipping to an end, completed a ruthless career by an act of strange brutality. In Gascony defections were occurring right, left and centre, but when the supposedly loyal Limoges 'went French' it was too much to bear. That the gates of the city had been opened to the French forces by the Bishop of Limoges, the godfather of the Prince's son Richard, added insult to injury. The Black Prince, a sick man, over-

Right: The keep of the castle of Dinan is one of the finest examples of the revival of castle building in France at the end of the fourteenth and beginning of the fifteenth century, which was the result of the defensive policy of King Charles V.

Left: Sunset over Saint-Malo. In 1373 Bertrand du Guesclin used Saint-Malo as a base for a raid on Jersey. In 1378 he negotiated, with Sir Hugh Calveley, the withdrawal of an English expeditionary force which used Saint-Malo as a landing stage.

Right: Edward III, from the effigy on his tomb in Westminster Abbey.

reacted totally. In 1370, he supervised a fierce siege from the litter in which he was forced to be carried, and when the town fell allowed a brutal sack and massacre. Historians have argued long about the rights and wrongs of the Prince's action. It has even been pointed out that the sack of Limoges was fully within the rules of war as they were accepted at the time. So it may have been. The important point about Limoges is that the Prince's action was totally unnecessary. It could never have achieved anything. If it were meant to terrorize other towns into confirming English rule, the Black Prince showed a deplorable lack of appreciation of the psychology of a populace who know they are winning. The following year he returned to England for the last time. In a brutal age he had controlled his savagery with wisdom and good sense, until this final, pointless massacre.

In 1372 the prize which had slipped from the Black Prince's grasp so soon after his classic victory of Najera was finally used against his country. The Earl of Pembroke, newly named Lieutenant of Aquitaine, sailed for the troubled province with an urgently needed relieving army. As his ships approached La Rochelle they were attacked by a dozen Castilian galleys. The battle lasted two days, and resulted in the total destruction of the English ships and the capture of the Earl of Pembroke. With the lines of communication cut on the direct sea route, the Gascon strongholds began to topple before the combined efforts of the Duke of Anjou, du Guesclin, and de Clisson. Poitiers (August 1372) and La Rochelle (September 1372) opened their gates to the French without resistance. In a battle at Soubise in that same August, the English suffered a further blow in the capture of Jean de Grailly, the Captal de Buch. For the first time in the Hundred Years War, military sense took precedence over the profit motive, and ransom was refused. This new policy of Charles V was highly unpopular among the French knights, and particularly so with the squire who

had actually captured him, but the decision was a sign of the times, and the unfortunate Captal remained in captivity in Paris until his death in 1376.

A LITTLE LOCAL DIFFICULTY

Du Guesclin's native Brittany remained the one place in the West where an English army could land relatively safely and where a raiding party could seek sanctuary. The continued existence of English garrisons in the Duchy resulted almost entirely from the Duke's less than total loyalty to the pledge he had made to Charles V. In 1372 he finally threw off his mask, repudiated his homage to the French King, and fled to England whence, in 1373, a 4,000-strong English army came to Saint-Malo, though the Duke was not with them. A rapid advance by du Guesclin from Rennes forced them to re-embark and sail round the peninsula to Brest, where they provided a welcome supplement to the garrison. Du Guesclin, however, had demonstrated to Edward III that the north coast of Brittany could not be relied upon as a staging-post for Aquitaine. He reinforced the point by taking the thorn in the flesh called Bécherel, which still dominated the peninsula, and in spite of attacks had resisted him since 1363. As a further gesture he used Saint-Malo as a base for a raid on Jersey.

Leaving Olivier de Clisson to continue the siege of Brest, du Guesclin hurried back to Paris in August 1373. John of Gaunt had landed at Calais, and was leading the largest and most destructive chevauchée that France had seen for many years. Gaunt appears initially to have had no great aim apart from the usual one of causing havoc and creating a 'presence', but it soon became evident that he planned to march right across France, over the Massif Central, to relieve Gascony. It is to John of Gaunt's credit that he actually did this and the arrival of his bedraggled army, depleted and harassed by du Guesclin, must have put heart into the defenders of Bordeaux. But the state of

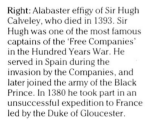

Right: Alabaster effigy of Sir Hugh Calveley, who died in 1393. Sir Hugh was one of the most famous captains of the 'Free Companies' in the Hundred Years War. He served in Spain during the invasion by the Companies, and later joined the army of the Black Prince. In 1380 he took part in an unsuccessful expedition to France led by the Duke of Gloucester.

Gaunt's troops, weakened and weary of the war, only showed in microcosm the general feeling on both sides. Charles V had restarted the war and was winning, but he feared that he had not the resources to finish it. In January 1374 du Guesclin concluded a local peace with John of Gaunt, which eventually spread to a general truce. In 1376 the Black Prince died, followed within a year by his father, the mighty King Edward III. On every hand men were tired of war.

For Charles V there remained a little local difficulty concerning the Duke of Brittany. In December 1378 the Duke was accused of treachery and Brittany was annexed to the French crown. Even though du Guesclin and de Clisson supported the King, the act proved to be an immense miscalculation. The population rose as one in support of the Montfort Duke, giving du Guesclin the unsavoury task of going to war against his own country-men. It is to his great credit that the Constable demon-strated an acute political skill which he had never before had the opportunity to employ. In a rare example of a negotiated settlement, du Guesclin managed to persuade an English army, which had landed at Saint-Malo, to return home without a fight. The commander, incident-ally, was none other than Sir Hugh Calveley. What conversation, what reminiscences, must have been exchanged by these two men – now the elder statesmen of their respective armies?

DU GUESCLIN'S FAREWELL

Following this temporary solution (the affair of the Dukedom still had a century to run) du Guesclin settled in Brittany, perhaps hoping for a well-earned retirement. He was, after all, nearly sixty years old, and had been fighting throughout his entire life, but a final call came from his King. The people of Languedoc had rebelled against the Duke of Anjou and formed 'Companies' which threatened the newly found stability of the area. It was to be du Guesclin's last campaign. Bidding farewell to Brittany at the Cathedral of Dol de Bretagne, where he reviewed his troops, he drove the brigands from Auvergne, and laid siege to a fortress called Châteauneuf de Randon. Here he was taken suddenly ill, and rapidly slowed down from the furious pace at which he had habitually lived his life. Forced to command the siege from his bed, he died there on 13 July 1380. The captain of the besieged castle, moved by the unexpectedness with which he had become part of a moment of history, brought the keys of the castle and laid them on du Guesclin's body.

So died the great, tough little Breton. His life was unique in its military style, breaking all the social conventions of the day, and even in death he aspired to a certain renown, for such were the demands for the honour of providing his last resting-place that his body literally had to be shared. Where as it was customary for the remains of Kings of France to be divided for burial in three places (the heart, skeleton and entrails) the Great Constable's were laid to rest in four. His entrails were interned in the Church of the Jacobins at Puy and his Flesh at Montferrand. It had been his wish to be buried at Dinan, in his native Brittany, but his heart was all that the King would allow. What was left of him was placed in Saint-Denis, beside the tomb which Charles V had prepared for himself, and which he was to occupy only two months later. Du Guesclin's heavy features and stocky build are well represented in the alabaster effigy of him, which is not that of the romantic, stylized knight, but of a sincere man of the people. At his feet, in place of the customary lion, is a dog, the symbol of fidelity.

Bertrand du Guesclin, unlike Joan of Arc, gave out no prophecies and suffered no martyr's death. But as she was to do half a century later, he seized the moment when France could reassert herself after black despair. If he heard any voice at all it was a quiet inner voice that spoke of his own greatness. He rejoiced, quite naturally, in the honours and titles heaped upon him: Count of Longueville, Duke of Molina, Earl of Trastamare, Con-stable of France, but always retained that common touch which enabled him to understand the mind of the ordinary soldier he had once been, whether to lead him or to oppose him. He was tireless and loyal, displaying the inspiration of Joan of Arc without her mystery. Had his patient strategy, when faced with the challenge of the chevauchée, been heeded and followed by those who came after him, Henry V's army would never have reached Agincourt in one piece, and the Hundred Years War would have been known by another name.

Below: The funerary effigy of Bertrand du Guesclin is far from the traditional stylized monument. Here is the simple man of the people, who rose from obscurity to the highest military honours that France could bestow. This cast of the original statue, which is in Saint-Denis, is preserved in the castle of Dinan.

6. Onward Christian Soldiers

TWO IMPORTANT concepts, central to the notion of chivalry, were briefly mentioned in Chapter Four: the idea of honour, and the noble expression of internationalism shown by the Crusade. As we come to examine the state of English knighthood following the painful withdrawal from France, these two topics stand out against the background of demoralization and decline.

KNIGHTLY HONOUR

King Richard II came to the throne of England in 1377 as a boy of ten, heir to the glorious military reputation of his father and grandfather, and heir also to the troubles that had arisen when that fearsome reputation began to decline. The Hundred Years War may have begun with the semblance of a civil war, a family struggle between Valois and Plantagenet, but by the 1370s it had become a war between nations, engendering a hatred between the two countries which in the years to come would so easily be rekindled into a renewed war. The very triumphs that Richard inherited made it difficult for him to obtain a peaceful settlement when peace was needed. The knights had returned with prisoners and booty. They expected success, and their honour demanded it.

The notion of honour was central to the concept of chivalry, and it was honour that provided the spur for a minor battle, which achieved little in itself, yet set the tone for the military policy of the reign. Its influence on foreign relations had a significance quite out of proportion to the reason for its being fought, for the Battle of Otterburn in 1388 was concerned with the possession of a small silken banner. Its only parallel is the Battle of the Thirty. Like the Breton encounter it was almost literally fought for the sake of fighting.

Opposite page, top: Montpazier, one of the finest examples of a fortified town, or 'bastide'. (Photograph by Daphne Clark) Opposite page, bottom: The Castle of Gravesteen, near Ghent, birthplace of Edward III's illustrious son, John of Gaunt. (Photograph courtesy of the Belgian National Tourist Office) Right: The ideals of chivalric behaviour have never been so well illustrated than in the pages of Le Gautier's *La Chevalerie*. In this engraving, the knight prepares to set off on a Crusade, and prostrates himself before the cross.

THE HOUSE OF DOUGLAS

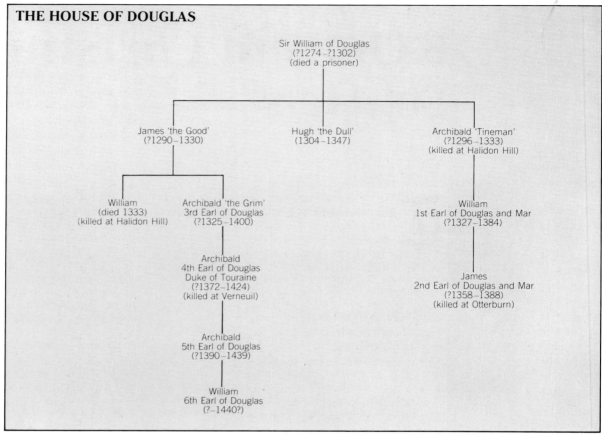

Otterburn arose from a raid across the border led by James, the second Earl of Douglas, who was the grandson of Archibald Douglas, Regent of Scotland, killed at Halidon Hill. Two armies had crossed the border. The larger had headed for Carlisle while the smaller, Douglas's host, poured down Redesdale, crossed the Tyne, and ravaged County Durham. Laden with booty, and perhaps a little over-confident, they advanced on Newcastle where they were met by Henry Percy, nick-named 'Hotspur'. The Percys were the major English family in the North, and we shall hear much of them in the pages to come. They and the Douglases were old rivals, and this encounter was nothing new. A skirmish ensued, from which the Scots managed to escape after some fighting. They did not, however, escape empty handed, but took with them the pennon from the end of Hotspur's lance, torn off during the mêlée. Was this a breach of the knightly code? Hardly, though the Scots would inevitably parade it as such on their return, like boisterous students brandishing a policeman's helmet. Henry Hotspur swore that he would recapture the pennon before the Scots crossed the border, and having made that vow, honour now entered very much into the situation. We can envisage this young man with the adrenalin pumping through his body, the impetous nature that gave him his nickname forcing him to respond dramatically to the youngster who had embarrassed him. The race was on!

There was equal determination on the other side to see the matter through. Douglas had returned the way he had come, up Redesdale, and failing to take Otterburn castle was advised by his companions to make good the lead they had on Percy and retire over the border with their booty. This advice he turned down. He was aware of the vow Percy had made and was determined to give him the opportunity of trying to fulfill it.

Percy's army was probably all mounted, consisting of about 2,000 men-at-arms and 5,000 mounted infantry, the 'hobilars' copied from the Scots. With these he continued to pursuit, and came upon the Scottish camp as it was getting dark on 19 August 1388. The surprise was total. Douglas and his men were 'dressed, unarmed, in gowns and long robes, ready for feasting' when the attack came, so there was little time to prepare: the Earl of Dunbar forgot to put on his bascinet and Douglas himself somehow armed himself though incorrectly (though Froissart is not specific). Henry Hotspur launched two attacks, one to the front and one, under Sir Thomas Umfraville, round the flanks whence he assaulted the camp, which had by now been vacated. Douglas rallied sufficiently to lead a counter-attack. This was unexpected by the English, and in the dark and at such close quarters their longbows were useless. In time the fact that the Scots had enjoyed food and rest began to tell in their favour. Henry Hotspur and his brother Ralph were captured and the English army drew away. Dawn found the Scots in undisputed possession of the battlefield, their victory made less than happy by the loss of James, Earl of Douglas, slain by an unknown hand, whose body was trampled by a thousand hooves.

It is often claimed that the Battle of Otterburn had no strategic significance. In fact it marked the first real Scottish victory over the English since Bannockburn, which is surely significance enough. It was as a direct consequence of Otterburn that Richard formally en-trusted the defence of the North to the Marcher Lords, a process that was ultimately to bring about his downfall, and is described in the following Chapter. It was also a factor in the suspension of the French Wars for the rest of Richard's reign: and all for the honour of a knight's banner!

CRUSADING – 14C STYLE

If wars had temporarily ceased between France and England, knightly virtues could find expression in other ways. Tournaments and Scottish raids were all very well, but of all the possible manifestations of the chivalric ideal, none encompassed more knightly virtue than the Crusade, and it is to this phenomenon that we now turn. To take the Cross and make war against 'the innumerable throng of Satan's satellites' was the epitome of everything in which the knight professed to believe. It added an odour of sanctity to the savage business of war, and gave a bizarre purpose to violence that was comprehensible to the medieval mind in a way that the long conflict between France and England could never be. When one monkish chronicler heard of the awful casualties at Crécy he lamented that the combatants had merely killed 'for the sake of an earthly kingdom', at which unhappy state of affairs there would be 'rejoicing at the event among the citizens of Hell'. How much better, he argued, if they had been 'stained in waves of their own blood by infidels, on behalf of the celestial kingdom and for the defence of the Catholic Faith'. The reader will recall that it was the wish of King Robert the Bruce that his heart be taken on Crusade.

In another way the Crusading ideal summed up the very genuine international brotherhood which knighthood had become. We have referred several times to the notion of the knightly class as an international élite, united by group solidarity, with a respect that transcended national boundaries so that every war could become effectively a civil war. A Crusade gave the opportunity for that ideal to be realized, as side by side, the forces of France and England would combat the 'lesser breeds without the Law'.

The great disadvantage of Crusading in the fourteenth century was that these 'lesser breeds' were becoming somewhat thin on the ground. The overt aim of the first Crusades had been to recover the Holy Places of Palestine from the invading Muslims, but so changed was the political structure of the Near East, and so debased had become the notion of a Crusade to the Holy Land by virtue of its use as a weapon of Papal politics, that the traditional destination for Crusading zeal had passed for ever. An alternative was needed.

As fortune had it, one alternative was provided by the advance westwards of the Ottoman Turks, the heirs to the military élite of Islam, under their first leader, Osman, active at the beginning of the fourteenth century, and his no less talented successors. Expeditions to halt this progress were carried out for a century and a half, and consistently ended in disaster for the Crusaders, who contrived to get themselves thoroughly beaten by the Turks, or neatly avoided coming within sight of them by the easy alternative of attacking someone else on the way. That most of the targets 'on the way' were themselves Christians threatened by the heathen seems to have mattered little to the Crusaders. In 1306 Crusaders captured Rhodes – from the Christian Greeks, and in 1366 Amadeus VI, Count of Savoy, took Gallipoli from the Turks and then proceeded to lose all this strategic advantage by attacking the Christian King of Bulgaria. The demands of national politics added an even more blatant streak of cynicism. The reader will recall the plans of Charles V of France to commission du Guesclin to lead a

Right: The ideal of chivalry in another scene from Le Gautier's *La Chevalerie*. The romantic notion of the Christian knight, fighting in a Crusade against the heathen, was a cherished aspiration which lasted throughout the time of the knight. Henry V's greatest ambition was to lead a unified Europe in a Crusade.

'crusading' army to fight the Turks for no reason other than to rid France of the mercenary companies who would take part in it. Not that the threat from the Turks was anything but real. It just seems as if the only time the threat was taken seriously was when it suited local politicians to provide some form of diversion.

Edward III of England was consistently less enthusiastic about Crusading than his French counterparts. As one strand of the complex thread of politics woven around the Gascon question in the 1330s, Edward had proposed a joint Crusade. But once hostilities loomed he quickly appropriated the money collected for the Crusade to put towards the expenses of invading France. In 1335 Philip likewise proposed a joint Crusade to Edward, and received an identical snub. From that time onwards little is heard of any Crusading plans between the two countries. From Edward's point of view it suited his plans to let the Crusade ideal slowly die away, so that the notion of an international brotherhood, which they had hereto-

Right: A knight of the Teutonic Order dressed in the style of the late fourteenth century. He wears the traditional white mantle bearing the black cross. Crusades conducted on behalf of the Teutonic Order against Lithuania provided military experience for a generation of knights.

fore represented, could be harnessed as a means of national politics, expressed from then on as service to the monarch and reaching its consummation in the Order of the Garter.

England was but one country, and a nation at war, and there is evidence that even during the first phase of the Hundred Years War the Crusade could provide an honourable solution to the problem of conflicting loyalties. A certain Gascon knight, Sir Aymenion de Pommiers, resolved that instead of joining either the French or English party he would take the Cross and go as a pilgrim to Jerusalem and 'many other fair places'. Of course once war had ceased a 'real' Crusade, in the sense of a military expedition, became an increasingly attractive alternative to pillaging the countryside, enlisting as a mercenary, or the cut and thrust of court politics. The Turks posed a constant threat, and in 1365 a number of Gascon and English knights took advantage of the lull in the fighting occasioned by the peace of Bretigny to join King Peter of Cyprus in his expedition to Alexandria. The Turks, however, were an enemy that required an essentially large-scale response. For a knight who wished to see some action, collect some booty and receive remission of sins while doing so there was one theatre of operations in the fourteenth century which became almost an annual tourist attraction – the Crusades against pagan Lithuania. Chaucer sent his Knight on a Crusade to Lithuania. So popular did the venue become that no one seemed to notice when, in 1386, the Lithuanians became converted to Christianity, and the Crusades continued.

THE CRUSADERS IN LITHUANIA

The Lithuanian Crusades were originally the prerogative of the Teutonic Order of Knights, under whose auspices the nobility of western Europe enjoyed its annual foray. The Teutonic Knights were not an 'Order' in the more modern sense of the 'Order of the Garter', or the 'Order of the Star', but the hardy survivors of the earlier, original breeds of monastic military Orders from which the secular Garter took much of its inspiration. They had begun in 1190 as a makeshift field hospital in Acre during the Third Crusade, and quickly developed into a much smaller, German, version, of the two major Orders of monastic knighthood, the Knights Templar and Knights Hospitaller. Like their more numerous brethren, the Teutonic Knights were dedicated to the defence of the Crusader states of the Holy Land and Near East, but changes in their fortunes and the demands of their native land made them turn their attention in other directions, beginning with the conquest of Prussia, and continuing, from about 1283 onwards, with an interminable war against the Lithuanians. It was this war which their comrades were to join in ever-increasing numbers. By the early years of the fourteenth century the Teutonic Order was heavily committed in Lithuania. The fall of Acre in 1291 had made it impossible for them to continue fighting in the Holy Land, and the growing distrust and suspicion of the military Orders by the Pope, exemplified by the arrest and dispossession of the Templars in 1307, led to the Order withdrawing to Prussia, far from any secular monarch's rule, where campaigns against the heathen Lithuanians would demonstrate that the Teutonic Knights were doing the job that was expected of them.

The nature of Lithuania gave a crusading knight a unique experience of campaign life. Between the cultivated area of Prussia and Lithuania lay a 100-mile belt of deciduous forest and swamp, left wild as a natural defence. It was traversed by rivers so meandering that

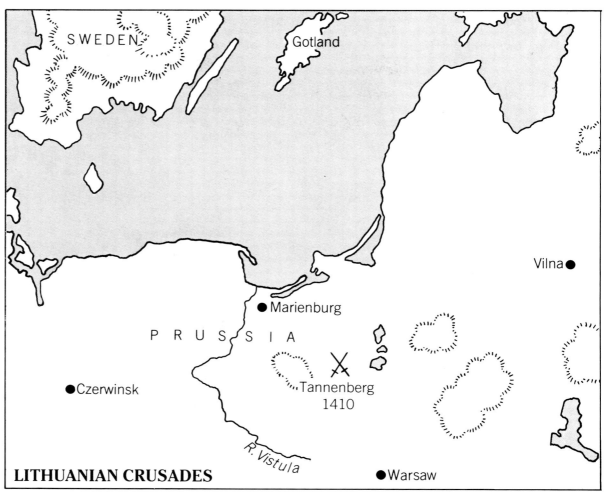

SWEDEN

Gotland

Vilna●

●Marienburg

P R U S S I A

✕✕
Tannenberg
1410

●Czerwinsk

R. Vistula

LITHUANIAN CRUSADES   ●Warsaw

traveller's tales spoke of some stretches where it was possible for boatmen to take a day to navigate a bend, and make camp at the same spot they had left the previous night. Extremes of rain and snow brought their own problems. A hard winter, with not too much snow, and cold enough to freeze the swamps, made communications and campaigning possible, as did a hot summer, which dried out the mud. But a summer in Lithuania could only be expected to last a month, and floods in summer or thawing ice in winter could trap an army, as in 1332 when King Wladyslaw III of Poland was trapped between two swollen lakes. In spite of, or perhaps because of all the challenges of terrain and winter the Lithuanian campaigns must have heralded a promise of adventure beside which the routine campaigning in Brittany or Aquitaine must have seemed mundane. As a young man, Marshal Boucicault of France went to fight beside the Teutonic Knights on three occasions 'Because there seemed to him that there was a great lack of warfare in France at that time.' Hungarians, Burgundians, Scots, Bohemians, Austrians and Italians all took part in the long-running enterprise. Henry of Lancaster, besieger of Rennes, and Thomas Beauchamp, Earl of Warwick, are among the earliest English names recorded.

Probably the most notable Englishman to go to Lithuania was Henry Bolingbroke, the son of John of Gaunt, who later became King Henry IV. It was said of him in his later years that, stricken by remorse for the part he had played in the deposition and death of Richard II, the one comfort that he could turn to was the thought that once in his life he had been on a Crusade. This atoning

event took place in 1390, during a lull in the fierce politics that were eventually to lead to him becoming the first Lancastrian King. He sailed from Boston, Lincolnshire, and landed in what is now northern Poland, whence with the Teutonic Knights, and allies from Livonia, he attacked and took the town of Vilna. Support such as this helped the Teutonic Order financially as well as militarily. Bolingbroke's expedition cost him £4,360, which was more than the Teutonic Order's budget for keeping the whole isle of Gotland. On occasion, rich adventurers like Bolingbroke tried to call the tune when it came to campaign objectives and strategy, but the vagaries of the Lithuanian weather placed their own limitations on inappropriate enthusiasm. If the weather were not right there could be no campaign, no matter how important might be the knight who was twiddling his thumbs on the battlements of Marienburg. Some, of course, were always prepared to risk disaster by going ahead under any conditions. When the Duke of Austria arrived one year, having made a vow to accomplish a Crusade before Christmas, the Grand Master put on a special 'token Crusade' to keep his important customer happy in case the weather did not improve.

Unlike the conventional view of war and profit in the Middle Ages, with vast fortunes to be made from ransom and loot, no one seems to have got rich out of a Crusade to Lithuania, except, perhaps, the Teutonic Knights themselves, who were quick to act once the custom of ransoming prisoners spread to these distant regions. They made a rule that any captured Lithuanian above the rank of knight had to be sold to the Order at a fixed sum,

after which the Grand Master would ransom him at an enormous profit.

What then accounted for its enduring popularity? Few knights other than those within the Order ever expressed religious feelings about the campaigns, and the Lithuanians could not be compared to the armies of Islam. There were no Holy Places to liberate, and any attempt by the Teutonic Knights to convert by conquest (not that they were particularly successful at conquering) was rendered rather prosaic by the acceptance of Christianity by Grand Prince Jogailo of Lithuania in 1386, a turn of events which had much to do with the fact that Jogailo had the previous year been elected to the throne of Poland, where he was now known as King Wladyslaw IV. It was partly this threat from a united Poland and Lithuania which led to the curtailment of much Crusading activity in the late 1380s and 1390s. The other reason for the apparent lack of volunteer Crusaders was that the old enemy had begun to reassert himself, and the Lithuanians were forgotten as the Turk began to move. With a fervour that had not been seen for decades, the international chivalric élite of western Europe began to set out on one of its greatest ever disasters.

NICOPOLIS

The European advance against the Turks was *real* Crusading on a grand scale. The multinational Christian army, 10,000 strong, under the general command of King Sigismund of Hungary, comprised English, French, Germans, Italians, Poles and the Knights Hospitallers. They were led by John of Nevers, son of Philip the Bold, Duke of Burgundy, and to be known to history as 'John the Fearless'. Spirits were high and many began to think in terms of not only driving the Turks out of Europe, but even of eventually recovering Jerusalem. The King of Hungary is supposed to have boasted that if the heavens fell his army would be capable of carrying the weight on their lances.

Sultan Beyazid, the Ottoman leader, was besieging Constantinople as the Crusader army made its way along the Danube, capturing Bulgarian towns as they went. He allowed them to penetrate deeply into his newly won Balkan territory, until a town called Nicopolis withstood a 16-day siege, and Beyazid realized that it was time to take the offensive against the Christians. In fact the Turkish army managed to get within two or three miles of the besieging Crusaders without being spotted, an extraordinary feat which is partly accounted for, according to some authors, by Marshal Boucicault's orders that anyone found guilty of spreading alarm and despondency among the army by announcing the approach of the enemy would have his ears cut off. This did little for the morale of the sentries, and the morale of the entire army was hardly better served when a quarrel arose as to which nation should have the honour of leading the attack.

The result was as devastating as Crécy or Poitiers. The Crusader army was decimated. The King of Hungary escaped in a ship, while John of Nevers was captured and ransomed for a considerable sum. The time it took to raise the money allowed the Burgundian propagandists to prepare carefully their version of the story of what had happened, and the future John the Fearless was welcomed home as a conquering hero, thus putting Valois Burgundy firmly on the map. But such was the nature of the Crusade in the fourteenth century. Its great advantage was that it brought its leader power, renown and prestige regardless of whether he had achieved anything. Considering that the Crusaders usually achieved nothing except the sacrifice of thousands of innocent lives, it was probably just as well it brought good to someone and it certainly explains the enduring, interminable struggle for Lithuania.

TANNENBERG – THE WATERLOO OF THE TEUTONIC ORDER

By the time the memory of Nicopolis had been suitably embellished, or forgotten, depending upon the particular needs of the time, the situation in the north of Europe was changing rapidly. As the fifteenth century began, the character of the warfare altered from being a Crusade against the heathen, to a defensive action in a campaign begun by Poland and Lithuania to reconquer the territories which the Teutonic Knights and their annual adventurers had taken from them. In 1407 the Order lost its Grand Master, Conrad von Jungingen, who died a most unusual, self-inflicted martyr's death. His doctor had prescribed sexual intercourse as a cure for gallstones, from which von Jungingen was suffering. The chaste knight refused to comply, and suffered the consequences.

He was succeeded by his brother Ulrich, who haughtily refused to believe that the Poles and Lithuanians could effectively unite against him. He also expected his ally, the King of Hungary (late of Nicopolis), to support him against them, but King Sigismund did nothing, and in July 1410 King Wladyslaw IV of Poland and his cousin, Grand Duke Witold of Lithuania, joined forces at Czerwinsk on the Vistula, and invaded Prussia. Ulrich and his knights, supported by that year's crop of Crusaders, who obviously realized they were going to get far more than they had bargained for, marched to meet them, and on 10 July the two armies met in battle at a village called Tannenberg.

The Battle of Tannenberg was the Waterloo of the Teutonic Knights. In this one engagement the long story of the Lithuanian Crusades came to an end, and great was the slaughter. The respective numbers engaged were probably in the region of 11,000 Teutonic, 16,500 allies, though among other claims to fame this decisive battle is outstanding for the greatest over-estimation of participants in history; the author of the Lübeck Chronicle estimates the strength of the allied army at 5.1 million men!

While the Poles were saddling-up a messenger arrived from Grand Master von Jungingen challenging the Polish King to single combat. The offer was refused, and a sudden thunderstorm signalled the dramatic start to the proceedings. The Poles and Lithuanians attacked in one huge mass which even the bravery of the Order could not withstand. Their casualties were heavy. The Grand Master, the Marshal of the Order, many other high officers, and more than 400 knights were killed on the field. The rest were either killed in the pursuit or captured. Tannenberg would not have been such a disaster had it been possible to represent it as a defeat of Christianity by the forces of Satan. Such an interpretation would have brought a further flock of volunteer adventurers to Prussia. But Europe did not see defeat by other Christian Kings as martyrdom. The old excuses had gone. In fact the Lübeck chronicler blamed the defeat on the Order's pride, saying that it was God's will. Other chroniclers, farther afield, got the whole business thoroughly mixed up. The French chronicler, de Monstrelet, to whom the word 'Crusade' meant only one thing, records that the Order was defeated by the Saracens.

For the knights of Europe, Tannenberg was the end of an era. The Crusade to the Holy Land in the twelfth century had involved going and winning. In the fourteenth it was sufficient merely to go in order to guarantee oneself a name in the annals of knighthood. After Tannenberg it was no longer possible even to go on a Crusade, and the bold adventurers of the Baltic lands were replaced by 'armchair Crusaders', who regularly took the Cross, but never actually went anywhere. The Burgundian Court in the 1450s was a particular example of a Crusading craze – but no one actually went to fight.

The young son of Henry Bolingbroke, whose 1390 efforts had earned him immediate renown and lasting comfort, cherished throughout his short life the burning desire to go on a Crusade and emulate the deeds of his father. As this young man was King Henry V of England it is fascinating to speculate what might have happened in 1415 had pagan Lithuania still been able to provide an outlet for lusty young energies, rather than have them directed once more at the Kingdom of France.

Left: The much ruined castle of Monmouth, birthplace of Henry V, from a Victorian engraving.
Right: The knight in this engraving, which is based on the tomb of Count Gunther von Schwarzburg, wears a full-skirted surcoat gathered at the waist.

7. The Sorcerer's Apprentice

ARS in distant lands for God or for King brought their own problems and their own rewards. The maintenance of peace in one's own country provided a different challenge. Since the victory over the Scots at Neville's Cross in 1346, England did not greatly fear a large-scale war with its northern neighbour. If a major invasion were mounted it tended to waste itself on sieges of Carlisle, Berwick or Norham, which allowed time for an English army of commensurate size to be raised and deployed. The need in the late fourteenth and fifteenth centuries was for what was basically a policing operation. This 'police presence' had to be large enough to cope with a raid of Otterburn proportions, and have sufficient local knowledge to prevent excesses from the English side during times of truce. As the English sovereign could not afford to maintain a direct military presence in these distant parts, the local soldiery had to be recruited and led by leaders they would respect and follow. There was, therefore, little alternative to entrusting the guardianship of the Scottish border to these 'Marcher Lords'.

From the King's point of view the great disadvantage was that he had so few Marcher Lords to choose from. In fact the choice was effectively between two families – the house of Percy and the house of Neville, a fact of northern life which was to extend until Tudor times. John Harding wrote in the fifteenth century that the Percys 'have the hearts of the people by north and ever have', while a later Tudor chronicler commented that the people of the north knew no king but a Neville, a Percy or a Dacre. The Dacres, however, like the Cliffords of Skipton and the Scropes of Wensleydale, were in the second division of border politics, and in time of trouble tended to attach themselves to one of the two major families.

The Percy family was one of the most remarkable knightly families of the later Middle Ages. Successive generations provided personal service, and large armies, for battles from Crécy to Barnet. In five generations no less than eight Percys met violent deaths, and the catalogue of their involvement reads like a chronicle of the fifteenth century. They became Earls of Northumberland in 1377, and owned large estates and manors on the East Coast of Yorkshire, the vale of York, and in Lower Wharfedale, where their castle at Spofforth was the only one of their residences that was not first and foremost a fortress. Spofforth, which was the birthplace of the most famous Percy of all, Henry 'Hotspur' of Otterburn fame, was twenty miles south of the great defensive chain of northern castles which stretched from the Pennines at Richmond, through Middleham and Castle Bolton, to the royal castle by the sea at Scarborough. With such a defence in depth in front of them, Spofforth could be allowed a little luxury. Like the Percys, the Nevilles

acquired their title during Richard's reign, Ralph Neville becoming the Earl of Westmorland in 1397. Also, like the Percys, we may record a succession of warrior deaths during the following century. The Nevilles owned lands in County Durham, Cumbria and Yorkshire.

To entrust the maintenence of law and order in a remote but very sensitive area of the kingdom to such warlike families was a risky business. One safeguard against either family becoming too powerful was to divide the border command between them and endeavour to arrange that their periods of responsibility alternated. In their military duties the Warden of the Marches acted like a Contract Captain under Edward III – for an annual payment from the King he undertook to raise troops as and when necessary. This system, and the policy which lay behind it, lasted until 1489, during which time there were Nevilles in the West March for 59 years, and Percy Wardens of the East March for 81 years in total.

Right: Spofforth Castle, near Wetherby, was the birthplace of Henry Hotspur. Although associated with Northumberland, the Percys held many lands in Yorkshire, and Spofforth was one of the their least well-defended castles because of its position so far south from the Scottish border.
Far right: Lionel Plantagenet (of Antwerp), Duke of Clarence, the third son of Edward III, from the gilt-bronze effigy on the side of Edward III's tomb in Westminster Abbey.

Beyond the duty to the King, the Warden was given virtually a free hand to make the best use of his resources, which included forays into Scotland for personal reasons, and much private feuding on the English side, where their methods were very similar, as noted by an observer of a gang of Westmorland men who carried out an operation against a local enemy near Kendal in 1388. They behaved 'like the Scots', creating such an uproar that the local inhabitants, well-trained in their reaction to a Scottish raid, took to the hills, and this was in a town fifty miles from the border!

The Percys reached the zenith of their powers during the 1390s. Between 1391 and 1396 Henry Percy, Earl of Northumberland, was Warden of the East March while his son Hotspur was Warden of the West. They ruled their territory like independent Princes, until Richard II, wary of their independence, tried to curtail their power by giving the Penrith Estates to Ralph Neville. Soon this threat was overtaken by the Percys' playing their part in a much larger drama: the deposition of the rightful King.

THE RISE OF LANCASTER

The coup, which placed ex-Crusader, Henry Bolingbroke on the throne of England as Henry IV, the first of the Lancastrian dynasty, occurred while Richard was in Ireland. As Richard had no heir he had named his successor before he left on a previous campaign, lest any disaster befall him. As Richard's line, from his father the Black Prince, was the senior one, it was not unnatural that he chose the second most senior surviving line to provide his heir – that from Lionel, Duke of Clarence, the Black Prince's younger brother. Lionel had been survived by a daughter, who had married into the powerful family of Mortimer – as formidable on their Welsh border as the Percys were on the Scottish one. The Mortimer heir was a young boy, Edmund. But the Mortimer line claimed

priority through a female descent. The next senior line was the House of Lancaster, whose heir was Henry Bolingbroke, son of John of Gaunt. Having been banished from the realm by Richard, Henry Bolingbroke took advantage of the King's absence to return in force to claim all the titles and lands of which Richard had deprived him. This may have been all he desired – but the support of the Northern Lords, in particular the Percys, made him play for higher stakes. Richard was arrested, and Henry was proclaimed King Henry IV.

The actual coup was bloodless. The problem facing Henry IV and his Percy allies was what to do with the rightful, anointed King, and the heir whom he had named. Young Mortimer was the easier to deal with, and was kept securely in a place of safety. For Richard there was the horror of the gloomy Pontefract castle, where he was placed under the care of a staunch Lancastrian official, Thomas Waterton. The precedent to give guidance was obviously the deposition of Edward II – but in that case there had been a son to put in his place whom the people would accept. Now there was no son, and an imprisoned heir. There seemed little alternative to keeping Richard in Pontefract and waiting for him to die.

Below: The remains of the keep of the great castle of Pontefract, for centuries the most important royal castle in the north of England. It was the place of imprisonment and death of Richard II, and the fortress where Edward I gathered his troops prior to the crossing of the nearby River Aire and the great victory of Towton. Although much destroyed, Pontefract is enjoying a thorough excavation which is likely to yield much information about this pre-eminent castle.

Rarely has a King's reign begun so inauspiciously as that of Henry IV. Mistrusted even by his allies, the one sure support Henry had during his short reign, beset throughout with rebellion and revolt, was his son Henry, Prince of Wales, Shakespeare's 'Prince Hal'. The enduring tradition which has his younger days spent brawling and carousing comes from a very early source. The Brut Chronicle tells us that when he was Prince of Wales, 'he fell and inclined greatly to riot, and drew to wild company'. His military exploits do not seem to have suffered from any excesses, if such did actually occur, and it was from an early age that he took service on his father's behalf, when the first threat came from Wales.

THE REVOLT OF OWAIN GLYNDWR

There was born in about 1359 a man called Owain Glyndwr, whose name is usually Anglicized as Owen Glendower. He had been both a law student and a knight during the latter half of the fourteenth century, and took up arms against Lord Reginald Grey of Ruthin in 1400, ostensibly over disputed lands on the Welsh border. This local quarrel soon took on the elements of a Welsh revolt, and in September his followers proclaimed Glyndwr as

Prince of Wales. Throughout that month he attacked Denbigh, Ruthin, Rhuddlan, Flint, Hawarden, Holt, Oswestry and Welshpool, only to be temporarily halted by an army of shire levies somewhere along the River Severn.

The situation was sufficiently serious to demand direct intervention at the very highest level. Prince Henry and Henry Hotspur (the Percys were loyal supporters) took charge of North Wales. Conwy Castle was attacked by Welsh rebels in 1401, and while they were thus occupied Glyndwr himself carried his operations to South Wales, where he defeated an English army at Hyddgen, and in 1402 scored another victory at the Battle of Bryn Glas when the Welsh archers in the English army turned against their leaders. Edmund Mortimer (the uncle of the boy of the same name who was the rightful heir to the throne) was captured by Glyndwr along with many others, and for days no Englishman dared go near.

The Welsh border was now in a higher state of tension than the Scottish border had been for many a year. In September Henry IV advanced from Shrewsbury in search of Glyndwr, and was caught in a terrific rainstorm which collapsed the tent in which he was sleeping. He would probably have suffocated had it not been for the fact that

Left: Sir Robert Waterton, depicted here on his tomb at Methley, Yorkshire, was a staunch Lancastrian who had charge of the deposed sovereign, Richard II, during the latter's captivity and death at Pontefract Castle.

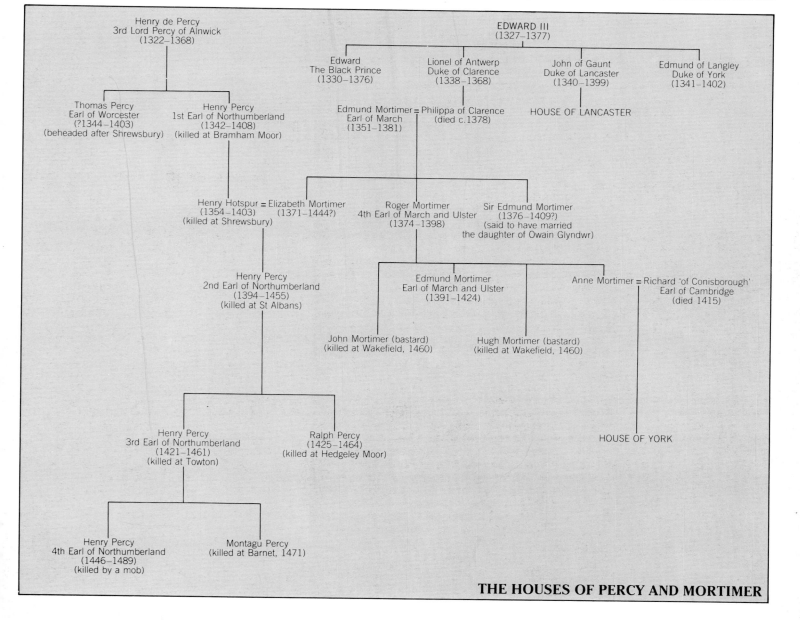

THE HOUSES OF PERCY AND MORTIMER

he was sleeping in his armour. Glyndwr's continuing success, and in particular his uncanny ability to disappear after a battle, quickly gave him the reputation of being a magician. By way of complete contrast, Henry's reputation had now reached rock-bottom. The only thing that saved him from total disgrace was a victory against the Scots at Homildon Hill in Northumberland, where the Percys destroyed another Scottish raiding army. The Scots were led by a Douglas, in this case Archibald, the Fourth Earl of Douglas grandson of 'James the Good', and victory was secured when the Scottish knights charged the English archers. The Battle of Homildon Hill was undistinguished, but was very important politically. Douglas was captured by the Percys, who naturally enough wished to ransom him in revenge for Otterburn. But Henry wanted Douglas kept as a lever for future negotiation with the Scots, which infuriated the Percys, turning them against him for the first time since the coup of 1399. Henry was also in no hurry to ransom Edmund Mortimer, captured at Bryn Glas, judging wisely that any Mortimer was safer in captivity. It soon proved that no ransom for him would be demanded, because Edmund Mortimer stayed happily in Wales and married Glyndwr's daughter, after Glyndwr had promised to help Mortimer secure the throne for his nephew. Now Glyndwr began to court the disaffected Percys. As Henry Hotspur was married to Edmund Mortimer's sister the plotting against Henry IV became quite a family affair!

A very clear exposition of the situation is contained in a letter which Sir Edmund Mortimer wrote to his tenants explaining why he was joining Glyndwr:

'Owain Glyndwr has raised a quarrel, of which the object is, if King Richard be alive, to restore him to his Crown, and if not, that my honoured nephew who is the right heir to the said Crown, shall be King of England, and that the said Owain will assert his right in Wales. And I, seeing that the quarrel is good and reasonable, have consented to join in it . . .'

Rumours that Richard II was still alive, and planning to lead the Scots in war were so prevalent, that Henry was forced to make a public proclamation against 'false reports', and stating that Richard was indeed 'mortuus et sepultus'.

Dead or alive, the deposition of a rightful king was sufficient reason to form any number of conspiracies, and the three-way plotting of Sir Edmund Mortimer, Glyndwr and the Percy family, father and son, was the most serious threat Henry IV had to face. It is to his great credit that he had the boldness to strike while the conspirators were divided. Henry was in Staffordshire when he heard the news of the alliance against him, and his adversaries were separated from one another by several hundred miles. Henry Percy, the Earl of Northumberland, was on the Scottish border; his son Henry Hotspur was in Chester, while Glyndwr and Mortimer were in South Wales. The pivot of the strategy had to be Shrewsbury, the

main crossing-point on the upper reaches of the Severn, and presently within Shrewsbury was a small army under the Prince of Wales, which had just carried out a raid on North Wales, and was now dangerously isolated from the King's main forces. Henry Hotspur reached a similar conclusion at the same time, and the opening moves of the revolt became a race for Shrewsbury. It was a race which King Henry won, entering the gates of Shrewsbury to join his son only hours before Hotspur, who now became the one left dangerously isolated. He had with him his uncle, Thomas Percy, the Earl of Worcester, but there was as yet no sign of the Welsh of Glyndwr. The only safe course was to withdraw to Chester, via Whitchurch to the north, but the Royal army would try to prevent him. Across the road which led out of Shrewsbury to the north was a ridge, and here he resolved to make a stand. It was not the rash decision of an impetuous youth, even though Shakespeare would have us believe that Hotspur and Prince Hal were of the same age. In fact, Henry Hotspur was 39, and the wild days of his youth at Otterburn were distant memories. His stand at Shrewsbury was a calculated risk, not a gamble for chivalric honour.

The Battle of Shrewsbury was fought on 21 July 1403, a 'sorry battle between Englishmen and Englishmen'. It had one unique feature – a contest between rival armies, both of which had longbows. It must have been a strange experience for the archers. The accounts of the battle give the impression of the two front ranks of archers nervously approaching each other and letting fly at their counterparts. Hotspur's army had the better of the encounter. The archers whom he had recruited in Chester, the prime breeding-ground for bowmen, overcame their rivals, allowing Hotspur to lead an advance on the King's centre division with the aim of capturing the monarch himself. But Prince Hal on the left wing had not suffered from the archers' fire, and was able to lead his wing in a flank attack on Hotspur, and a huge mêlée ensued. An arrow, fired by an unknown hand, transfixed Henry Percy, called Hotspur. Their leader dead, the rebels collapsed.

The site of the battle of Shrewsbury is today marked by a church, raised by Henry IV as a chantry. An effigy of the victorious king crowns the gable end, while all around are gargoyles, whose faces are supposed to represent the rebels. Shrewsbury thus deprived Glyndwr of two allies, for Thomas Percy, Earl of Worcester, was to be beheaded shortly afterwards. The old Earl of Northumberland remained an ally, biding his time in the Marches, while his son's and brother's places were taken by armies of a very different kind – the French.

THE FORGOTTEN INVASION

The story of French support for Glyndwr's revolt is one of the most fascinating episodes in medieval history. It began with a number of raids on the south coast in 1403 and 1404. Targets included Plymouth, Dartmouth and the Isle of Wight, and achieved little, one Breton leader, the

Below: The site of the Battle of Homildon Hill (1402), looking up the slope of the hill past the boulder known as the Bendor Stone. It was partly arguments about ranson of prisoners captured at Homildon Hill that led to the split between King Henry IV and the Percys.
Below right: The charge of the Scottish knights at the Battle of Homildon Hill in 1402. The defeat of the Scots at the hands of the Percys was one of the few pieces of good news to come to Henry IV during a troubled year.

Sieur de Castellis, being killed by local people during the Dartmouth raid. In November 1403 the Welsh, perhaps accompanied by a small French expeditionary force, attacked Edward I's mighty castle at Caernarfon, leading to the following pathetic letter being received by Henry IV from the Constable of Chester:

'. . . Robert Parys, the Deputy Constable of Caernarvon Castle, has informed us through a woman, for neither man nor woman dare carry letters on account of the rebels of Wales, whom Owen Glyndwr, with the French and all his other power, is raising up to assault the town and castle of Caernarvon . . . And in the castle there are not in all more than twenty-eight fighting men which is too small a force, for eleven of the abler men who were there at the last siege of the place are dead . . .'

The Welsh castles at this time were very meagerly garrisoned. An extant document refers to the numbers at Conwy being fifteen men-at-arms and sixty archers, 39s 2d being allowed daily to keep them. Conwy, in fact, was next to feel threatened, followed by Harlech, Beaumaris and Aberystwyth. Harlech and Aberystwyth fell early in 1404, giving Glyndwr sufficient confidence to call a parliament, and undertake a further conference with the French. So dramatic were his successes that the County of Shropshire arranged a 3-month truce with him, recognizing Glyndwr's Wales as an independent state.

By 1405 the Percy/Mortimer/Glyndwr Alliance was given a more formal aspect, combining in one grandiose scheme the prophecies of the Welsh bards, the share of spoils, and a very complicated division of territory. It arose from a conference between Glyndwr and one Hopkin ap Thomas, whom Glyndwr held to be 'Master of Brut', meaning skilled in the prophecies of Merlin. According to Hopkin ap Thomas the present combatants were all to be found in these prophecies. Henry IV was 'the mouldewarp accursed of God'; Glyndwr was the dragon, Percy the lion, and Mortimer the wolf, the three who would divide the mouldewarp's kingdom among them. Mortimer's nephew was to be placed upon the throne, and then the kingdom was to be divided up very precisely. At this point Hopkin ap Thomas seems to have taken a back seat. Owain Glyndwr was to rule a 'Greater Wales', Percy the north of England, and Mortimer the rest. They even agreed the boundaries between their respective territories. 'The north' was to consist of all of England north of the Trent, plus Leicestershire, Northamptonshire, Warwickshire and even Norfolk. 'Greater Wales' was to stretch 'along the Severn to the north Gate of Worcester, thence to the ash trees on the main road from Bridgnorth to Kinver, thence by highway to the source of the Trent, then to the source of the Mersey and along to the sea'. In fact, the loss of Henry Hotspur had probably sealed the fate of any such grandiose scheme, and although Glyndwr controlled several of the major Welsh castles, he began to suffer defeat in field battles. Henry IV found further encouragement in the swift crushing of the northern revolt led by no less a person than the Archbishop of York. Seeking to make an example Henry had the Archbishop beheaded outside the city of York. His tomb is in the Minster, the scene of many miracles from that day on. As if in heavenly judgement, Henry IV fell ill.

Meanwhile the French responded wholeheartedly to Glyndwr's call, setting sail on 22 July 1405 for Milford Haven, where they landed early in August. The army consisted of 2,600 men, including 800 knights and 600 crossbowmen. Joining Glyndwr's 2,000 Welshmen, they captured Haverfordwest and Carmarthen and advanced across the border and through Herefordshire. The place where they made a stand was Woodbury Hill, near Great Witley in Worcestershire. This quiet wooded hill in the heart of England thus has the distinction of being the site of the farthest penetration by an invading force in the whole of English history since 1066. Henry IV entered Worcester on 22 August. There was some skirmishing between English and French/Welsh troops, then Glyndwr, taking the French with him, withdrew to his mountains.

It was a tactic which the French could not understand, and their support began to wane. By Lent 1406, the French had left. Gradually Henry and his son fought back. Aberystwyth castle was attacked in 1407, an action notable for the first appearance on the scene of a knight who was later to make a great name for himself in France – John Talbot. Further encouragement came with the defeat of another Percy revolt. In a last attempt at overthrowing Henry, the Earl of Northumberland, Hotspur's father, marched south with a Scottish army. Sir Thomas Rokeby, High Sheriff of Yorkshire, held the bridge at Knaresborough against them, and pursued Percy when he headed off to cross the Wharfe at Wetherby. He caught up with him at Bramham Moor, between Leeds and

Far right: The castles established in Wales by Edward I are well-known as excellent examples of the development of fortifications. Conwy, in this artist's impression, shows how well the castle was integrated into the defences of the town. In spite of its size, Conwy was completed in four years – 1283-87, and there are records of 1,500 men working on Conwy during the summer of 1285. The cost, £20,000, was the biggest sum spent by Edward I on any castle in Wales.
Right: Beaumaris shows how an inner curtain wall structure could provide an alternative to a keep. It was the last of Edward I's Welsh castles, and remained uncompleted even after thirty-five years' work. Its almost perfect concentric design was considered impregnable, but this was never put to the test, and Beaumaris never suffered siege or attack of any kind throughout its long history of decay. The entire castle is surrounded by a wet moat supplied by the waters of the Menai Strait.
Below: The battlements of the Eagle Tower at Caenarfon are a small detail from the fortress which Edward I intended to be his showpiece. The inspiration for its design came from the walls of Constantinople, which Edward I had seen while on the Seventh Crusade. Caernarfon's layout is vast and majestic, with well-planned defensive systems.

Right: Woodbury Hill in the County of Hereford and Worcester is the little-known site of the furthest penetration on to English soil of a French army. A total of 10,000 troops, including 600 crossbowmen, had landed at Milford Haven in August 1405 in support of the revolt of Owain Glyndwr. Henry IV marched to Worcester to oppose them, and after some minor skirmishing the French, who had captured Haverford West and Carmarthen, withdrew and Glyndwr's support began to ebb away.

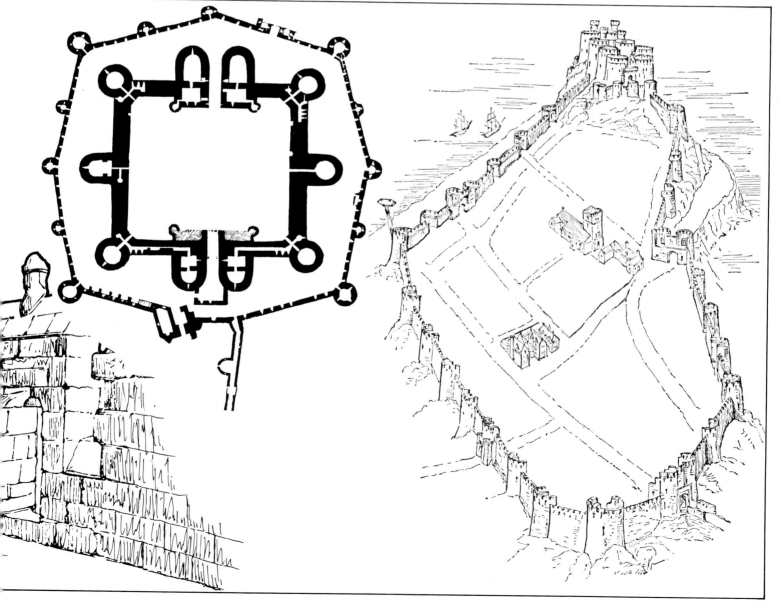

Opposite page, top left: Richard II, from his tomb in Westminster Abbey.
Opposite page, top right: The lion rampant of the Percys, beautifully captured in stone on the wall of the keep of Warkworth Castle.
Opposite page, bottom: The hills of the Welsh Marches, so peaceful now, yet during the Middle Ages a disputed land, fought over as fiercely as the Scottish marchlands. This particular area, viewed from the keep of Wigmore Castle, was also the scene of much fighting during the Wars of the Roses.

CAMPAIGNS OF OWAIN GLYNDWR AND WARS OF HENRY IV

Top left: This martingale, bearing the arms of Owain Glyndwr, was discovered during excavations at Harlech Castle.
Top right: Henry IV, first monarch of the Lancastrian House, from his tomb in Canterbury Cathedral. (Photograph courtesy of Dunstan Gladthorpe)
Bottom: Bramham Moor, between Tadcaster and Leeds, was the scene of the defeat of Sir Henry Percy, the first Earl of Northumberland. His son, Hotspur, having been killed at Shrewsbury in 1403, the defeat of Bramham Moor marked the final eclipse of a Percy-inspired challenge to Henry IV. The Earl was captured and beheaded on 'The Pavement' at York.

Tadcaster, and in a 'sharp, furious and bloody' battle the old Earl was captured, and afterwards beheaded on 'The Pavement' in York. In 1409 Aberystwyth and Harlech castles were recaptured, and at Harlech Edmund Mortimer was killed.

The following year Glyndwr led his last raid into England with an attack on Shrewsbury. He then vanished from history, to live on in legend. With his disappearance the House of Lancaster seemed secure. Young Edmund Mortimer, in whose name so much had been attempted, was a virtual prisoner, so the Mortimer line seemed amost certain to die out. He only had one legitimate sibling, a sister, Anne. She married the Earl of Cambridge and in 1411 gave birth to a son, but by a strange combination of fate and fortune this young man was to inherit both the Mortimer claim to the throne and another through his father. For this baby was Richard Plantagenet, the future Duke of York. The white rose had begun to flower.

8. The Picardy Affair

Right: Henry V, from the tomb in his Chantry at Westminster Abbey. The head is a modern reconstruction recently restored to the wooden effigy.

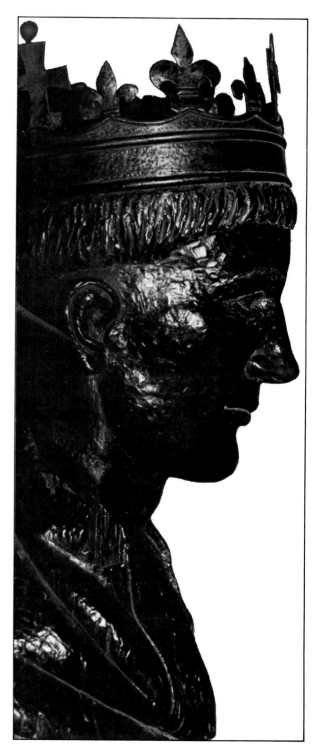

ENRY V's invasion of France, the unexpected and crushing victory of Agincourt, and the diplomatic success of the Treaty of Troyes, which effectively gave him what had been denied to his great-grandfather, Edward III, are among the best-known events of the Hundred Years War. In this chapter I intend to examine more closely how all this was achieved. What factors enabled Henry V to gain such a sweeping victory? What had happened to the reforms of Charles V and du Guesclin, and the lessons supposedly learned in the 1370s?

The France which Henry V invaded in 1415 was a very different place from the proud yet tired nation whose guerrillas had harried the last manifestation of chevauchée raiding in the fourteenth century. Charles V's successor, his son Charles VI, was subject to periodic bouts of insanity, which lasted throughout his long reign. Lacking a firm ruler, the French Court became a battleground for personal rivalries, particularly between two men: Charles's uncle, Philip the Bold, Duke of Burgundy, whose inheritance had been secured by du Guesclin's victory of Cocherel, and Charles's brother, Louis, Duke of Orléans. The seniority of years which Burgundy possessed controlled the balance of power in his favour until his death in 1404, when he was succeeded by his son, John the Fearless, whom we last heard of being defeated in the Crusade of Nicopolis. The new Duke of Burgundy needed all the bravery of his nickname to counteract his rival. For three years the quarrel continued until the Duke of Orléans was murdered by Burgundian agents in 1407. The new Duke being of tender years, command of the 'Orléanist' faction was taken by Bernard of Armagnac, whose daughter married the young Duke in 1410, and a civil war began between the 'Burgundians' and the 'Armagnacs'. John the Fearless was driven out of Paris and, in a fateful step, appealed to England for help.

Under Henry IV English policy had been that of playing off one faction against the other. Henry IV was now dead. He had laid the foundations of a dynasty by blood and intrigue, leaving his strong, vigorous son to inherit his throne of England and his attitude towards France. Under Henry V, this attitude took on the more cynical aim of delaying the start of the inevitable war until he had fully completed his preparations for it. This threat was so apparent that the Burgundians and Armagnacs in fact concluded an uneasy peace, neither side daring to suppose which way Henry would incline. But civil war had taken its toll. The Armagnac bands had caused even greater havoc and fear among their own countrymen than had the English soldiers or the Free Companies of the previous century. It was a stricken France which awaited Henry's incursions.

By comparison with France, England was a country blessed with unity. Opposition to the Lancastrian take-

Right: The standard of Archibald, Earl of Douglas, with the saltire of St Andrew.

Right: A gargoyle on the wall of Battlefield Church, Shrewsbury, depicting a knight loading a cannon.

Right: King Henry IV, victor of the Battle of Shrewsbury in 1403, immortalized in stone on the East gable of the church built on the site of the conflict.

Right: The standard of Henry Bolingbroke, Duke of Hereford, who was to become Henry IV. Note the red rose of the House of Lancaster, one badge among several, but the one that was to capture the imagination of a generation of later historians.

Below: The site of the Battle of Shrewsbury, looking westwards towards the church. Henry Hotspur's forces would have occupied the sloping ground to the right of the picture.

over continued, but with little effect. An attempt by Richard, Earl of Cambridge to put Edmund Mortimer on the throne was nipped in the bud while Henry's troops were preparing to embark, and did nothing to deflect the warrior King from his aims.

But what were his aims? Possibly his principle one was war itself. He had made his name as a war leader, and was determined to show his subjects that the traditional view of the king as a leader in battle, which Edward III had been, was alive and flourishing in his great-grandson. In the discussion earlier about du Guesclin's re-conquests in the 1370s it was noted how the ailing King and Black Prince had not been able to fulfil this role, and this perhaps offers a clue to Henry V's subsequent behaviour. He invaded France simply because it was expected of him.

He certainly seems to have been utterly convinced of the rightness of his claim to the French throne, and any consideration of the damage the pursuit of that claim might do to the country he purported to rule never entered his classic medieval mind. Throughout the negotiations which preceded his invasion he was talking in terms of 'recovering his just inheritance', and if any preference was made as to what that inheritance consisted of it seems to have concentrated on Normandy and Aquitaine. It may be that the latter was considered as a possible military objective, at least early in 1415, but Aquitaine was a long distance to travel with the large army he was assembling, and there was always the threat from Brittany which could cut his lines of communications. Normandy was nearer. It had many castles and fortified towns which could be used as bases, so his original plan appears to

Right: Sir Simon Felbrygge on a monumental brass dated 1416, wears armour typical of that worn during the Agincourt campaign. It is 'alwite' armour, i.e., complete plate armour without the heraldic gipon or surcoat. The rigid helmet, although affording considerable protection to the neck, had the disadvantage that the knight could not turn his head independently of his body.
Left: Thomas Swynborne's armour has no gipon, so we can see clearly how well-articulated it was. The bascinet and its aventail of mail has given way to the great bascinet, and the sword is worn slung from the hip.

have been a march to Bordeaux, capturing Rouen and Paris on the way. Perhaps the story of his grandfather, John of Gaunt's 'Grand Chevauchée' was taunting him to achieve great things.

The major obstacle proved to be much nearer home. He landed at Harfleur, a port on the Normandy coast now swallowed up in the modern complex of Le Havre. It was the key to Normandy, and Henry must have totally underestimated the resistance that would be brought against him when he attempted to reduce it. The resulting siege took five long, hard weeks which proved as expensive in casualties as in time. The vigour and determination of the French defenders was of the highest order. They repaired by night the damage Henry's guns wrought by day. Meanwhile the English soldiers, encamped in the unhealthy salt marshes, were debilitated by an epidemic of dysentery so severe that many had to be ferried home to recover.

The eventual fall of Harfleur looked like a disaster, a far cry from Shakespeare's 'Once more unto the breach. . .' The garrison had surrendered by negotiation, having set a date for relief, but with so many of his army dead, sick or deserted Henry was forced to consider his next move very carefully. He could have garrisoned Harfleur and gone home, but that was not what was expected of a hero king. Nor would it persuade Parliament to make further monies available if that were all he had to show for his efforts. A march to Paris, let alone Bordeaux was out of the question. The French army, he understood, had concentrated in the capital, and he now had only 900 men-at-arms and 5,000 archers available. Henry's resultant action was in a sense a compromise, but a compromise on such a daring scale that the majority of his Council recommended strongly against it. He would carry out a chevauchée. To Edward III it had been the most useful way to displaying one's mastery. In Henry's case it must have been this 'bravado' aspect of a chevauchée, rather than the devastation it could cause, which attracted him. He had taken a long time to reduce a fortress in a country he claimed was his own. A different gesture was required, and to march with impunity through France to Calais would be that gesture. This view, of a 'proud' march, is supported by the fact that during Henry's ensuing march his troops were kept under very tight discipline, and looting, burning and rape were forbidden. It was very different from Edward III's day, when such activities were the *raison d'être* of the chevauchée, and astonished the French, who had regularly suffered all three at the hands of their own countrymen, the Armagnacs.

I cannot accept the view that Henry was trying to provoke the French king into attacking him. The whole course of his subsequent march looks as though he were trying to avoid the French army, rather than to bait it. Henry was very well-informed of the potential of the French leadership. The older men, in particular the Duke of Berry, had personal memories of the later chevauchées of the 1370s, and firsthand experience of the success of Charles V and du Guesclin's tactics of avoiding pitched battles and harrying a column from a distance. Such men would be unlikely to be drawn into battle, but Henry's force, isolated and weakened, would be a prime target for harassing tactics. Besides, whatever Henry's personal view of his own capabilites or those of his army, the fact remained that they would be heavily outnumbered.

The long march which eventually ended at Agincourt was a military feat that brought credit to both sides. Credit to Henry because, even if Agincourt had not taken place, it was quite an achievement to have established on

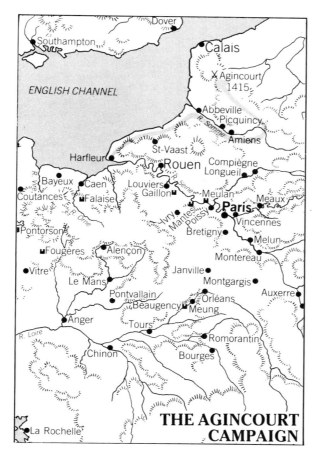

THE AGINCOURT CAMPAIGN

THE BATTLE OF AGINCOURT, 25 October 1415

French soil an alternative base to Calais, and linked the two by a well-disciplined march. To the French goes the credit for having responded so decisively to the challenge, and of having reacted so intelligently to Henry's activities. Marshal Boucicault, disgraced at Nicopolis, showed himself now as a good commander, and when Henry reached the Somme he found all the crossing-places heavily defended for miles upstream from Blanchetaque, where Edward III had crossed before Crécy. So he turned right, and headed upstream, while the French army, which had crossed at Abbeville, followed his every move on the far bank.

Amazingly, Henry managed to give them the slip. Either he had a rudimentary map of the area, or a reliable source of local knowledge, but having approached the bridge at Corbie the English army turned sharp right to gain advantage of a similarly orientated bend in the river. The gamble paid off. The French army hurried round the course of the Somme, the English set off across country, and used a ford upstream from Peronne. Henry may have crossed in safety, but his way to Calais was now barred by the French advanced guard, who were prepared to resist him, if necessary without the support of their main body. This is indicated by a recently-discovered battle plan drawn up, probably by Boucicault himself, to oppose Henry should he attempt to cross the Somme. It is interesting to note that it imitates the usual arrangement of the English army by placing dismounted men in the centre, archers in the front and mounted knights on the flanks. So determined was Boucicault to oppose Henry at Peronne that he proposed mounting servants and grooms on the unused horses of the dismounted knights. However, his total force was only slightly more numerous than Henry's, and only about a fifth of what could be assembled by joining the French main body, and it

was this consideration that led the French to withdraw northwards.

They must also have made the observation that the English army appeared to be in a very weak state. It had now marched for a fortnight, and there must have been considerable numbers of stragglers. The discovery of the bodies of dysentery victims on the way, and reports of continuing desertions, must have led to the inevitable conclusion that the time was ripe to strike in force. In this light the decision to fight what was to become the Battle of Agincourt can only be seen as an eminently sensible one.

AGINCOURT

The great Battle of Agincourt might so easily have been fought elsewhere. The French had had the opportunity of choosing their ground and as we have seen, abandoned it in favour of more certainly uniting their forces. But they still held the advantage in numbers and morale. The English army had now marched for 17 days with only one day's rest. The French had covered 180 miles in ten days, but they were nearly all mounted. Above all, the odds of four to one against struck home to the English troops, and it was Lord Hungerford who actually voiced the opinion of 'needing more men', to which Shakespeare, in his *King Henry V*, puts the words, 'We few, we happy few, we band of brothers' into the King's mouth for reply. Such heroic sentiments may have been far from the King's thoughts on the day, for we know that prior to the battle he offered terms to the French, stating that he would return Harfleur in exchange for safe conduct to Calais. It was perhaps only after these proposals had been summarily rejected that the 'do or die' attitude, which is the best-remembered feature of Agincourt, really came into being. To the French it would be more than revenge for Poitiers – it

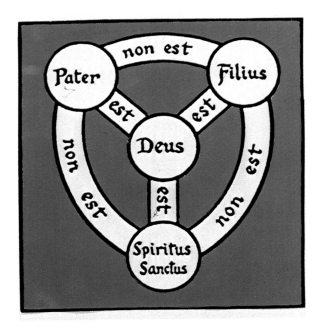

would be just recompense for the years of captivity suffered by their King John – for here was an English king for the taking.

As noted above, we now know that the French had worked out a plan of battle, which was based upon the successful English model that had been previously used against them. It was a tragedy for them that the narrowness of the front they were compelled to take did not allow for the correct deployment. In fact, so totally were Boucicault's original ideas overruled – indeed, his plan was abandoned – that the archers and crossbowmen were placed at the rear of the wings and took little part in the subsequent action. The English drew up in a 1,000-yard front between two woods, straddling the Calais road. The knights stood four deep, shoulder to shoulder with the archers. There was no reserve except for a small baggage guard. For four hours there was no movement by either side, then the English advanced, planted stakes, and fired arrows to provoke the French into attacking. At last a response came from the French knights on the flanks who funnelled in towards the English lines, ignoring the archers and concentrating on the dismounted knights. At once they were hit by volleys of arrows, which forced them to turn in on the ranks of their own advance guard, causing great confusion as their charge got under way. But this charge also was halted by the archers, and amidst the confusion of dead and dying horses and men on the muddy ground a huge mêlée developed in the centre. The archers left their bows and joined in with knives and swords. Within half an hour a wall of French dead had begun to build-up across the field, a phenomenon that had not been seen since the Battle of Dupplin Moor, where the field had been much more restricted. So fierce was the crush that men could not move to fight. As one chronicler later commented, 'Great people of them were slain without any stroke.' One such was the Duke of York, suffocated in the press, and found later without a mark on his body.

The more nimble archers began to take prisoners and escort them back to the baggage train. But one part of Boucicault's original plan remained: a separate French attack on the baggage train. The sight of the French third line preparing to join the attack, and unlikely to join the mêlée in the centre, led to Henry's order that all the

prisoners be killed, a decision for which he is always heavily criticized as an example of his bloodthirsty nature. Such nature was probably never in doubt, but I cannot see how the killing of the prisoners at Agincourt is evidence of that. In the circumstances he probably had no choice, nor did he have much time to make a careful decision about anything. During the battle he fought off attacks from eighteen individual French knights, and at one time stood guard over his fallen brother, Humphrey, Duke of Gloucester. Killing the prisoners was no mere act of vindictiveness, such as had motivated Edward III after Halidon Hill. Once this responsibilty was removed the battle was as good as won.

That such a complete victory should be won once again by archers overcoming armoured knights is particularly ironic in view of the great strides made in defensive armour since the last disaster. Using monumental effigies as our guide, it is clear that by the early years of the fifteenth century the gipon style of surcoat was going out of fashion, and examples of the period show us the complete plate armour beneath. The most visible addition had taken place with the helmet. The flexible aventail of mail which hung down from the edge of the bascinet, was now replaced by one or more solid plates that rested on the shoulders, in a combination of helmet and neckguard known as the great bascinet. It was the most complete protection yet devised, but had the disadvantage that the knight could not move his head independently cf his body, a hindrance which must have been very acutely felt at Agincourt, when the dismounted knights were set upon by the ligher-footed archers. It was the essential clumsiness of such armour, rather than any considerations of weight, that were its drawback.

Thus was accomplished the Battle of Agincourt, resulting in 10,000 French casualties and numerous high-ranking prisoners, among whom was the Duke of Orléans. But Henry's greatest benefit was less material than moral. It enhanced his reputation in England, and made his name abroad. It also served to consolidate his political position at home, and through him that of the Lancastrian dynasty. But in military terms it was the unexpected outcome of a modest raid, a welcome bonus to an otherwise pointless campaign whose only tangible gain was Harfleur, itself a potential drain on the English

Opposite page, left: The banner of the Holy Trinity, carried by Henry V at Agincourt. It illustrates the doctrine of the Trinity in a neat pictorial form.

Opposite page, right: The arms of John de Wodehouse, an English knight who distinguished himself at Agincourt, and was thereupon allowed to change his ermine chevron to the blood-spattered golden one shown here.

Above right: The standard of John, Duke of Bourbon, who fought at the Battle of Agincourt. The white cross on blue is the cross of St. Denis.

Below right: The spectacular fortress and monastery of Mont-Saint-Michel, the only fortified place never to be taken by the English during Henry V's campaigns in Normandy. (Photograph by Daphne Clark)

finance and manpower which would be needed to keep it defended. There were no long-term military consequences, except perhaps the most important of all – the fact that after the exhaustion of the 1370s England was back in France.

HENRY'S NORMANDY INVASION

In 1417 Henry returned to continue where he had left off, but in a very different vein. 1415 had been a raid, a gesture, a gambler's adventure. His new strategy shows greater deliberation, more long-term goals, perhaps even a certain maturity. He landed at Tonques, on the opposite side of the Seine from Harfleur, and decided that Caen would be his first target. In an action not dissimilar to that of Edward III's siege, he launched two simultaneous

assaults from the new town onto the old. Soon after the town had capitulated the castle followed suit. To consolidate his position he decided to establish a line of fortified towns from Verneuil to Alençon, which he carried out town by town, siege by siege, Falaise falling to a bombardment from 20-inch diameter cannon-balls. With lower Normandy firmly in his grasp the next major prize was the Norman capital, Rouen.

In Chapter One the siege of Berwick by Edward III was studied in detail for the unparalleled illustration it gives of the chivalric aspect of military life as shown by the gentlemanly courtesies of agreement and negotiation. Henry V's siege of Rouen between 1418 and 1419 is interesting because of the insight it gives into the conditions suffered by people at the opposite end of the

social spectrum. From the military point of view the siege of Rouen is no different from scores of others. It lacks the bizarre complexity of Berwick, and the dash of the defenders of Rennes. What Rouen has instead is a pitiable humanity, which brings the whole notion of knightly warfare down to an understandable scale.

The town was thoroughly blockaded by the English, who had surrounded it with the conventional palisade, but with the addition of a ditch in which traps and pitfalls were concealed. By October the tightness of the English grip, and the constant bombardment, had brought the townspeople to the verge of starvation. John Page, a gentleman of London, was an eye-witness, and recorded his touching observations in the form of a long poem. In one section he dwells particularly upon the shortage of food:

> They ate up dogs, they ate up cats
> They ate up, mice, horses and rats

For a horse's quarter, lean or fat,
One hundred shillings it was at.
A horse's head for half a pound,
A dog for the same money round.
For 30 pennies went a rat
For two nobles went a cat.
For sixpence went a mouse,
They left but few in any house.

Soon even these commodities became scarce:

> Then to die they did begin
> All that rich city within
> They died so fast on every day
> That men could not all them in the earth lay
> Even if a child should otherwise be dead
> The mother would not give it bread
> Nor would a child to its mother give
> Everyone tried to live
> As long as he could last
> Love and kindness both were past.

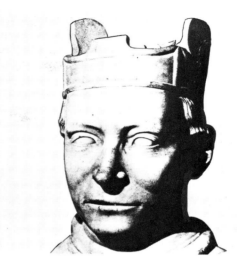

The English army had other considerations concerning supplies. King Henry wrote to the Mayor of London: 'And pray you effectually that, in all the haste that ye may, ye wille do arme as many small vessels, as ye may goodly, with vitaille, and namely with drink . . . for the refreshing of us and our said host.'

The mayor responded with 'Tritty botes of swete wyne, ten of Tyre, ten of Romeney, ten of Malvesey, and a thousand pipes of ale and bere, with thus thousand and five coppes for your host to drink.' Meanwhile the inhabitants of Rouen starved, and were driven out of the gates by the garrison who had no means for their relief. But Henry regarded them as the garrison's responsibility, and with the stubborness that was one of his chief characteristics would not let them through the English lines. It was a futile point to press. Other examples in history indicated that no honour was to be lost by allowing the refugees out. But Henry insisted. If the garrison would not take them back, in the ditch they would stay. And there they did stay, to perish from cold and hunger. They may have been in the ditch when John Page saw them for the first time. Perhaps he was one of the Englishmen who took them food and drink at Christmas time on the King's permission? Henry, after all, was a great Christian king.

Eventually a conference was held between besiegers and besieged, and a deal was struck. There were no complex clauses as at Berwick, simply that Rouen must be given up if no relief arrived within eight days. As Agincourt had effectively robbed France of its army, no relief could come, and the city fell, ending a long and bitter year for both sides. One chronicler relates a joust between an English and a French knight, but even this diversion sounds less than chivalrous. The Frenchman ran the other through with his lance, and the English had to buy his body back for 400 gold nobles.

All that could now stop Henry in his tracks would be an accommodation between the Armagnac and Burgundian factions whose rivalries had continued throughout his campaigns, making a concentrated effort against him impossible. In 1419 a meeting was arranged between the Dauphin Charles, son of the King, who now represented the Armagnacs, and John the Fearless, Duke of Burgundy. The suspicion that the two men had of each other is well-shown by the choice of meeting-place: the centre of the bridge at Montereau, which had been barricaded at both ends. The suspicion was justified. The Dauphin's attendants turned on the Duke of Burgundy and smashed open his skull with their battleaxes. Henry could have asked for nothing more than this disastrous piece of vengeance,

which was to keep the French ruling classes divided for years. Well has it been said that the English entered France through the hole in the Duke of Burgundy's skull. A formal Anglo-Burgundian alliance soon followed, and in 1420 a treaty was agreed at Troyes, which provided for Henry's marriage to Catherine, daughter of the King of France, and the establishment of a 'dual monarchy'. Charles VI, however, was to remain King of France until his death, so at a stroke of a pen the Dauphin, Charles's son, was punished for the action of his followers on the bridge by being effectively disinherited. From now on the Dauphin would be Henry's enemy.

THE AULD ALLIANCE

But where was the Dauphin to look for allies? Ranged against him were the joint forces of England and Burgundy. Following the Treaty of Troyes the victorious King had gone home with his French bride, leaving his brother, Thomas Duke of Clarence, and his able general, the Earl of Salisbury, in charge of the French campaign, so the Dauphin turned for support to Scotland, England's old enemy and a constant source of irritation. But this time his plans were not for a Scottish raid across the border to coincide with a French advance. Instead he welcomed into France a large Scottish army, and to the Dauphin's great advantage the absence of Henry provided the

opportunity for his lieutenants to indulge in the advancement of their own self interests. Whereas Henry had been content to control and advance his lines of communication, of which the successful siege of Melun in 1420 was a good example, Clarence endeared himself to his troops by conducting chevauchée-style raids to the south and south-west, which brought back large hauls of loot. But mobile raiding forces did not have the benefit of large numbers of English archers, and Clarence was to pay the price. In one such raid into Dauphinist territory just north of the Loire he was tracked by a Scottish army under the Earls of Buchan and Wigtown, and a French contingent under the Constable de Lafayette. An English foraging party captured some Scots and, as if this were a signal for a general pursuit, set off under Clarence's leadership, for the village of Bauge, where they fought the Scots for possession of the bridge. As John Hardyng's chronicle puts it, the Duke of Clarence '. . . arranged his troops in fear and hurried to Bauge, and would not rest even though it was Easter Eve . . .' As the victorious English began to ford the river, more Scots appeared on the brow of a nearby ridge, and the dismounted Clarence led his men in an impetuous charge uphill. What can have been his motives? Unsupported by archers, isolated from his comrades, Thomas of Clarence broke every precedent of English arms in France, and paid for it with his life.

Right: This fine equestrian statue outside the Town Hall in Vannes represents Arthur de Richemont, Duke of Brittany and Constable of France. De Richemont fought at Agincourt, was a companion of Joan of Arc, and played a decisive part in the great French victory of Formigny (1450), which drove the English from Normandy. The surname of this French hero is particularly ironic, as it is the French version of 'Richmond', the title bestowed upon the Dukes of Brittany by the English sovereign.
Opposite page, top: Falaise Castle, in Normandy, was the birthplace of William the Conqueror. In 1450 it became associated with another French hero when it was surrendered to Poton de Xaintrailles in exchange for the captured John Talbot, the leading English commander of his day. (Photograph by Ian Clark)
Opposite page, bottom: The Castle of Chinon, scene of the meeting between Joan of Arc and the Dauphin in 1429. (Photograph by Daphne Clark)

Left: The Tower of the Château de Vincennes near Paris, where King Henry V of England died, probably from dysentery, on 31 August 1422.
Right: Thomas, Duke of Clarence, killed at the Battle of Bauge in 1421 when his force was defeated by a Franco-Scottish army. His death was a blow to his brother, Henry V.

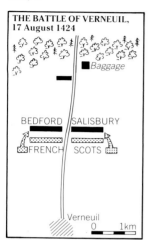

THE BATTLE OF VERNEUIL, 17 August 1424

The victory put new heart into Dauphin Charles. The Earl of Buchan was created Constable of France, and was joined in France by Archibald, Fourth Earl of Douglas, the veteran of Homildon Hill, whom the Dauphin created Earl of Touraine. New encouragement was given the following August when Henry V died after contracting what is believed to be dysentery while conducting the siege of Meaux. Many Englishmen thought him irreplaceable. He had returned to France to restore English fortunes after Clarence's death, and had begun the work speedily and brilliantly. Now his brother, John, Duke of Bedford, had to keep the operations going.

The following October the King of England was joined in death by the poor, mad King of France. Naturally enough the Dauphin proclaimed himself to be King Charles VII, but under the terms of the Treaty of Troyes the new King of France was the English infant Henry VI. One way of settling the matter was by war. In mid 1423 the Dauphin moved against Burgundy, and an army under Sir John Stewart of Darnley besieged Cravant. The army was chiefly composed of Scots, with the addition of levies from Lombardy and Spain.

It was a shrewd move on the Dauphin's part. The Burgundians were less formidable than the English, and Cravant was isolated from any English garrison. Bedford immediately sent 4,000 English to Cravant's relief under the general command of the Earl of Salisbury. Should the matter come to a pitched battle, it would be the first to be carried out by English and Burgundians working together, so a council of war was held in the cathedral of Auxerre to work out harmonious arrangements for co-operation. This shows good judgement on Salisbury's part, and it was certainly beneficial to the armies to know that such planning had taken place at all. The plans involved the welding together of the armies of two separate nationalities, which was not an easy task. As early as 1327 we noted the friction between English troops and foreign auxiliaries. The arrangements were drawn-up and made known to the soldiers. Among the details recorded are that each man was to carry two days' food and that no prisoners were to be taken until the issue of the battle

was decided – a wise precaution when arrangement of ransom took time.

The Anglo-Burgundian army found the Franco-Scottish army lining the far side of the River Yonne at Cravant. While the archers provided covering fire the English men-at-arms dismounted and, led by the Earl of Salisbury, began to ford the river, while the right wing, under Lord Willoughby, contested the bridge. In spite of being forced back initially by the Scots, the Anglo-Burgundians carried the day, the decisive push being provided by the castle garrison, who took the Scots in the rear. The Lombards and Spanish, as was the way of mercenaries, were the first to flee. John Stewart of Darnley lost an eye and was captured. It was a victory for careful planning, good communication, and dashing leadership, all of which had been demonstrated by the Earl of Salisbury that day.

The defeat at Cravant did not, however, destroy Charles's faith in the fighting qualities of the Scots, and in 1424 another army, this time consisting of 6,500 troops, landed at La Rochelle and joined forces with the Dauphin in the south, to be welcomed 'as another Messiah'. Unfortunately his countrymen did not take so kindly to this sudden incursion by thousands of foreign troops, whom they denounced as *sacs à vin* and *mangeurs de mouton*. One chronicler went as far as to say that their eventual defeat at Verneuil saved the French from being slaughtered by them. Verneuil, where the classic battle, often referred to as a 'second Agincourt', was fought, was a castle in Normandy, and it was the memory of that great defeat that brought Verneuil into the history books at all. A deal had been done with the defenders of Ivry, 30 miles west of Paris, that it would surrender if not relieved by a certain date. The relieving army was that of the Dauphin with its large Scottish component, whom the Duke of Bedford eagerly desired to catch in a pitched battle. There lay the French dilemma. Their leadership, naturally enough, wished to avoid another Agincourt, and was content methodically to capture as many English-held towns as possible, beginning with Verneuil, hoping thus to draw the English from Ivry. But the Scottish leaders were eager for battle, and their wish prevailed, so that on 17 August 1424, the allied army stood arrayed on the open plain one mile north of the castle of Verneuil. Leading the Scottish army was Archibald, Fourth Earl of Douglas, the veteran of Homildon Hill and Bauge, and now, by the grace of Charles the Dauphin, Duke of Touraine.

The 'second Agincourt' was so like the first as to require only brief details of its execution. The Duke of Bedford was a conventional soldier and not one for the surprise attack or the flank movement. His battle formation was therefore closely akin to that of his brother's at Agincourt, with the addition of a stronger guard on the baggage train, which he had arranged in a circle at the rear. The chronicler, Jean de Waurin, who was present at both battles, declared that Verneuil was the more strongly fought of the two. There was a worrying moment early in the fight when the French cavalry advanced on the English archers while they were still planting their trusty stakes – the French had obviously learned a lesson from Agincourt – but in spite of a day of fierce fighting, that initial charge did not decide the victory, and almost the entire Scottish army were killed, including Douglas, his son James, and his son-in-law, the Earl of Buchan. It was the last time in the Hundred Years war that a considerable Scottish army was to take the field. The Dauphin Charles was now totally isolated south of the Loire. Even his great fortress town of Orléans might now be taken, barring some miracle.

9. The Long, Losing War

THE CAMPAIGNS of the 1380s, masterminded by Charles V and Bertrand du Guesclin, and which brought to a halt the first phase of the Hundred Years War, came to an end from sheer exhaustion: an exhaustion of will, of resources, and of great leaders on both sides. In the 1420s, the decade from which the decline of English power in France is usually traced, any portents of a future collapse were either absent or unheeded. Henry V, whose meteoric campaign had re-established in a few years that which it had taken Edward III many to accomplish, was dead. But of great leaders there was no shortage on either side.

It is interesting to compare the 'long, losing war', which ended so successfully for the French in 1453, with the campaigns waged fifty years before by du Guesclin and de Clisson. Once again we see the emergence of talent on the French side from an unconventional direction. Poton de Xaintrailles began his career as a mercenary, like du Guesclin. So did his comrade in arms, Etienne Vignolles, called 'La Hire'. Jean Dunois, Count of Longueville, bastard son of the Duke of Orléans, overcame the handicap of his illegitimacy to lead French armies to glory. Others had more exalted backgrounds. Arthur de Richemont, brother of the then Duke of Brittany, and son of the Duke victorious at Auray, was created Constable of France in 1436. It is worth spending a few moments discussing this character, who will appear prominently in the chapter. His name 'de Richemont', is in fact the French version of the English title 'Richmond'. We noted earlier that the lands of the 'Honour of Richmond', which included several estates in North Yorkshire and the castle of the same name, had been originally given to a knight of Brittany by William the Conqueror. Throughout the centuries they remained in the gift of the sovereign, bestowed upon successive Dukes of Brittany, or withdrawn from them depending upon the incumbent's allegiance. At the time when Arthur of Brittany was born

Opposite page, top: Poton de Xaintrailles, one of the companions of Joan of Arc, who carried on the war against the English after her death. He was one of the commanders of the vanguard at the Battle of Patay in 1429, and recaptured Falaise Castle from the English in 1450. (An original painting for this book by artist, Anthony Beasley)

Left: This photograph shows the interior of the main gate to the castle of Fougères, one of the three fortresses on the border between Brittany and the rest of France.

Right: Sir Richard Redman's tomb at Harewood in Yorkshire bears this monumental effigy of a knight dressed in a suit of armour typical of that worn in the years of the 'Long, Losing War'. His helmet is a great bascinet, and he wears a collar of the supporter of the House of Lancaster, which consisted of a series of 'S' 's. He died in 1425.

Far right: Jean Dunois, Count of Longueville, bastard son of the Duke of Orléans, was a companion of Joan of Arc and played a prominent part in the long campaign against the English.

the Montfort Dukes were very much in favour, so the man who was to become the scourge of the English bore throughout his life an English name.

On the English side the war flung into prominence one name above all others – that of John Talbot, who from 1442 onwards held the title of Earl of Shrewsbury. Though almost forgotten by popular history today, Talbot's personality was larger than life during his heyday, and he left a reputation for ruthlessness which continued long after his death. As recently as the nineteenth century children in Gascony were checked by telling them that 'The Talbot' was coming, a vivid illustration of how a figure can enter into legend.

John Talbot was born in about 1387, and may well have received his first taste of action at the Battle of Shrewsbury in 1403. We know he was present at the sieges of Aberystwyth in 1407–8, and Harlech in 1409. His time in Wales was marked by no great victories, but showed a grim determination in the military sphere, and a ruthlessness that marked the beginning of his legendary aura. He served at Melun and Meaux under Henry V, but it is on his

return to France in 1427 that the phase of his career begins for which he is best remembered and feared. His first engagement was at the capture of Pontorson by the Earl of Warwick. At the subsequent siege of Montargis he was forced to withdraw, and hearing that La Hire had captured Le Mans marched to its rescue with only 300 men. His small band arrived outside the walls just as dawn was breaking, and swiftly assaulted the sleepy guards. The surprise was complete. Le Mans was re-taken, and Talbot acquired a reputation for rapid action that was to endear him to the soldiers who fought under his banner. He was shortly to be tested in a series of attacks which were the preliminary to what was planned as the major English advance since Henry V's Normandy campaign.

ORLEANS
By the year 1428 the Dauphin Charles had reached his lowest ebb. Since the English now occupied all the area between the Seine and the Loire, the latter river now marked a very genuine frontier between their Anglo-

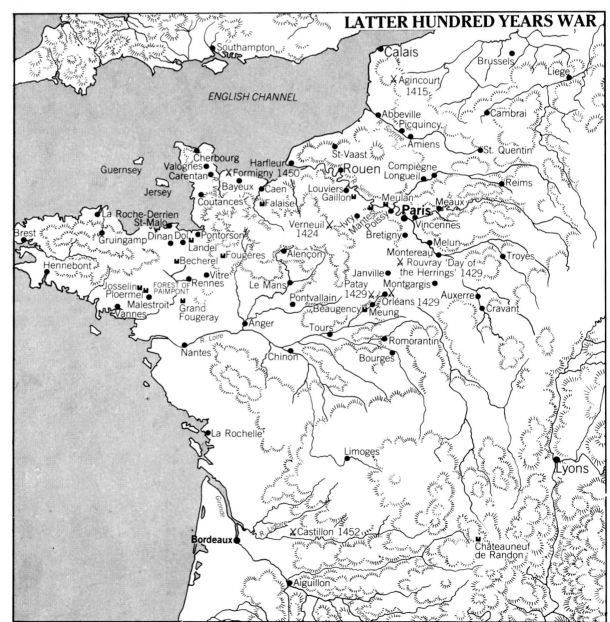

Right: The Tour Magdaleine at Le Mans. The retaking of Le Mans in 1427 from the French knight, Etienne Vignolles, called La Hire, was one of the first exploits of Sir John Talbot in France. The operation was achieved with only 300 men, and acquired for Talbot a reputation for rapid action that was to endear him to his followers.

Burgundian occupied territory and his 'French' Kingdom of Berry. For the English conquest to continue, and in particular for the late Henry's long-term aim of removing the rival king from the throne of France, the Loire had to be crossed and the fight taken to him in his own territory, whence he dared not venture. From all the available crossing-points the Duke of Bedford boldly selected one that would have tremendous psychological effect in additon to its military advantage – the city of Orléans.

Orléans lies midway between Paris and Bourges, and is the nearest point to Paris on the River Loire. Strategically it had much to recommend it – English armies advancing south from Orléans could be easily supplied from Paris. Its capture would be as great a boost to English morale as it would be depressing to the French. The decision to attack was therefore taken, after a brief pause for consideration of a moral point. Orléans, apparently, did not belong to Charles VII, but to his brother, Charles, Duke of Orléans, who had been held captive in England since Agincourt, awaiting ransom. It was an act without precedent in what remained of the 'rules of war' to attack the territory of a knight held captive, but it illustrates the importance in which Orléans was held that this particular objection was brushed aside. Needless to say, no further 'moral' objections were raised.

The summer of 1428 was spent in raising the army, which eventually numbered about 5,000 men under the command of Thomas Montagu, Earl of Salisbury. Salisbury was the experienced soldier, a veteran of Agincourt, who had commanded at Cravant, and his excellent eye for strategy is well-illustrated in the pre-liminaries to his campaign. His first major objective was to capture the town of Janville, which lies fifteen miles north of Orléans, to use it as a forward base for what he foresaw as a long siege. Janville fell after a brisk attack, enabling Salisbury to begin the isolation of Orléans by water, by capturing Jargeau upstream and Beaugency and

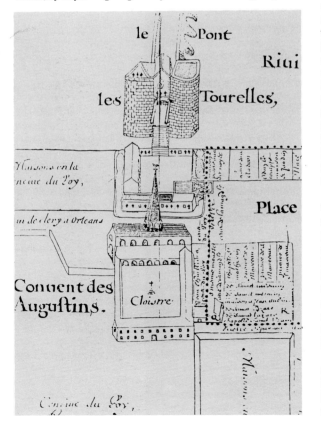

Meung downstream. The road to the latter two towns passes quite close to Orléans, so on 8 September the city had its first glimpse of the English army in the form of a small detachment guarding the road along which the artillery train must pass. As it happened Meung surrendered at the threat of artillery fire, but Beaugency proved a much more difficult operation. Its castle and its abbey, which had been fortified, were just within range of the long bridge. A siege of the castle began on 20 September, and on the 25th a simultaneous attack was launched on the castle from the north, and on the opposite end of the bridge from the south, the possession of Meung having enabled the English army to cross the river. There was a fierce hand to hand fight on the bridge (pieces of armour have been dredged from the river) and with the bridge in English hands the garrison surrendered the following day. A week later Jargeau, the fortress upstream from Orléans, surrendered to Sir William de la Pole and the isolation was complete. The English army joined forces and made camp on the southern bank of the Loire opposite the city of Orléans.

The defences of Orléans matched its strategic import-ance. It was naturally strong, the river being 400 yards wide where it was crossed by the bridge to the south. The city had an extensive wall, with five fortified gates and several towers. It was also well-provided with artillery and ammunition. No fewer than 71 guns were mounted on the walls, and there were numerous heavy-calibre siege pieces. The garrison consisted of about 2,400 men, augmented by an equal number from the civilian populace.

The closest defended area to the English encampment was, of course, the bridge. This consisted of nineteen arches, and, as a sensible defensive measure, did not quite span the river at its southern side. Instead the southernmost of these arches boasted a fort called 'les Tourelles', with twin towers, from which a drawbridge could be lowered to complete the crossing. On the southern bank itself was the most recent of the defensive works, an earthwork barbican. Salisbury began by attack-ing the barbican and the river fort, pounding both with artillery fire until he judged the time to be right for an assault. Resistance was fierce, but eventually the French abandoned both the barbican and les Tourelles, destroyed two arches of the bridge, and withdrew to the northern bank. One chronicler suggests that the reason for their withdrawal was Salisbury's attempt at mining the fort, but as the fort was in the river this seems hard to believe! The most likely explanation would be a decision to concentrate the forces on the northern bank, and create a wider 'moat'.

The capture of les Tourelles gave the English a valuable vantage-point, the twin towers commanding a good view of the city. One day the fort was being used for this purpose by the commander himself, and as Salisbury stood gazing towards Orléans a shot was fired from a French cannon across the river. Salisbury withdrew from the window as the noise of the report reached him. But he was too late. The cannon-ball struck the window and dislodged an iron bar, which spun across the room and removed half his face. The severely wounded com-mander was taken to Meung where he died eight days later.

The death of the Earl of Salisbury deprived the English army of its most valuable leader. He was succeeded by the Earl of Suffolk, who was joined by Talbot and Lord Scales when the army was withdrawing to winter quarters. But the late Earl had done his work well. The morale of the defenders was low, and with great patience the investing army began to construct siegeworks round the city's northern perimeter. This was a huge operation, because the line of the walls was 2,000 yards long, and to construct a defensive perimeter at least 700 yards away required a line of about 4,000 yards. This massive work was begun on the western side of the city, covering the approach from the direction of the Dauphin's castle of Chinon.

By the following February the line was still far from complete, and small contingents of reinforcements were managing to get through. That month there occurred an incident which shows how the ingenuity of the individual knight could occasionally manifest itself. It became known as the 'Day of the Herrings'. On 12 February 1429 Sir John Fastolf was escorting a convoy of 300 wagon-loads of herrings intended for the English army, whose Lenten observance forbade the eating of meat. At Rouvray they were attacked by the vanguard of a French army. Suspecting that the main body would be soon upon him Fastolf arranged his wagons into a 'laager' – a familiar enough tactic in later years, but almost unique in the 1420s. The French commander, Clermont, responded to the tactics in an equally enterprising way, by subjecting the 'wagon train' to small-calibre artillery fire. Many of the wagons were holed by the cannon-balls and the herrings spilled out. Had his tactic been persisted with there might have been a notable victory – the surrender of an English army to field artillery fire. However, a patient reduction on this scale did not appeal to the more chivalric-minded among his troops, in particular Sir John Stewart of Darnley, whom we last heard of captured at Cravant. Ignoring Clermont's orders, he advanced his Scots knights to the attack, and met a hail of English arrows. Clermont had no choice but to support the assault, which had equally disastrous results. Fastolf counter-attacked, and scattered the French/Scottish army.

Sir John Fastolf probably did not realize it at the time, but his good fortune, and ability to react to the opportunity it afforded, had unexpectedly destroyed the very army sent by Charles VII to relieve Orléans. With this force destroyed the city's fate appeared to be sealed, and negotiations for surrender began. It was at this point that, out of the blue, another relieving army appeared before Orléans, and one very different from any armed host the English had so far encountered. Priests marched with it, the soldiers sang, and, strangest of all, it was being led by a girl.

THE COMING OF THE MAID

The phenomenon of Joan of Arc, Saint and saviour of France, is a puzzle as difficult to comprehend in the military sphere as it is in any of the other aspects of her brief and tragic life. The whole of her 'public career', from her first visit to the Dauphin Charles, to her cruel death at the stake in 1431, encompassed little more than two years. Yet in that brief space of time she somehow achieved that of which none of her contemporaries seemed capable – the complete reversal of the power balance between England and France – and she did it in a way that made a final English withdrawal inevitable.

Few lives so short (she was nineteen when she died) have been so well-recorded and studied. We know that she was a country girl, born in the village of Domremy in Lorraine, the Anglicizing of her name as 'Joan of Arc' concealing her surname, 'd'Arc'. In the summer of 1424, when she was in her thirteenth year, she began to hear the voices which were to speak to her for the next five

years. She was convinced the voices were from God, and equally sure of the message they were proclaiming: that she had been chosen to restore the kingdom of France, and drive the English out of her country. Later she was told to accomplish this by going to see the Dauphin at Chinon, raising the siege of Orléans, and crowning him King of France at Reims. As to the great siege, the winter operations had been going on for some time when Joan acted. Her interview with the Dauphin at Chinon, during which she convinced him of the genuine nature of her mission, took place in late February, about a fortnight after the 'Day of the Herrings', a time when French morale was at its lowest. As his original relieving army had been cut to pieces by what was virtually the guard of a baggage train, the Dauphin's decision to raise another army, with or without Joan at its head, represented a considerable act of faith. This alone illustrates the confidence he placed in her.

The assembling of the new army took time, a fact which irritated Joan, for she was eager to be in action, and they eventually left for Orléans on 27 April 1429. As a collection of fighting men, some 4,000 strong, it was nothing remarkable, but as a cohesive group of inspired individuals it was unique in history. The army marched with the devotion of pilgrims, happy and elated. Whatever the ordinary soldiers thought she was, saint, mascot or magician, she gave them an inspiration they had never had before, and a strict discipline. Swearing was forbidden, prostitutes were banned, and everyone attended Mass and made confession. In a spirit of confidence and

ecstasy the army advanced. But what effect did this have on the English soldiers? Prior to Joan's arrival at Orléans the effect was probably negligible, because only the most senior knights are likely to have heard of her, and any information they had probably came from a letter Joan wrote to the Duke of Bedford before setting out, in which she called upon him to surrender all the English acquisitions in France. Assuming that the contents of the letter were made known to the Orléans commanders, one expects that the attitude of those awaiting Joan's army must have been largely one of great curiosity.

Joan's soldiers carried all before them. Her army, with its train of supplies, marched proudly on to Orléans, through the incomplete English lines, and she began to inspire the defenders of the city by her self-confidence. Perhaps inevitably, however, the deep trust in her did not extend as far as the French commanders, whose charisma she had totally supplanted. They may have been demoralized by recent events, but their years of experience as hard-bitten soldiers made them very reluctant to accept Joan's military advice or direction. Certainly they recognized her contribution to morale, her role as a figurehead and an example, but she was not admitted to their councils of war. For example, one problem facing the French forces was the need to get a further large train of supplies safely into Orléans. The plan worked out by the Duke of Alençon, supposedly in command of Joan's army, and Dunois of Orléans, the commander of the garrison, was for a number of barges to be brought a few miles upstream, loaded away from the English lines, then floated on the current downstream to the city, while Alençon's army proceeded along the southern bank. The scheme worked perfectly, but the presence of Joan of Arc has tended to obscure a straightforward and successful military operation for which Dunois and Alençon deserve more credit than they have ever received. There are

Left: A tapestry in the Museum of Orléans, depicting Joan of Arc with her famous banner, entering Orléans in 1429.

Right: Another statue of Joan of Arc at Orléans marking the site of the unexpected English defeat.

Below: The city of Orléans was the strategic and psychological prize which was the aim of the Duke of Bedford in 1428. The River Loire, shown in the foreground, marked a definite border between the northern part of France, controlled by the English army of occupation, and the 'Kingdom of Berry' under the Dauphin Charles.

several points to note. First, that the plan was worked out without consulting the Maid. Second, that her inspiring presence no doubt greatly helped the operation, and may well have been 'built in' to the plan by the commanders, and thirdly, how the whole event has been embellished. Later interpretations, swallowed whole by some chroniclers, claim that Joan prayed for a change in the wind to bring the boats back to Orléans, and a miracle occurred. To add this totally unnecessary rider to a straightforward story adds nothing to Joan's reputation once the actual circumstances are understood.

If Joan wrought any miracle at Orléans it was in the hearts and minds of the ordinary French soldiers and civilians – and that was wonder enough. As she had transformed the relieving army so she transformed the inhabitants of Orléans from a broken-down, wearied, starving mass into a fighting community. The very day that she entered the city an attack was being mounted on the English Fort Saint-Loup, probably as a diversion to cover the arrival of the rest of the supplies. Joan galloped out of the town and so heartened the attackers that they actually captured and burned the fort, probably greatly surprising themselves into the bargain. Admittedly Saint-Loup was isolated outside the English lines, evidence indeed of the disdain the English had for the French military capacity prior to Joan's arrival, but once smoke was seen rising from the fort, Talbot, who had advanced with a small relieving force, prudently withdrew.

The capacity of the French to fight was dramatically confirmed a few days later. South of the bridge was

an English fortress converted from the Convent of the Augustins. In a well planned operation the Orléans army moved against this fortress and the mid-river fort of les Tourelles. Under the direction of Dunois a bridge of boats was constructed from the little island of Saint-Aignan to the southern bank, while the Tourelles garrison was engaged. After a day of fierce fighting, led by the Maid, the Augustins fort was captured, and the following day the full strength of 4,000 French troops was launched against les Tourelles, which with the remnants of the Augustins garrison numbered about 500 men. The barbican earthwork was first to fall, and as the English retreated across the drawbridge to les Tourelles it collapsed under their weight. A poignant touch was provided by a gallant English knight called Glasdale, who was cast into the river and drowned, bearing in his hand the banner of the late great English captain, John Chandos. It was a symbolic fall. The French were able to redouble their attack by constructing a temporary bridge across the arches they had previously destroyed. Les Tourelles was

taken. The English were now isolated on the southern bank, and within a few days they decided to raise the siege. Enough was enough.

Orléans was the turning-point in the long, losing war. The miracle that was Joan of Arc had shown that victory was not only possible, but inevitable. Years later her companion in arms, Dunois, was willing to testify that prior to the coming of Joan of Arc two hundred Englishmen would put to flight eight hundred or a thousand Frenchmen. Now all was changed. Such a transformation is nothing less than miraculous.

One other transformation now occurred – in the attitude of the French commanders towards her. She had 'won her spurs' at Orléans, and could be trusted and consulted. Thus began a furious week of campaigning and fighting, as Joan speedily retook the fortresses along the Loire which Salisbury and Talbot had so methodically reduced before Orléans. Jargeau was the first to be liberated. Three shots from the great mortar 'la Bercere' practically demolished one of the main towers, and at

Joan's insistence an immediate assault was mounted, during which the Maid herself ascended one of the scaling ladders. The Earl of Suffolk was captured on the bridge as the English army escaped, and like a true knight, enquired anxiously of his captor if he too were a knight. When the Frenchman confessed that he was only a squire, Suffolk knighted him on the spot, and surrendered.

Beaugency fell after a short artillery bombardment of its huge twelfth-century keep. To shorten the range some guns were floated by barge into the middle of the river. But the vital factor was the presence of Joan of Arc which seems to have brought the domino theory into effect. On hearing the news that Beaugency had fallen, the garrison at Meung lost heart and withdrew towards Patay, eighteen miles due north. At this point Joan received reinforcements in the shape of 1,000 Bretons under Arthur de Richemont, Constable of France. It was his first meeting with the redoubtable Maid, and his words as she embraced him give a vivid illustration of the ambivalent

attitude of the French commanders towards her: 'Whether you are sent from God I know not: if you are I do not fear you, for God knows that my heart is pure. If you come from the Devil I fear you still less.' In common with all his contemporaries he would use Joan, but he could not understand her. She was too strange, too different to fit any category known to him. Sent from the Devil? The definition of a witch was far wider than we appreciate today, and saints did not dress up in men's clothing and lead assault parties. One senses all along the fear that the powers she had used against the English might just possibly be turned against the French too, as if she were being driven by some impersonal force that was not her own, and not herself.

Once again Joan's boldness prevailed, and the French army, now about 6,000 strong, set off in vigorous pursuit of the retreating English. As the latter were encumbered by a slow baggage-train the French rapidly gained ground, and Sir John Fastolf decided to make a stand near Patay. While Fastolf deployed his troops on a ridge, Talbot stationed himself with a company of archers to the south. Both knew the precarious nature of their position. Theirs was the only English field army in France at the time, and they were being approached by a large French force elated after a week of victories.

For some reason Joan did not lead the attack at Patay. This may well have been a wise precaution in view of the number of English archers who would be operating unencumbered by siege works, and any of whom would be eager to bring down the 'witch' who had plagued them. Instead La Hire and Poton de Xaintrailles led the vanguard, followed by the main body under Alençon and Dunois, with de Richemont and Joan of Arc at the rear. La Hire and Xaintrailles led the French knights in a well-conducted cavalry charge, which swept round the archers' stakes to attack them from the flanks. It was a bold move which paid off. The unprepared archers were caught, and the main body lay open to attack. The engagement was over very quickly. Sir John Talbot was captured, as was Lord Scales, and Sir John Fastolf led an ignominious withdrawal with the survivors. Defeated and disgraced, he was deprived of his Garter, but this spiteful and unnecessary attempt to make a scapegoat of him was later revoked.

The triumphal week which began at Orléans and culminated at Patay was Joan's work. On 17 July, after a march in strength that was more like a military parade, Charles the Dauphin was anointed and crowned King Charles VII at Reims Cathedral. It was a political masterstroke. According to the English, the rightful King of France was a boy of seven who held court in London and whom his so-called subjects had never seen. The legitimacy of the new Charles VII was a statement of intent to the French people and to the Burgundians who had English sympathies. Could anything now stop his progress?

Had the king been willing to risk the hazards of war against the English a little longer, the campaigns might well have gone from strength to strength, but he preferred to receive the surrender of Burgundian towns, hoping thereby to prise Burgundy from his English allies. In September Joan led an attack on Paris. While Alençon maintained observation over the Porte Saint-Denis, Joan launched her army against the Porte Saint-Honoré. This time things did not go her way. Wounded in the leg by a crossbow bolt, she lay in the open until dark, none of her erstwhile companions coming to her rescue. As winter approached, Charles VII disbanded his army, leaving the

Below: The keep of the castle of Beaugency, on the Loire. Beaugency was an important factor in the defence of Orléans. It was captured by the English as a preliminary to their siege of Orléans, and retaken by Joan of Arc in the week of victories which followed the raising of the siege in 1429.

conduct of the war to a few garrisons and mercenary bands, whom Joan was permitted to lead. But the spirit which she had earlier supplied in the cause of France did not work with these forces. In May she took part in a sortie from the beleagured town of Compiègne. The French lingered to pillage, giving the Burgundian troops time to rally. They put the French to flight, and the commander of Compiègne, fearing that the Anglo-Burgundians would enter the town, was forced to close its gates before all his army had returned. Joan of Arc was one of those left outside. Soon she was in the hands of her enemies.

The subsequent story of Joan, of her imprisonment and trial, and execution at the stake, is a familiar one from which no one emerges with any credit. The most amazing and disgraceful feature is that King Charles VII made no attempt to negotiate for her, or in any way to liberate her. There exists the possibility that Charles may have considered exchanging Joan for Talbot, who had been captured at Patay, because it is recorded that Charles 'bought' Talbot in May, shortly after Joan's trial began. But nothing was set in motion, and Talbot was not in fact liberated until 1433, when he was exchanged for Poton de Xaintrailles.

For their part, the English regarded the capture of the Maid as an event of immense importance. They sensed that the spell could be broken, perhaps even interpreting that in the literal sense, considering the reputation she had acquired. A brief attempt was made to assert English kingly authority by arranging for Henry VI's coronation in Paris, but the event, though carefully stage-managed, lacked the authenticity which the pious masses demanded, and achieved nothing. The trial of Joan had greater potential. If she could be denounced by an ecclesiastical court as a witch and a heretic, her achievements would be degraded along with her own reputation. This is what happened, notwithstanding the fact that within a few years the witnesses had been denounced as false, the trial exposed as a sham, and Joan's name cleared to become the heroine and saint she is to this day. But by then she was dead, and the immediate objective had been attained.

THE COMPANIONS FIGHT ON

Though deprived of her presence, the Maid's companions continued her work. In February 1436 Arthur de Richemont attacked Paris and began a carefully planned siege. A well-timed riot in the city enabled the French troops to enter unmolested, and the English garrison, who had taken refuge in the Bastille, were allowed to withdraw. At the same time as the submission of Paris came the long-awaited and planned reconciliation with Burgundy. The English in France were now totally isolated, yet the war had nearly twenty years left to run.

During these twenty years France gradually recovered from two crises. The immediate one of the expulsion of the English was a long, slow process, the Government's exhaustion allowing it to take little initiative, but rather to wait for the English generals to make the first move, either in a show of strength from the garrisons or by expeditionary forces from across the sea. The other crisis was more insidious. The long-lasting plague of unemployed mercenaries continuing their own private wars for their own ends once again threw the people of France into terror. The changed nature of their origin, as compared to the late fourteenth century, is hinted at by their nickname. They became known as 'les Ecorcheurs', 'the Skinners', in place of the previous appellation, 'les Anglais'. The French peasantry knew very well that

the majority of these bands were their own countrymen. Several of the great names who had fought beside Joan of Arc, including La Hire and Xaintrailles, had brief reigns as mercenary Captains, but always in the King's name. To his credit Charles VII attempted to grapple with the problem, reinforcing the ordinances of Charles V, and adding several of his own on the control and recruitment of troops. In November 1439 an ordinance set out to establish a royal monopoly on recruiting, limiting the maximum strength of companies to one hundred men, each company being based in a castle. In the confused situation of fifteenth-century France it was obvious that such reform would not take instantaneous effect, but with stricter control by the military authorities, and better and more regular pay for the men, order gradually became restored as the years went by.

The big test for the reforms came in 1444. In that year was concluded the Treaty of Tours. It achieved a truce (a lasting peace was still out of the question) and a marriage between England's King Henry VI, now twenty-three, and

The most important technological development in armour during the Later Middle Ages was the gradual replacement of mail by plate. Chain mail consisted of hundreds of small rings linked painstakingly together. A mail coat was heavy and ungainly to wear, the weight being borne excessively by the shoulders. The first of the two figures shows a knight of about 1375, by which time about half the mail has been replaced by plate. Attached to his helmet is an aventail of mail, which provides protection for the neck, yet allows freedom of movement. The decorative surcoat hides a body armour of plate beneath.

The second figure, dating from about 1430, represents a further development. The aventail of mail has now been replaced by a solid plate neckpiece, which has the disadvantage of restricting freedom of movement – a technical problem which was only solved later in the century. Note the elaborate defences provided for the weak points of elbow, knee and shoulder. Very little mail can now be seen.

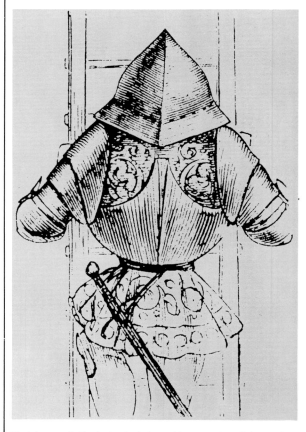

The 'chapeau de Montauban', a helmet with an extra-large brim, used while climbing scaling ladders, redrawn by the author from a manuscript in the Bibliothèque Nationale, Paris, dating from about 1420.

Charles VII's niece, Margaret of Anjou. It was a match well-regarded on both sides of the Channel, none suspecting the effect it would have in England in the years to come, as the pious King Henry acquired a headstrong and ambitious Queen. The military innovation which followed the Truce of Tours was that for almost the first time the French army was not disbanded. If it had been, no doubt fresh bands of brigands would have been set free. Instead relatively large forces were maintained under arms. At first all dubious elements in the army were removed, and the best of the remaining troops were formed into 'Companies of the King's Ordinances'. Each consisted of one hundred 'lances' comprising one man-at-arms with five more lightly armed attendants. The planned strength of the lances was not always met, but there were always about twenty companies active. Their numbers were furnished by towns and districts of France, which also had to delve into their own pockets for the men's upkeep. There were the usual grumbles which taxation produces, but it was the lesser of two evils.

THE END IN NORMANDY

When the war resumed in what was to prove its final phase, it was the French king who took the initiative by besieging Le Mans. His new standing army was impatient for action, and his counsellors were impatient for results. England was presently undergoing the internal political turmoil which was shortly to emerge in armed conflict as the Wars of the Roses. In 1450 a new Lieutenant of Henry VI arrived in France – Edmund Beaufort, Duke of Somerset. No doubt in order to influence English public opinion, he embarked upon a rash policy of provocation, which suited ideally the French king's aims. Instead of withdrawing the ousted English garrisons of Maine to Caen or Rouen, he moved them to erstwhile neutral territory on the borders with Brittany. He also entrusted an Aragonese leader of mercenaries, François de Surenne, with a revenge attack for Maine. In March 1449 de Surenne captured the border fortress of Fougères in Brittany, owned by the Duke of that province, whose uncle, Arthur de Richemont, had already done so much for the French

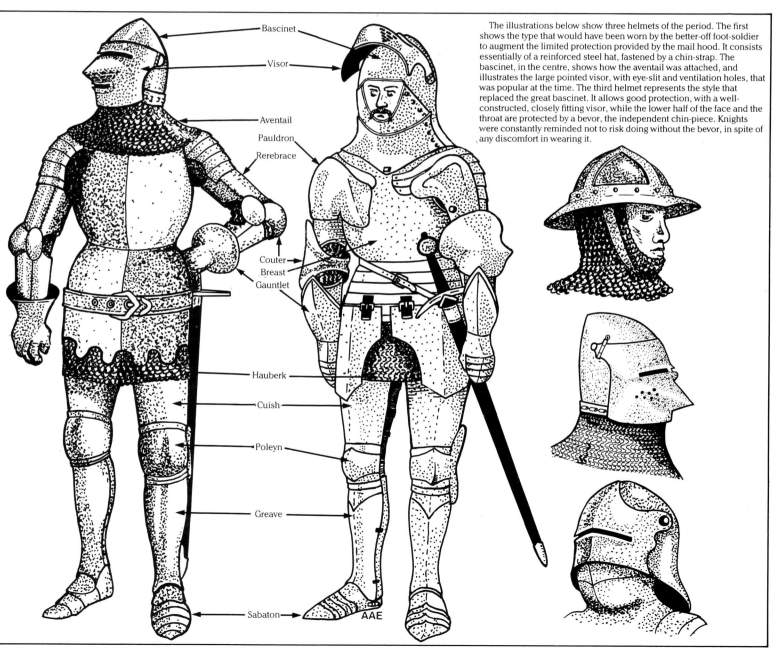

The illustrations below show three helmets of the period. The first shows the type that would have been worn by the better-off foot-soldier to augment the limited protection provided by the mail hood. It consists essentially of a reinforced steel hat, fastened by a chin-strap. The bascinet, in the centre, shows how the aventail was attached, and illustrates the large pointed visor, with eye-slit and ventilation holes, that was popular at the time. The third helmet represents the style that replaced the great bascinet. It allows good protection, with a well-constructed, closely fitting visor, while the lower half of the face and the throat are protected by a bevor, the independent chin-piece. Knights were constantly reminded not to risk doing without the bevor, in spite of any discomfort in wearing it.

Bascinet
Visor
Aventail
Pauldron
Rerebrace
Couter
Breast
Gauntlet
Hauberk
Cuish
Poleyn
Greave
Sabaton
AAE

Opposite page: A tower on the outer defence works of Mont-Saint-Michel, whose walls are among the best-preserved and most evocative of medieval military architecture in France. Right: One of the two large bombards captured by the French from the besieging English at Mont-Saint-Michel. Its size may be gauged by comparison with the author's son standing beside it.

cause. The capture of Fougères was the final break between England and Brittany. After prolonging negotiations for a short time while his captains continued the Brittany affair in his name, Charles VII entrusted a final campaign to the veteran Dunois of Orléans, in a bid to drive the English out of Normandy. For twelve months the French progressed steadily in a campaign of brief sieges that was everywhere successful. Three columns operated separately but in concert: the Counts of Eu and Saint-Pol in the North; Dunois in the centre, supported by the Duke of Alençon; and in the west, where Normandy borders Brittany, Arthur de Richemont and his nephew, the Duke. This latter company had the satisfaction of re-taking Fougères in November. Rouen had fallen in October, and as winter wore on it was joined by the symbolic prize of Harfleur, Henry V's first victory on French soil.

English resistance was feeble. Talbot tried to harry the French armies, but his resources were insufficient, and in March 1450 reinforcements under Sir Thomas Kyriell had to be sent to Normandy. Kyriell's army consisted of a mere 2,500 men. Note how it was commanded by a commoner – just as in the chevauchée of 1370 led by Sir Robert Knowles. Perhaps no one of noble birth was willing to risk his reputation by leading what was likely to be a forlorn hope. He made a bad start. Instead of advancing on Bayeux he responded to local requests to reduce the town of Valognes, which he accomplished, though not without the help of reinforcements sent from other parts of Normandy, which the beleaguered forces could scarce afford. But the loss of time far outweighed any gain. Four weeks had elapsed since his landing, giving time for two separate French armies to advance on the Cotentin peninsula in search of him.

The first French army was under the command of the Count of Clermont, based at Carentan, twenty miles west

of Bayeux, and numbering about 3,000 men. Being outnumbered by Kyriell's augmented force, it made no attempt to stop his advance across the estuary of the River Vire, where the English army was for a time delayed by the high tide. Instead he waited to be joined by the other army, commanded by Arthur de Richemont. His 2,000-strong contingent was about twenty miles south-west of Clermont's, at Coutances.

By 15 April 1450, Kyriell's army was encamped by the little village of Formigny, within a few hours' march of Bayeux. Yet during that morning the English army did not continue on its way. Perhaps Kyriell wished to emulate his predecessors at Agincourt and Verneuil, and destroy Clermont's army in a field battle. What, of course, he did not know was that he was opposed not by one army but two, the second of which was moving towards him with great rapidity. The communications between Clermont and Richemont must have been of the highest order by any standards, and remarkable by medieval ones, for as Clermont advanced from the west de Richemont seems to have pinpointed the exact spot where Kyriell would be, and moved upon it, shadowing his comrade's moves perfectly. Sir Thomas, for his part, formed a line of battle strikingly similar to that employed at Agincourt, and prepared to meet the threat from the east.

The analogy with Agincourt might well have extended as far as another crushing English victory, had the day continued the way it began. The headstrong young Clermont, disregarding the advice of his older colleagues, led an impetuous attack on foot against the lines of English archers. The archers managed to hold them off, and after two hours of fighting, during which a counter-attack by the archers captured two French field guns – an ironic comment on Charles VII's modernization programme – the French army began to give way.

At this point de Richemont appeared, from the south approaching Kyriell's left flank. With great difficulty Kyriell redressed his line to face the new threat – but the fresh troops carried the day.

The battle of Formigny sounded the death-knell for the English occupation of Normandy, and the remaining fortresses fell like houses of cards. Caen, held by the Duke of Somerset, capitulated to four columns of troops and artillery fire. Falaise surrendered to Xaintrailles as an exchange for the captured John Talbot – quite a ransom! Finally Cherbourg collapsed under a remarkable bombardment from the artilleryman Jean Bureau, who waterproofed his shore-based guns before every high tide by covering them with tallow and hides. On 11 August 1450 English rule in Normandy came to an end.

FAREWELL TO AQUITAINE

Charles VII's army entered Bordeaux as liberators, but were received as invaders. Aquitaine, after all, had been English for three centuries, and the burgesses sent a request for help to Henry VI. His response was to send to them his greatest soldier – John Talbot, since 1442 Earl of Shrewsbury, and now in his mid sixties. Henry VI could scarcely afford to let him go, because the turbulent events which later became known as the Wars of the Roses were beginning to cast a shadow across his realm. The army which Talbot took to Gascony was small, about 3,000 strong in all, but was considered sufficient for the job. Gascony welcomed him and most of the western parts of the province were back in English hands by the autumn of 1452. During the winter Charles VII gathered his forces for a final reckoning with the man whose name had already become a legend, and three separate French armies converged on Bordeaux. The centre column was under the command of Jean Bureau, who had already made his name for good artillery work, and it was with a considerable artillery train that Bureau's army approached the small walled town of Castillon.

Even though Bureau's army was formidable (some chronicler's claim he had 300 guns with him), the reputation of Talbot was sufficient to make him adopt a fundamentally defensive posture before Castillon. Instead of attempting to surround the town his men constructed a palisaded earthwork to the south, out of range of the defenders' guns. It was a considerable work, using the little River Lidoire as one side, with deep ditches and ramparts on the others. The numerous guns were placed around the perimeter and the base was ready for an assault on the town, or to resist an attack by the famous Talbot. Talbot's advance on Castillon was rapid and tiring. His army left Bordeaux in the early hours of 16 July, and marched throughout the day and most of the night. At daybreak on the 17th, the French advance guard (mostly archers) which was located in the Priory of Saint-Laurent were taken completely by surprise and overwhelmed. It was a fitting climax to the long and difficult march.

Could the impetus be continued? Sensibly, Talbot decided to let his men rest, while his scouts investigated the dispositions of the French main body in their earthwork. Their respite was short-lived because just as Talbot was preparing to attend Mass prior to setting out again, a report arrived that the French were abandoning the position and moving away. It was too good a chance to miss – to catch the French army while they were withdrawing. But Talbot had placed too much faith in the Intelligence he had received. What the scouts had actually seen was servants riding the horses away from

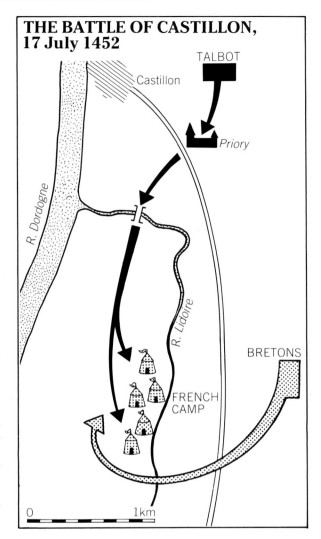

THE BATTLE OF CASTILLON, 17 July 1452

the French camp to make room within for the archers fleeing from the Priory.

The French army with all its guns, secure behind its ditch and palisades and outnumbering the English by six to one, must have provided a chilling sight, almost, one might say, a unique sight for the period. Talbot could not bring himself to call a retreat. Instead he led an attack in the teeth of cannon fire. Such a move could ultimately have only one result, but the struggle continued for some time, until a detachment of Bretons, whom the French had stationed some distance away, took Talbot in the right flank. As he fought to organize a withdrawal Talbot's horse was struck by a cannon-ball, the animal fell, trapping the aged knight beneath it, and a French soldier seized the opportunity to drive his battleaxe into Talbot's skull. That was the end of the battle. The Anglo-Gascon army dispersed, and the long history of England's first colony came to an end. The body of the Earl was found the next day, recognizable only because a certain tooth was missing. His remains were taken home to England, and interred at Whitchurch.

The Battle of Castillon effectively ended the Hundred Years War. The names of The Black Prince, du Guesclin, Henry V, Joan of Arc and Talbot were consigned to history. England had its own difficulties approaching in the shape of the Wars of the Roses, but Castillon, though won by the modern arm of artillery, had given what western Europe was not to see again, an armed clash between the knights of France and England.

Top right: King Charles VII of France, whose throne was secured by the activities of Joan of Arc. Although history reviles 'Dauphin Charles' for abandoning the Maid, it was he who began a long, slow series of reforms in French military life which prepared the country for its time of greatness in the succeeding century.

Top, far right: The seal of Henry VI of England. Son of the warrior King Henry V, the pious and studious Henry VI presided over the English withdrawal from France, and suffered the upheaval of the Wars of the Roses.

Below: John Talbot, Earl of Shrewsbury, killed at the Battle of Castillon in 1453. So disfigured was his corpse that the herald could identify him only by his teeth. This cast of his effigy is in the Victoria and Albert Museum.

10. The War of the Old Men

SYMBOLISM is a powerful force in human society. By the use of symbols concepts are simplified and more readily communicated. But as the reality on which traditions are based fades into obscurity, the symbols which represent that reality become stronger. In Japan children playing games habitually divide into 'red' and 'white' teams, subconsciously recalling the identifying colours of the opposing sides in a civil war. In England the supposed 'two sides' in the civil wars of the fifteenth century are also seen as red and white, but in a stronger, more poignant symbolism as the colours of rival roses, fragrant and beautiful, identifying the great dynastic struggle of Lancaster and York.

When Henry Tudor succeeded to the English throne in 1485, he took as his badge the 'Tudor Rose', which, in heraldic terms, is parti-coloured red and white. It symbolized his marriage to Elizabeth of York, a union popularly regarded as 'uniting York and Lancaster' that it came to symbolize the end of an era is because of Henry's considerable skill in political propaganda, and the efforts of his Tudor successors to portray him as a peacemaker, uniting two warring factions symbolized by the two roses. But to some extent such a union had already occurred when the first 'Yorkist' King, Edward IV, married the widow Elizabeth Woodville. Her family had been staunch Lancastrians, and her late husband had been killed at St Albans fighting for the Lancastrian King. Strangely enough, Queen Elizabeth's coat of arms included a red rose, not actually of Lancaster, but from her mother Jacquetta of Luxembourg – so Henry's white and red allusion could have been made earlier – if anyone had thought to make it.

Where Henry's allusion left off, popular history continued the theme. Shakespeare's lively but highly inaccurate history plays presented the various struggles of the fifteenth century as one unified conflict. There is still some controversy as to who first coined the phrase, 'The Wars of the Roses'. Sir Walter Scott has been suggested, but his actual words, in the novel *Anne of Gierstein* are: '... the civil discords so dreadfully prosecuted in the wars of the White and Red Roses', which is not quite the phrase we are used to. (Note the absence of the capital letter for 'wars'.) Nevertheless, it has passed into common usage, leaving generations of schoolchildren convinced that it was all something to do with Yorkshire and Lancashire, and commemorated every year by a cricket match.

The Wars of the Roses are difficult to understand, perhaps for the simple reason that they did not in fact actually happen. St Albans 1455 was a York v. Beaufort conflict; Northampton: largely one of Neville v. Bucking-

Opposite page: A fifteenth-century merchant's house from Bromsgrove, now rebuilt at the Avoncroft Museum of Buildings, Bromsgrove. The timber frame is of oak which is infilled with wattle and daub. Split hazel branches were woven to form a frame-work and then daubed with a plaster made from mud, cow-dung, lime and chopped straw and coated with a wash of lime, cow-dung and boiled mutton fat. The hall would originally have had a hearth in the middle of the floor.

Top right: Heraldry has been called 'the shorthand of history', and nowhere is the allusion better illustrated than in the coat of arms of Richard Neville, Earl of Warwick and Salisbury, called 'the Kingmaker'. On this one shield we see combined the previous arms of noble knights, acquired by inheritance and marriage. In the second quarter are the quartered arms of Montague and Monthermer, borne by his grandfather Thomas, Earl of Salisbury, killed at the siege of Orléans. In the first quarter are the quartered arms of his father-in-law, Richard Beauchamp, Earl of Warwick, which Beauchamp bore after 1423 with an inescutcheon of Clare quartering Despenser, now seen in the Kingmaker's fourth quarter. The third quarter displays the arms of Neville differenced by a label for Lancaster.

Right: Wigmore Castle, now almost completely ruined and overgrown, was in the Middle Ages a major fortress on the Welsh Marches and associated largely with the family of Mortimer, the Earls of March.

ham; Mortimer's Cross: York *v.* Tudor; Barnet: York *v.* Nevilie; Hexham: Neville *v.* Beaufort – all a little like a football fixture list, while the supposed climax at Bosworth involved the majority of nominal 'Yorkists' or 'Lancastrians' standing by to see which side won.

The red rose was, in fact, a very ancient badge of the House of Lancaster. The golden rose was brought into English heraldry by Eleanor, Queen of Edward I, and was used as a badge by Edward II and Edward III. Edward I's brother, the first Duke of Lancaster, changed the colour to red for his own badge. It was flown on the standard of Henry Bolingbroke, who became Henry IV, but little, if any use seems to have been made of it during the 'Wars of the Roses' until the astute Henry Tudor advanced his claim, largely because no one during this period was actually 'Duke of Lancaster'. The 'Lancastrians' fought and died under the banners of the King of England.

There were, however, Dukes of York, who used the white rose, obtained originally from the Mortimers, so of great potency in advancing kingly claims. But it was one badge among many others, including the sun in splendour and a rather fine looking falcon. It was the happy coincidence of two similar badges that led to the association being made, and the clever brain of Henry Tudor to realize the power of explanation it could have.

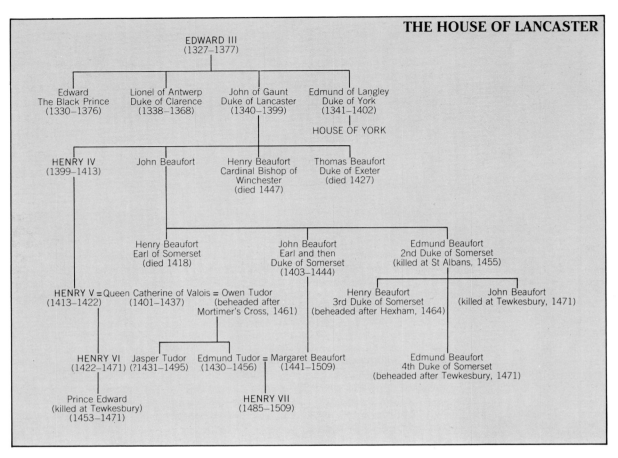

THE HOUSE OF LANCASTER

EDWARD III
(1327–1377)

Edward
The Black Prince
(1330–1376)

Lionel of Antwerp
Duke of Clarence
(1338–1368)

John of Gaunt
Duke of Lancaster
(1340–1399)

Edmund of Langley
Duke of York
(1341–1402)

HOUSE OF YORK

HENRY IV
(1399–1413)

John Beaufort

Henry Beaufort
Cardinal Bishop of
Winchester
(died 1447)

Thomas Beaufort
Duke of Exeter
(died 1427)

Henry Beaufort
Earl of Somerset
(died 1418)

John Beaufort
Earl and then
Duke of Somerset
(1403–1444)

Edmund Beaufort
2nd Duke of Somerset
(killed at St Albans, 1455)

HENRY V = Queen Catherine of Valois = Owen Tudor
(1413–1422)   (1401–1437)   (beheaded after
                               Mortimer's Cross, 1461)

Henry Beaufort
3rd Duke of Somerset
(beheaded after Hexham, 1464)

John Beaufort
(killed at Tewkesbury, 1471)

HENRY VI   Jasper Tudor   Edmund Tudor = Margaret Beaufort
(1422–1471) (?1431–1495)   (1430–1456)   (1441–1509)

Edmund Beaufort
4th Duke of Somerset
(beheaded after Tewkesbury, 1471)

Prince Edward
(killed at Tewkesbury)
(1453–1471)

HENRY VII
(1485–1509)

So much for the 'Roses'. What of the 'Wars'? Was England split in two for a generation, the country laid waste, and trade suspended? Apparently not. An analysis of the fighting during the 'Wars' shows brief, sporadic outbreaks of activity, confined largely within short periods. The longest continuous period which could be called a 'war' lasted just one year, from the landing of the Yorkists in Kent in June 1460 and the advance on Northampton, to the final 'mopping-up' after Towton the following April and May. The floods which occurred in November 1460 probably caused more disruption to normal life. The suggestion that most of England was very peaceful during the latter half of the fifteenth century is in fact supported by the Burgundian Commynes (1447–1511) who commented that '. . . out of all the countries which I have personally known England is the one where public affairs are best conducted and regulated with least damage to the people . . .' Compared to the long struggles of Burgundy, England must have seemed a paradise.

One final myth about the period will be briefly mentioned here, as it forms the underlying theme of the following chapters, – that during the Wars of the Roses England was isolated from the mainland of Europe in a political sense and in the field of military development, and that the Wars were an anachronistic, parochial struggle fought with outmoded tactics and weaponry. It is strange that this idea should ever have been formulated, considering that England had been fighting in Europe for a century. In the following pages I hope to show that the Wars of the Roses (it is impossible to avoid the term), by their nature as civil struggles, helped to change earlier ideas of warfare, learned almost totally in France, to something more appropriate. Thus not only did England witness a progression in warfare, helped greatly by

relations with Burgundy, but the Wars laid the foundations for England's later return to the European stage, which would have been impossible had military thinking not had the impetus of the Wars of the Roses.

The first 'War' is usually regarded as having its origins in the First Battle of St Albans in 1455. This engagement was so brief as to hardly deserve the title of battle. The 'St Albans Incident' was merely one more example of a process which had occurred several times before – the attempt by an aggrieved baron to put his case before the King. York had, in fact, tried a similar exercise in 1451, and in spite of raising a large army was forced to abandon his plans before any fighting took place. Where the 1455 incident differed from the much larger strategic conflict of 1451 was in the way it ended – in violence. The 1451 affair had ended with the humiliation of the leader of the protesting party – the Duke of York. Note that this was two years before the Battle of Castillon. English armies were still engaged in France while this domestic quarrel was going on. In fact, John Talbot, Earl of Shrewsbury, was instrumental in bringing it to a peaceful and successful conclusion in favour of the King. But by 1455 he was dead, and York had less to fear, so before considering the military lessons to be learned from the Wars of the Roses, let us take a brief look at the main protagonists.

YORK AND LANCASTER

Richard Plantagenet, Duke of York, was born in 1411. Before he reached his sixth birthday both his father and his uncle had met violent deaths. His father, the Earl of Cambridge, was executed by Henry V in 1415 following the failure of a conspiracy to put Edmund Mortimer on the throne. (Cambridge had married Mortimer's sister). By way of contrast, Richard's uncle, the Duke of York, paid for his staunch loyalty to Henry V by being suffocated to

death on the field of Agincourt. He died childless, so the title of Duke of York passed to the boy Richard.

In 1424 Richard's other uncle, Edmund Mortimer, in whose name so many rebellions had been plotted and so many lives already lost, also died childless. The two separates lines of descent from Edward III – via Clarence/Mortimer, and via York, now came together in Richard's inheritance. He was the sole personification of the union between York and Mortimer, the sole legitimate Mortimer heir, and the sole York heir. He received the Earldom of March to add to his titles, the castle of Wigmore, and the Mortimer's Earldom of Ulster – giving a useful sanctuary in Ireland should he ever contemplate rebellion.

More influence was to come. In 1438 he married Cecily Neville, of the powerful Marcher family who were the Percys' great rivals. She gave Richard children, and a collection of relatives who would alternately help and hinder the House of York for the next thirty years. Among these Richard acquired a brother-in-law, the Earl of Salisbury, who was to fight beside him at Wakefield, and a young nephew of ten, another Richard, who in time would inherit the titles of Salisbury and Warwick, and with the epithet of 'Kingmaker', play a decisive part in the fate of his uncle's house.

During the English withdrawal from France Richard served with distinction. He was Henry VI's Lieutenant in France in 1436–37, and 1440–47. By 1452 he had become the richest magnate in England. The statue of him at Wakefield, a faithful copy of a contemporary effigy formerly in Shrewsbury, shows a proud man, successful in war and peace, and the only man in England with the lineage to seriously threaten the overpowering legitimacy which the Lancastrian line had by then secured for itself.

The only serious rivals to York were the Lancastrian branch who had become the Dukes of Somerset. They were the Beaufort family, descended, like York, from Edward III, but through John of Gaunt. The Beauforts were originally Gaunt's illegitimate offspring, legitimized by his marriage to their mother following the death of his first wife, Blanche of Lancaster, the mother of Henry IV. Just as the Mortimer and York families had come together in the person of Richard, so would the Beaufort and the main 'Lancastrian' line do the same years later, when Margaret Beaufort married Edmund Tudor, son of Owen Tudor and Queen Catherine, widow of Henry V, and produced the future Henry VII.

York's present concern was not with Margaret, but with her uncle, Edmund Beaufort, the second Duke of Somerset. He and Richard of York were the main candidates for the position of Protector of the Realm during Henry VI's periodic bouts of insanity. Their fortunes varied, and each fell into and out of favour. In 1448 Edmund Beaufort replaced York as Lieutenant in France, and York was posted to Ireland – an unfortunate choice for a virtual exile, as here were the large Mortimer estates of Ulster. So the rivalry continued, the 'Yorkist' faction taking the offensive by suggesting that the new Prince of Wales, Prince Edward, born to Queen Margaret and her chaste, saintly King, was in fact the son of Edmund Beaufort. The truth, or otherwise, of the suggestion, was never established, but such a liaison could well explain the almost fanatical attachment the Beauforts had to the main Lancastrian line.

In May 1455 the political struggles between Beaufort and York broke into physical violence at St Albans, the protagonists in the brief conflict little suspecting that to future historians they were launching the Wars of the Roses. St Albans represented an attempt by York to secure

Left: The clock tower at St Albans.
The brief Battle of St Albans in
1455 was fought in the streets
around this tower.
Right: The last survivor of the
former seven gates of the town of
Ludlow. The grooves for the
portcullis are still visible. The
Lancastrian army entered by this
gate after the Battle of Ludford
Bridge in 1459.

Right: Ludford bridge, which crosses the River Teme below Ludlow. This is the actual medieval bridge over which was fought the brief 'Battle of Ludford Bridge' in 1459, when the Lancastrians forced their way into Ludlow.

Below: The castle of Ludlow viewed from Whitcliffe Hill. Ludlow was one of the two great Yorkist fortresses of the Welsh Marches.

the person of the King, then under the protection of Edmund Beaufort, and St Albans is where the Yorkist army caught up with King Henry and his Lancastrian supporters.

The First Battle of St Albans was unlike any other battle in the wars to come. It was, first of all, extremely brief, and fought entirely within the confines of the historic town. We have been left a description of it written by the Abbot of St Albans Abbey, John Whethamstede. It may well be a literal eye-witness account, for one can imagine the worthy Abbot stationed on top of the great Abbey gateway, noting every detail of the conflict raging below.

When the approach of the Yorkists was noted the Lancastrians began to fortify the town as best they could, dropping tree trunks across the streets, and reinforcing the old town ditch. The attacks began at ten o'clock, and

were held off until the Duke of York's nephew, Richard of Warwick ('the Kingmaker'), found a weak spot in the defences, apparently by breaking through some houses beside the Chequers Inn. Their sudden arrival in the market-place, caused great alarm, so a warning bell was rung to call every man to arms (this was probably the bell in the fourteenth-century clock tower, which still exists). Once the Yorkists were in the main streets a fierce mêlée developed. The Royal banner was flung to one side, and the King himself was wounded in the neck by an arrow. In the thick of the action fell the very man on whose behalf – theoretically at least – the fighting had taken place. Edmund Beaufort, second Duke of Somerset, had received a prophecy that he would die at Easter. Easter had passed, but he had since had a recurrent dream of Windsor Castle, a place which he had subsequently

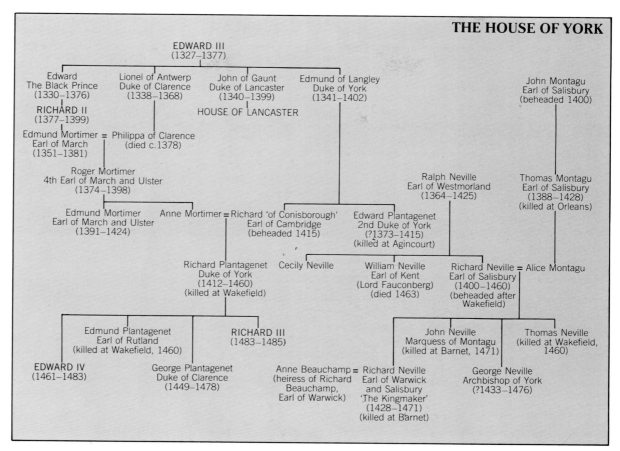

THE HOUSE OF YORK

EDWARD III
(1327–1377)

Edward
The Black Prince
(1330–1376)

RICHARD II
(1377–1399)

Lionel of Antwerp
Duke of Clarence
(1338–1368)

John of Gaunt
Duke of Lancaster
(1340–1399)
HOUSE OF LANCASTER

Edmund of Langley
Duke of York
(1341–1402)

John Montagu
Earl of Salisbury
(beheaded 1400)

Edmund Mortimer = Philippa of Clarence
Earl of March   (died c.1378)
(1351–1381)

Roger Mortimer
4th Earl of March and Ulster
(1374–1398)

Thomas Montagu
Earl of Salisbury
(1388–1428)
(killed at Orleans)

Ralph Neville
Earl of Westmorland
(1364–1425)

Edmund Mortimer
Earl of March and Ulster
(1391–1424)

Anne Mortimer = Richard 'of Conisborough'
Earl of Cambridge
(beheaded 1415)

Edward Plantagenet
2nd Duke of York
(?1373–1415)
(killed at Agincourt)

Richard Plantagenet
Duke of York
(1412–1460)
(killed at Wakefield)

Cecily Neville

William Neville
Earl of Kent
(Lord Fauconberg)
(died 1463)

Richard Neville = Alice Montagu
Earl of Salisbury
(1400–1460)
(beheaded after
Wakefield)

Edmund Plantagenet
Earl of Rutland
(killed at Wakefield, 1460)

EDWARD IV
(1461–1483)

RICHARD III
(1483–1485)

George Plantagenet
Duke of Clarence
(1449–1478)

John Neville
Marquess of Montagu
(killed at Barnet, 1471)

Thomas Neville
(killed at Wakefield,
1460)

Anne Beauchamp = Richard Neville
(heiress of Richard   Earl of Warwick
Beauchamp,   and Salisbury
Earl of Warwick)   'The Kingmaker'
                              (1428–1471)
                              (killed at Barnet)

George Neville
Archbishop of York
(?1433–1476)

Left: The massive square keep of the castle of Brougham in Cumbria, owned by the Clifford family. Their involvement in the Wars of the Roses was to prove disastrous for this staunch Lancastrian family. Thomas, the Eighth Lord, was killed at the Battle of St Albans. The Ninth Lord, Thomas 'The Butcher', killed the son of the Duke of York on the bridge at Wakefield, then perished himself while attempting to hold the northern bank of the River Aire against the Yorkist advance northwards, a move which led to the Battle of Towton. Following his death all the Clifford lands were confiscated.

avoided. When the battle was over he was found slumped in the doorway of the Castle Inn, beneath a swinging sign bearing a picture of Windsor Castle.

THE RAISING OF ARMIES

The St Albans affair begs one particular question. How was it that a wealthy landowner could so easily raise an army to oppose the King, when for a generation it had been the monarch alone who had raised armies for the wars in France? What had changed since the days of Shrewsbury? Were lords such as York so powerful that they had a standing army which would fight for them alone? The surprising answer is yes, they did [effectively] possess a standing army, or at least one that could be quickly assembled. Even more strange is the fact that they were able to muster troops more easily than could the King himself.

This stange paradox arose out of the organizational arrangements set up during the latter part of the Hundred Years War, and now transferred from the need for foreign invasion and occupation to purely domestic quarrels. We have noted earlier the system of raising armies by contract, originally the brainchild of Edward III for launching his campaigns in France, but which proved its real worth in the ease with which armies could be quickly raised and garrisons maintained. To sum up the original working of the system: a number of Contract Captains, usually nobles, settled individual terms of service by negotiation with the King, drawing-up a fairly standard form of contract specifying rates of pay, profit to be expected from plunder, etc. The reader will recall that quite early after such systems were adopted Sir John Chandos had acquired a reputation for being a 'good boss'. Such men would have no difficulty in finding troops for the King's service.

But one side in the Wars of the Roses were not for the King, and it is a measure of how successful the system had been in producing 'instant armies' that the loyalty properly due to the King could be channelled elsewhere, or rather, halted at an intermediate stage. To be seen to respond quickly and loyally to a King's demands had always been a good recommendation for advancement, so there was an incentive to take measures that would ensure a permanent supply of troops for the Contract Captain. The practical result was that the Captain would quite simply contract for the service of soldiers for life. Thus when trouble arose there was no need of lengthy negotiations. The contract had already been agreed for service in 'peace and war', and the men whose loyalty was thus 'retained' (hence the term 'retainers') received a retainer fee, sometimes a quite substantial sum. In this way, Sir Edward Grey, who died in 1457, was contracted for life to Humphrey Stafford, the First Duke of Buckingham, who was to meet his death at Northampton. Grey's contract had lasted from 1440, when he had 'signed terms' of £40 per annum. His was the best-paid. Two other knights received £20 per annum, and the remaining seven knights in Buckingham's personal retinue received £10. The esquires were more numerous and were paid at a lower rate. Each of these knights and esquires could themselves sub-subcontract for archers and men-at-arms, many of whom would be personally known to the hirer, so there was a potential for creating a large cohesive army. In the case quoted of the Duke of Buckingham, we know that prior to the Battle of St Albans 2,000 badges of the 'Stafford knot' were produced and distributed to Buckingham's men.

There was, however, one great disadvantage in the 'civil' Wars of the Roses compared to the Hundred Years War, and this was the time factor. A contract captain who

Right: Standard of Henry, Second Duke of Buckingham, beheaded by order of Richard III in 1483. The 'Stafford knot' was the badge worn by the Stafford retainers at St Albans and Northampton, where Henry's father, and later his grandfather, met their deaths.
Below left: The arms of the town of Ludlow commemorate its associations with the Yorkist kings. The white rose and the Lion of March were both badges used by the House of York.
Below right: The recently cleaned and restored face of the effigy of Sir Richard Croft in Croft Church, Hereford and Worcester. Sir Richard Croft was Edward IV's tutor in his childhood, and later fought alongside him in the Wars of the Roses, It is probably to Sir Richard's experience and local knowledge that Edward owed his victory of Mortimer's Cross.
Opposite page, top: The bridge over the River Lugg, site of the Battle of Mortimer's Cross, 1461.
Opposite page, bottom: The huge fortress of Bamburgh, Northumberland. From the end of 1463 Lancastrian hopes centred on this castle, where Henry VI held solitary state, but in 1464 it fell to a fierce artillery bombardment conducted by the Earl of Warwick.

undertook to raise armies for France could expect weeks, perhaps even months, to select and train his troops, and for the soldiers to get to know their commanders. Once the First War of the Roses began, events moved at such a rapid pace that armies were hastily recruited and equally hastily used. The presence in such a force of experienced, well-trained veterans of the French Wars was a godsend to a desperate commander, provided that their speedily sought allegiance remained steadfast. We will see several occasions in the following pages when it did not. But there were literally thousands of such men to be called upon, and their usefulness was fully recognized.

For experienced soldiers and recruits alike, loyalty to the point of death had a strong mercenary aspect. There is a recorded case, in 1464, of the wages for Henry VI's army being intercepted near Newcastle. The army which the King had assembled were fully equipped and ready to move off, but '. . . would not go one foot with him till they had money . . .' If financial considerations could hinder a King's army what had become of the loyalty due to the sovereign's person? Did the King have no troops on whom he could depend?

The position was that the only permanent military forces were those concerned with guarding England's

borders. One thousand of these were permanently stationed in Calais, defending the last possession of Henry VI in France, while others, based respectively at Berwick and Carlisle, kept a constant watch on the Scots. To a large extent, therefore, the King had to 'go to the market-place' for his armies as did his rebellious subjects, with perhaps the slight advantage that early on in the Wars of the Roses the name of the King still had a considerable influence on professional troops, as the Earl of Warwick was to find when he took the Calais garrison to oppose the King at Ludlow. From 1461, of course, there were two kings demanding absolute loyalty.

In addition to the contract captains, there were two other ways of raising armies. The first was the employment of foreign mercenaries. These had been used in domestic conflicts before, and against the Scots. The reader will recall the brawling between English and Hainaulters shortly before Halidon Hill. The Earl of Warwick employed Burgundian handgunners at St Albans in 1461, and both sides employed the specialist, and expensive, German gunners when artillery came into the Wars in the mid 1460s. Large numbers of Swiss and Flemings, armed with their characteristic pikes, were also recruited. The chroniclers of the period give us little

indication of how they were used – or, for that matter, how any troops were used, but the lack of reference to them indicates that conditions were inappropriate for their use as a phalanx of pikes. This method was most effective against cavalry, but the English tended to fight on foot. Also the skilled English archers were very good at breaking-up large bodies of troops, which rendered pikemen ineffective.

On one occasion, at least, during the Wars of the Roses the paid foreign troops included Scots. In 1462 Henry VI, whose military operations were by them confined to the north, came to an agreement with George Douglas, the Earl of Angus, for the supply of troops. Within a month of winning, Henry promised, Douglas would receive a Dukedom in England, with a value of 2,000 marks, which he would be free to hold in time of peace or war (war no doubt referring to the ever-present likelihood of hostilities between England and Scotland). In the latter case, Douglas would be entitled to send twenty Scotsmen to govern his lands, who would be treated as 'honorary Englishmen'!

A final means of raising armies, that of a 'Commission of Array', was, strictly speaking, only available to the King, a consideration that was subject to some interpretation after 1461 when there were in fact two kings. Commissions of Array were the ancient means of raising troops for 'the defence of the realm', and were revived by Henry VI in 1459 on the grounds that his realm was in peril from rebellion. It was something of a haphazard affair compared to the methods of contract captaincy. The quality of troops arrayed depended almost totally on the enthusiasm and loyalty to the sovereign of the person appointed as Commissioner. Nor was there any guarantee that the army subsequently arrayed would be used in the manner for which it was intended. A bizarre case occurred in 1460 when the Duke of York, declaring himself the loyal servant of King Henry, desirous of rescuing the King from his enemies, claimed 'defence of the realm', and gave one of his more distant Neville kinsmen the job of commissioning an array. This the Neville did, then used the troops so arrayed to attack York on the King's behalf!

Arrayed men depended upon the Commissioner for their military equipment. Some were very poorly kitted-out, the chroniclers referring to them as 'naked men'. Other contingents were well-served, their equipment exceeding the minimum standards laid down by regulation. The surviving account of a muster of this sort at Bridport in Dorset indicates a reasonably equipped army for one so hastily assembled. Of 180 men arrayed, 100 had some form of weapon, including about 70 with bows and arrows. Seventy had some or all of the following: a sallet (helmet), jack (reinforced coat), sword, buckler (small shield) and dagger. Ten of the muster had all of the items mentioned. There were also a sprinkling of poleaxes, spears, axes and one handgun, together with odd bits of armour. Such were the ways in which the armies of the Wars of the Roses were formed, but whatever means the commanders used to persuade, shame or pay men to join them, there was certainly no shortage of the basic raw material. The end of the French Wars had seen the return of large numbers of men whose only trade was that of soldier. Bored, unemployed and disillusioned by the transience of their achievements and the decline in their own skills, they were readily available to the recruiting officer.

THE FRENCH CONNECTION

Warfare has many aspects. There was much more to the Wars of the Roses than two lines of levied men, lined up facing one another for a series of battles. Civil war was a matter of political chicanery, desperate strategy, and subtle manoeuvring on and off the battlefield. The personality and experience of the commanders played a vital part. When the Wars began, the commanders on both sides shared a common experience – that of fighting in the Hundred Years War. They respected the power of the English longbow. They understood the strength of a fortified position, and had the patience needed for the formalities and discomfort of siegework. They knew the limitations of heavy cavalry. They knew how to select and train loyal troops, and had never experienced the insult of desertion. How, therefore, would these old soldiers react to a totally new situation, where archer was to be pitted against archer, where troops had to be raised in days, where few massive fortifications existed, and where the enemy were the troops of a neighbour beside whom they had lived and fought in France?

After the St Albans incident, four years went by before fighting restarted and it was the King's side which took the initiative. York was seen to be gathering his forces once more, but the armies were divided geographically. Richard of York was in Ludlow, with an additional garrison at nearby Wigmore. His brother-in-law, Richard Neville, Earl of Salisbury, was at Middleham Castle in Yorkshire, while the third Richard of the trio, Richard of Warwick, Salisbury's son, was serving a term as Captain of Calais. For the two Earls to join forces with the Duke they would have to pass through the Midlands. Henry VI accordingly raised his standard at Coventry and tempted the rebels to take the bait by launching a fragmented attack on the royal castle of Kenilworth, one of the best-defended fortresses in the land. The Royalists could then hit them when they were divided.

For such a plan to succeed required considerable political manoeuvring to ensure that York could not obtain help more local than his distant kinsmen, and in this context Queen Margaret had already been active. She had entrusted the awakening of Lancastrian sympathies in Wales to a Welsh family with royal connections – the Tudors. The Tudor rise to power had begun with Owen Tudor's marriage to Henry V's widow, Queen Catherine, binding the family as close to the Lancastrian line as the Beauforts. Owen's son Edmund was therefore Henry VI's half-brother, whom the King honoured by investing him as Earl of Richmond. He began Margaret's scheme in 1456, only to die soon afterwards, just two months before the birth of his son Henry, who was destined to raise the Tudors to undreamed of heights. Edmund's work was continued by his brother Jasper, a skilled politician and one of the few major leaders in the Wars of the Roses to see their completion. By 1459 he had managed to secure most of west and south-west Wales for the Lancastrian cause, including the fortresses of Carmarthen and Aberystwyth, and heard his praises loudly sung by the Welsh bards, who emphasized his royal blood, his Welsh ancestry and his efforts to unite Wales for the King.

Meanwhile, Queen Margaret directed her own energies towards improving her position in Cheshire and North Wales, thus progressively isolating York in the Marches. In the spring of 1459, we read, the Queen 'allied unto her all the knights and squires of Cheshire for to have their benevolence, and held open household among them; and made her son the Prince give a livery of swans to all the gentlemen of the countryside'. In an age that appreciated omens, in a 'little town in Bedfordshire' there fell a 'blody rayne', the red drops appearing on sheets which a woman had hung out to dry.

Richard, Earl of Warwick, was preparing to come to the aid of his father and uncle with 600 men of the Calais garrison, a rather bold gesture, considering that the Yorkist faction were already regarded as rebels, and the Calais garrison were the only 'official' Royal standing army. This was also the interpretation put upon it by Warwick's followers, who were most reluctant to accept his bland statement that the Yorkists were acting solely in self-defence. Eventually they sailed for England leaving Warwick's uncle, William, Lord Fauconberg, in charge, but only after Warwick had sworn an oath that he would not lead them against their King. Warwick's father, Richard of Salisbury, was likewise on the move, hurrying from Middleham Castle across England to Ludlow. His route took him through Staffordshire on the road to Shrewsbury, where the Lancastrians caught him, just as they had planned, isolated from any other Yorkist support, at a field called Blore Heath.

The battle which followed, however, did not go as the Lancastrians would have wished. After heavy fighting, from 'one of the clock till five afternoon', the Earl of Salisbury was able to continue his journey under cover of darkness. It is evident that at Blore Heath Salisbury did not encounter the full Lancastrian host, for we read that Queen Margaret was with the main body only five miles distant, and presumably entrusted the stopping of Salisbury to a detachment thought sufficient for the purpose. The commander of the force, Lord Audley, was slain during the battle, the presumed spot where he fell being marked by a stone cross. The fullest account of Blore Heath, in Gregory's Chronicle, gives part of the credit for Salisbury's escape to a certain Friar Austin, who remained on the battlefield and 'shot guns all that night', to cover the retreat. By the time the Lancastrian main body dared to sent scouts to investigate the mysterious artillery fire, the victorious Salisbury was well on his way, leaving the ambushers with the problem of what to do with the obstinate friar, who calmly explained that he had stayed there all night because he was afraid to move!

A major Yorkist army had slipped through the net which the Lancastrians had been so patiently weaving. Two days later Richard of Warwick did the same; his army, clad in red jackets with the badge of the ragged staff, avoided a Royal ambush near Coleshill. By the end of September 1459, the Yorkists were safely within the twelve-foot thick walls of Ludlow Castle, and had dispatched a letter to their King, claiming that they bore him no personal malice, but stressing their determination to fight for what they saw as their cause. '. . . having regard to the effusion of Christian blood, . . . which that God defend which knoweth our intent, and that we have avoided . . .'

THE LUDLOW INCIDENT

From Worcester the King's army advanced on Ludlow for the reckoning. According to Gregory's Chronicle there were 30,000 'harnessed men', together with 'naked men that were compelled to come with the King' – an obvious reference to poorly equipped levies. The road to Ludlow from the south crosses the River Teme by a fine four-teenth-century bridge, almost within sight of the castle, at Ludford. It was at Ludford Bridge, rather than from within Ludlow itself, that Richard of York prepared his position, digging 'a great deep ditch and fortified it with guns, carts and stakes'. Had the delay at St Albans made him consider such a defensive line, or was it perhaps the awful lesson of Castillon – the 'updated Agincourt' that had so devastatingly removed the English from France? No doubt the Lancastrian commanders would have ascended Whitcliffe hill on their left flank, to gaze down upon the mighty fortress and consider how, having disposed of York's field fortifications, they might besiege it. But military skill was not to be the decisive factor at Ludlow. There was some fighting on the bridge, raids and skirmishes against the Yorkist line, and an exchange of fire, but Yorkist morale was running low, and their rivals brilliantly exploited the situation. With a particular eye to the Calais troops, Henry proclaimed a Pardon to any Yorkist who would join him. In desperation the Ludlow commanders turned to bluff, telling their troops that Henry was dead. But they were not fooled. As darkness fell on 12 October 1459 the first Yorkist deserters began to slip across Ludford bridge to the King's peace.

Once the Calais men followed them the débâcle was complete. Led by Andrew Trollope, another veteran of the French Wars, they abandoned Warwick and his muddled, apparently motiveless 'rebellion' for the security of their

Left: The cross commemorating the death of Lord Audley at the Battle of Blore Heath in 1459. Blore Heath arose from Queen Margaret's attempt to intercept the Yorkist forces under the Earl of Salisbury who were marching to join his brother the Duke of York in Ludlow. Because of the unusual position of the cross, halfway down the hill, and invisible from the road which passes the site, it is more than likely that it represents the actual spot where Lord Audley was killed.

Above: 'This worm-eaten hold of ragged stone' are the words Shakespeare used to describe Warkworth Castle, battered into surrender by Henry IV following the death of Hotspur at the Battle of Shrewsbury. Within a few years Hotspur's father was to provide a last gasp attempt at Percy control of the Lancastrian hegemony.

Right: Threave Castle, in Dumfries and Galloway, was built in about 1370 by Archibald 'the Grim', Third Earl of Douglas. In 1454 or thereabouts, Threave's defences were dramatically improved by the building of the first artillery wall in Britain. One of the corner towers of this unique wall is illustrated here. Its efficacy was soon put to the test when Threave was besieged by King James II in 1455, using the latest available cannon, including the famous 'Mons Meg'.

Far right: Dunstanburgh Castle, built on rocky cliffs on the Northumberland coast. Much work was done on Dunstanburgh by John of Gaunt in the 1370s and 1380s. The castle was severely damaged during the 'Northern War' of the Wars of the Roses, when it was bombarded by the Earl of Warwick.

These plans illustrate three castles in the North of England: Alnwick, Norham and Scarborough. They developed over the centuries from the Norman style of keep and bailey into complex late medieval patterns.

Alnwick was the foremost stronghold of the Percy family, and successive generations of the family contributed to its much-restored buildings which can be seen today. Alnwick began as a motte castle in the eleventh century, and in the early twelfth century a stone keep was added. In 1138 the castle is described as being 'very well fortified'. The Third Percy, Earl of Northumberland, who was killed at the Battle of St Albans in 1455, built the fine Barbican gate in the south-eastern corner.

Norham, its massive keep rising from a central mound, makes good use of the River Tweed as a natural moat. It would be from this direction, the Scottish border, that attacks would be expected. Like Alnwick it began as a castle of wood, destroyed by the Scots in the 1140s. It was rebuilt in stone in the 1160s, and as a front-line fortress has endured the most punishing treatment over the years. The great tower was extended in the fifteenth century, and surrendered to James IV of Scotland days before his defeat at Flodden in 1513.

Scarborough, a Royal castle, marks the eastern boundary of the defensive chain running across North Yorkshire via Castle Bolton in Wensleydale, and Richmond. It is notable for its triangular barbican, built in the 1240s, which has its entrance in a large twin-cylindrical turreted gateway. Scarborough saw military action at a time much later than this book. It was besieged in 1536, during the Pilgrimage of Grace, and twice during the Civil War. It also sustained damage from German ships during the First World War.

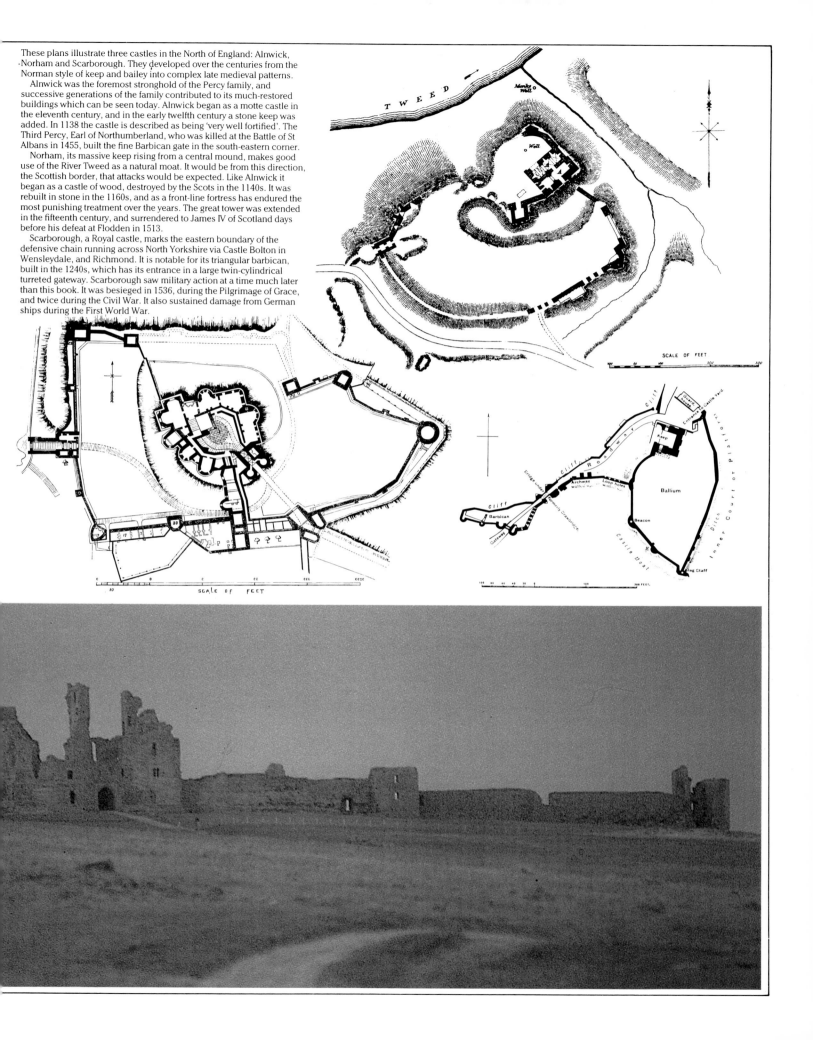

monarch. It is not difficult to see why. As Captain of Calais, Warwick was a King's man; but, seeing the danger to his father and uncle, the needs of his family had overridden his normal duty. Once the point had been made, he would have been able to assure the king that the Yorkist quarrel was not with him but with the evildoers who advised him, just as they had at St Albans. However, the Ludlow campaign had not been speedily settled, and to an ordinary soldier from the Calais garrison, the feeling that they were engaging in rebellion must have grown from day to day, until the choice had to be made between the immediate leader and the ultimate object of their loyalty. Seeing his army disintegrate about him, Richard of York had little choice. To stay within Ludlow was to offer himself as a prisoner by siege, so that night he too slipped away and 'fled from place to place in Wales, and broke down the bridges so that the King's men should not come after them'.

By morning the Yorkist army had disappeared, and the Lancastrians took their revenge for Blore Heath on the town of Ludlow, which was 'robbed to the bare walls'. Another account tells how the Royalist troops went on a drunken spree, 'and when they had drunken enough of the wine that was in the taverns and other places, they full ungodly smote out the heads of the pipes and hogsheads of wine, that men went wet-shod in wine, and then they robbed the town, and bare away bedding, cloth and other stuff, and defouled many women'. To the veterans from France it must have seemed like old times again.

Ludlow was essentially a triumph for Queen Margaret's Tudor-led propaganda, which, when tried, proved to have neutralized York's local support. It is also likely that Jasper Tudor was advancing on Ludlow with an army when the defections occurred, for we know he was late arriving at Coventry on 20 November, where a Parliament was held, and passed an Act of Attainder against the Yorkist leaders. The Act proclaimed:
'. . . that the said Richard, Duke of York, Edward, Earl of March, Richard, Earl of Salisbury, Edmund, Earl of Rutland, etc., for their traitorous levying of war against your said most noble person, at Ludford specified above, be declared attainted of high treason against your most noble person . . .'
Defeated, outgeneralled, and now officially attainted with treason, the Yorkist leaders dispersed far and wide. Richard of York went to Ireland, Warwick back to Calais, where he was harried by the latest Beaufort, Henry, who had succeeded to his late father's Dukedom of Somerset.

THE OLD SOLDIERS FADE AWAY
Richard Duke of York remained in Ireland when his kinsmen returned to take up the challenge once more. In the summer of 1460 the Earl of Salisbury landed at Sandwich with his son Warwick and his nephew, Edward, Earl of March, Richard of York's heir, and a promising soldier. They had returned to an England sodden by the wettest summer the country had experienced in many years. Communications everywhere were difficult, horses and men becoming mired in the mud of the ill-made roads. Warwick's father, Salisbury, remained behind in London, besieging the Tower, while the younger warriors of York set off to capture the King. Henry, perhaps in direct response to the invasion, had moved his headquarters south from Kenilworth to Northampton. His army, under Humphrey, Duke of Buckingham, whose son had been killed at St Albans, had constructed a formidable field fortification on a bend in the River Nene, cutting into the river banks to flood a moat in front of the palisades. We know that these fortifications bristled with guns, as at Castillon, because it is recorded that they were brought from Kenilworth, and the difficulty of transporting them is probably why Northampton was chosen for a stand. When Richard of Warwick ascended the rising ground which overlooks the position he must have recalled Ludford bridge, but this time the defensive army was holding an artificial position, not merely strengthening a natural one with a fortress behind. The river, traversed by a small bridge, was at their back. Even though the earthen walls looked formidable, the pouring rain indicated that the guns, brought at such enormous cost in time and manpower, were probably sinking into the mud and would be unworkable.

On 10 July 1460, the Yorkists attacked. Edward, Earl of March, carrying the banner of his absent father, took the left flank, William Neville, Lord Fauconberg (Warwick's uncle and a veteran of France) the right, and Warwick himself the centre. They advanced on a narrow front, waded the ditch under heavy archery fire and the occasional ball from the few guns left in action, then slipped and squelched their way up the slimy embankment to the Lancastrian defenders. At first there was fierce hand to hand fighting, but suddenly the Lancastrian right wing, under Lord Grey of Ruthyn, signalled to the Earl of March to advance unhindered. Hands reached down to help his exhilarated troops scale the palisades. Field fortifications were pushed over, and the united Yorkist left and Lancastrian right turned on to Buckingham in the centre. The panic-stricken Lancastrian troops fought one another for the narrow passage of the bridge. In the confusion the Duke of Buckingham was killed, and the King was taken prisoner by the Yorkist faction.

Northampton was a victory for the younger generation of the House of York; Richard of York was still in Ireland, and Richard of Salisbury was besieging the Tower when the fight took place. The hero of the hour was Warwick the Kingmaker, and it was largely a Neville government that was formed out of the survivors and victors of Northampton. Ludlow and Northampton had two points in common. First, they involved the use of a fortified camp which controlled local communications, with the object of challenging an enemy to launch a costly assault or talk terms. This defensive approach had worked well in France, but now we come to the second point. This was civil war, and in both cases defeat had come about because certain bodies of troops changed sides. This remorseless self-interest, ensuring one's survival by ending up on the winning side – which, because it then held the king's person, became the Royal party – was to become a feature of the wars.

If Henry VI had had no son, the Wars of the Roses would have ended at Northampton. An Act of Parliament carried by the Yorkists, reversed the Act of Attainder, and proclaimed the loyal Richard of York, heir of the Mortimer line and the York line, as Henry's successor. Richard returned to England in September 1460, to await his succession. But Henry, of course, did have an heir, Edward, Prince of Wales. More importantly he had a wife, the indomitable, talented French-born Queen Margaret. From the moment that the Act was passed her devotion to the cause became passionate. The older Lancastrian leaders, Buckingham, and her supposed lover, Beaufort, were dead. The new ones now had a cause, and a fierce spokesperson in the Queen, who would suffer any hardship for her son's throne. She was determined to prove that in disinheriting him, the Yorkists had made a rod for their own backs.

Queen Margaret, already skilled in propaganda in Wales, set about recruiting a new army. This time she concentrated on the north of England and Scotland, helped by the Percy family, whose long rivalry with the Nevilles was rapidly coming to a head. As the army grew in size she tried it out by raiding and skirmishing in Yorkshire, York's second power base, where the destructive presence would have the maximum psychological effect. It was a challenge Richard of York could not long ignore, and in December he headed north accompanied by his brother-in-law, the Earl of Salisbury. The young lions remained in the south, Warwick in London, and Edward of March 'showing the flag' in the border country whose name he carried. York's march was a double challenge – to Margaret, busily arranging a Lancastrian rendezvous at Hull, and whose rough troops were pillaging York's estates, and to Warwick, to assert his seniority and military skill which had been somewhat eclipsed by his son's and nephew's dash at Northampton.

THE END AT WAKEFIELD

The events which followed marked the end of an era in the Wars of the Roses. Perhaps York, in his determination to get to his 'capital' instead of settling for safer havens at Doncaster or Nottingham, overreached himself. But his pride dictated that he alone should rescue his tenants from the intimidating assaults of the Lancastrians, and he needed to show the next generation of Yorkist leaders that he was still the old master. He spent a merry and peaceful Christmas at Sandal castle, even though the countryside was swarming with Lancastrian warbands, supplied from the massive Royal fortress of Pontefract scarcely ten miles away. Sandal was much smaller, and it is quite likely that the Lancastrian army were prepared for a full assault. Somehow that assault never took place, because on the fields between Sandal castle and the city of Wakefield was fought a battle which decimated the Yorkist army, and totally wiped out the older generation of Yorkist leaders. Why did it happen?

There are various accounts of the Lancastrian attempts to lure York out to fight. One holds that Sir Andrew Trollope, who had changed sides at Ludlow, led a large contingent of Lancastrians flaunting spurious badges and claiming to be a reinforcement from Warwick, and that the Battle of

Wakefield took place when the defenders moved outside the walls to greet them. Others suggest that the Yorkists were caught while out foraging, or that the Lancastrians 'taunted' York into attacking an isolated group of Lancastrian soldiers. What these accounts have in common is the implication that here was a new, aggressive young Lancastrian leadership, able to employ psychological warfare and play upon the fear and pride of an old soldier. They also make it clear that when the Yorkists were lured out of Sandal the main body of the Lancastrians was being kept well out

Far right: Sir William Gascoigne, who died in 1465, was one knight of the Wars of the Roses who received his knighthood on the field of battle. In William's case it was bestowed upon him at the Battle of Wakefield in 1460. He must have continued to support the House of York until his death, for his collar bears the alternate suns and roses of the Yorkists.
Right: The ruins of Sandal Castle, near Wakefield, looking north towards the city. The slopes leading from Sandal down to the River Calder were the site of the Battle of Wakefield in 1460.

of sight of the castle. Their leader was Henry Beaufort, third Duke of Somerset, whose father had been killed at St Albans. As the year 1459 drew to its close, the troops of Richard of York burst through the Lancastrian vanguard. It was then that the main body, under Thomas, Earl of Clifford, whose father had been killed by York at St Albans, emerged in the poor light, catching York 'like a fish in a net'.

Richard of York fell on the battlefield and a savage pursuit began as the Yorkists fled in all directions. York's second son, Edmund, Earl of Rutland, the only one of his children to be present, headed for Wakefield, crossing the Calder by the city's main bridge to the south. Projecting from it, its foundations in the river bed, was a small chantry, its fine west front part of the bridge itself. It promised sanctuary and a hiding-place, but before the young man could scramble inside he was seized by Clifford. Plunging a dagger into Edmund's back, 'The Butcher', as he came to be known, added another chapter to the long saga of York and Clifford rivalry.

So perished a young member of the House of York at Wakefield. For his uncle, Richard Neville, Earl of Salisbury, an equally savage fate was in store. Taken to the dungeons of Pontefract, to await a possible ransom, he was dragged from his brief incarceration by a mob and beheaded. His grizzled old skull joined the severed heads of his brother-in-law and nephew, on the Micklegate in York. 'York', said the vengeful Lancastrians who had spoiled the county, 'may now look upon York.' The man who had been declared heir to Henry was crowned in death – stuck high on a gate, and the crown was of paper.

From the Lancastrian point of view the Battle of Wakefield shows a new flair, a more dramatic style of waging warfare, in contrast to the plodding defensive fiasco of Northampton, where the remainder of their 'Old Guard' had been destroyed. At Wakefield the Lancastrians had achieved what they had failed to do at Blore Heath. They had caught the Yorkists while they were separated, and destroyed them. As to how total had been that destruction only time would tell.

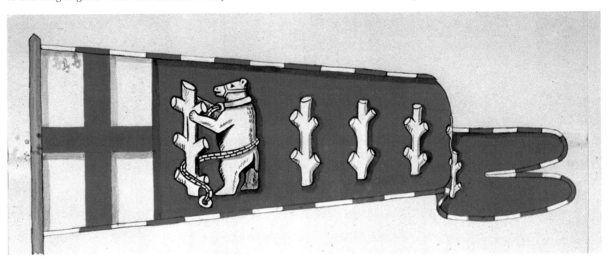

Right: The bestowing of knighthood upon a man was sometimes carried out on the field of battle. Here the senior knight 'dubs' the newcomer with his sword.

Left: The standard of Richard Neville, Earl of Warwick 'the Kingmaker', showing the bear, a ragged staff badge of Warwick, and the ragged staves used as badges by his troops during the Wars of the Roses, on a field of red.

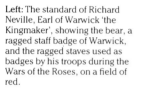

Right: The chantry on the bridge over the River Calder at Wakefield. Following the Battle of Wakefield, Edmund Earl of Rutland, son of the Duke of York, was murdered by Thomas 'The Butcher', Earl Clifford, on the bridge outside the chapel.

Left: Warwick Castle, seat of the Earls of Warwick and one of the most perfectly preserved castles in England. The line of domestic buildings seen to the left of Caesar's Tower date mainly from the fourteenth century.

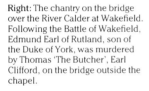

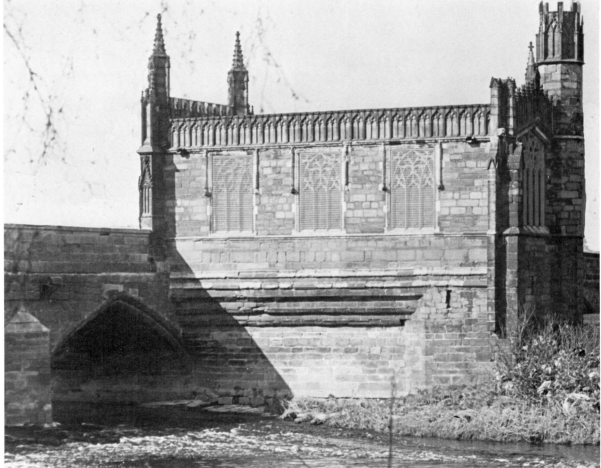

Right: A knight arming *c.*1450. The manuscript depicts Sir John Astley, assisted by his squire, a boy training to be a knight and acting as a servant. (The term 'esquire' denoted a fighting man of a rank lower than knight).

Right: A late fifteenth-century helmet for a foot-soldier. It is German, and is in the Wallace Collection, London.
Far right: Suit of armour. (Wallace Collection, London)

ARMOUR IN THE WARS OF THE ROSES

Developments in armour continued the trend towards total plate armour that has been discussed throughout this book. In an army consisting of veterans of the French campaigns hungry for work, and hastily recruited levies who kept the odd helmet in the barn in case of action, the notion of a 'suit of armour' was probably meaningless to ninety-five per cent of the soldiers engaged. Armour was always expensive, so parts of armour that were serviceable and comfortable would be retained, and broken pieces replaced. If the knight could afford it he would choose the latest development, and if he were fashion-conscious, perhaps seek out the latest style from Germany or Italy. Throughout the fifteenth century, however, it was practical considerations which produced new fashions. The attractive fluting on the surfaces of the so-called 'Gothic' style of armour, exemplified by the well-known mounted figure in the Wallace Collection, helped to give additional strength and deflected blows aimed at it.

The most noticeable innovation in armour at this time was in the helmet. The 'great bascinet', which prevented the knight from turning his head independently of his body, was finally replaced by something more suitable for the foot soldier. This was the armet, a round helmet which fitted closely to the head. Perhaps not allowing much more sideways movement than the great bascinet, but without its ponderous weight. The sallet resembled a modern infantryman's helmet. It was fastened with a strong chinstrap, and additional protection for the lower face was provided by a bevor, a reinforced chin and neckpiece which came up to the mouth. In combat several knights abandoned the bevor and suffered the consequences of a throat or neck injury. As in all periods of warfare, armour was always an attempt to reach a compromise between protection and movement.

The remarks made earlier about freedom of movement in armour are even more strikingly illustrated in these later suits. They were superbly articulated, the weight being more evenly distributed than ever. A reasonably fit man would have experienced little restriction of movement from weight alone, but prolonged bouts on foot would have caused him to sweat profusely which would have weakened him very quickly. This is what happened at Towton, even though snow was falling.

The completeness of plate armour, and its strengthening by fluting, led to the decline of the sword as a cutting weapon and its relegation to use as a piercing weapon for delivering the *coup de grâce*. Grappling between knights would be carried on with a variety of weapons designed to crush armour surfaces rather than cut mail or thin plate. Various combinations of axehead, hammerhead and spike were used.

A well-equipped army must have been a daunting sight – the measured, sinister advance of armoured knights, bolts and arrows bouncing off their burnished armour, or tearing into embroidered surcoats. I find it hard to believe that in a civil war knights would have gone into battle without some form of personal identification in the form of a surcoat. Livery colours were practically universal for foot soldiers, and it would have been even more important that a commander could easily identify his costly men-at-arms. Funerary monuments and brasses may indicate plain burnished armour, but this can be misleading. Several surviving effigies of the period do indeed display the tabard, the contemporary form of surcoat, gathered at the waist. The free-flowing version would have been something of a hindrance in battle and was probably only worn in camp.

11. The Sun in Splendour

AKEFIELD did for the House of York what Northampton and St Albans had done for Lancaster: it deprived them of the older generation of commanders. From the beginning of 1461 onwards the Wars of the Roses entered a new and savage phase. The leaders were young, unhampered by ideas appropriate only to foreign wars, and were playing for much higher stakes than merely to be in the King's favour. The new spirit showed itself first on the Lancastrian side, as Queen Margaret launched what can only be described as a chevauchée in her own country. The soldiers she had recruited in the north were rough, hard men used to border raiding and feuds. In the depths of winter they began to sweep southwards like a horde of ravaging locusts, towards London, still held by the Yorkists. As Whethamstede's Chronicle relates: '. . . they robbed, despoiled and devastated, and carried off with them whatever they could come upon or discover, whether garments or money, herds of cattle or single animals, sparing neither churches nor clergy . . .'

When they were only a week's march from the capital, Warwick set out to meet them. It must have been difficult for him to decide how to combat such a heterogeneous band, moving on a 30-mile wide front. He had no shortage of troops, because the fear of the approaching northerners had made recruitment very easy. But such a large, hastily assembled army was difficult to garrison in London, where Warwick might have been safer. His cousin Edward would be on his way from the Marches, eager to avenge his father's death, and the Lancastrians had shown how they were now able to pounce on an isolated Yorkist position and destroy it quickly before reinforcements could arrive. His uncle had paid with his head for abandoning a fortified position at Sandal, but Warwick himself had overcome one at Northampton! What was he to do? Warwick's final decision, to move to St Albans and erect field fortifications on a wide front, smacks of compromise.

Perhaps he relied on bringing the northern army to a pitched battle on ground of his choosing. If they encountered the Yorkist army, the Lancastrians would surely engage; to by-pass it and continue towards London would invite attack from the flank. He would at least slow down the Lancastrian advance, perhaps until his cousin Edward, Earl of March, and now of course Duke of York, could come from the Welsh Marches to join him. Warwick had no means of knowing that Edward was on his way, still less that he was in fact advancing to meet Warwick having just fought and won a decisive battle.

THE BATTLE OF MORTIMER'S CROSS
The background to this surprising improvement in Yorkist fortunes is as follows. Edward, Earl of March, was in Gloucester when the news reached him of his family's tragedy. He immediately began to levy troops from various shires, and succeeded in assembling a large host, surprisingly perhaps in view of the Queen's previous efforts. However the Marches proved loyal, and the Lancastrian behaviour at Ludlow can only have inclined any local waverers to follow the dashing young Duke. Edward also had the advantage of being well-known in the vicinity. He had spent his boyhood in the Marches, under the tutelage of Sir Richard Croft, whose simple castle of Croft, a few miles from Wigmore, had become a second home for the Yorkist heir. Thus many local knights flocked to his standard, in particular Sir William Herbert, Sir Walter Devereux and Sir Roger Vaughan. All were veterans from France and familiar with the Marches. Herbert and Vaughan in particular could appeal with effect to Welsh sentiment, a much needed counter to the Tudor propaganda from the other side.

It soon proved that the Tudors were Edward's nearest and deadliest threat. Having set out eastwards to seek Margaret's army, Edward was forced to turn and engage the force that had appeared in his rear. It was a motley band, consisting of Welsh troops under Jasper Tudor, Earl of Pembroke, accompanied by his father Owen, and Irish, French and Bretons who had probably been brought in via Milford Haven by James Butler, the Earl of Wiltshire.

The two armies came face to face at a crossroads known as Mortimer's Cross, about six miles from Leominster, and not far from the castles of Wigmore and Croft. Here Edward fought his first battle as Duke of York under the azure and murrey standard of his house, ornamented with the white rose. Early in the morning of 2 February 1461 his troops were startled by a strange dawn phenomenon, probably caused by mist in a frosty sky. They saw 'three suns in the firmament shining full clear, whereof the people had great marvel, and thereof were aghast'. For a brief moment the three suns shone, then came together as one. Seeing his men discomfited, and knowing the psychological value of a good omen, 'the noble Earl Edward them comforted and said, "Be thee of good comfort and dread not; this is a good sign, for these three suns betoken the Father, the Son and the Holy Ghost, and therefore let us have a good heart and in the name of Almighty God go we against our enemies." '

The reaction of the Tudor army to the three suns is not recorded, but it seems to have been an equally positive one for they were the first to move into the attack. Little is known of the details of the battle, but we may assume that Edward drew up his army on the east bank of the River Lugg, using it, and the Wig marsh on its west bank, as natural defences between them and the Lancastrians, who descended from the hills which sweep down to the Wigmore road. The attack was fiercest from the Tudor left

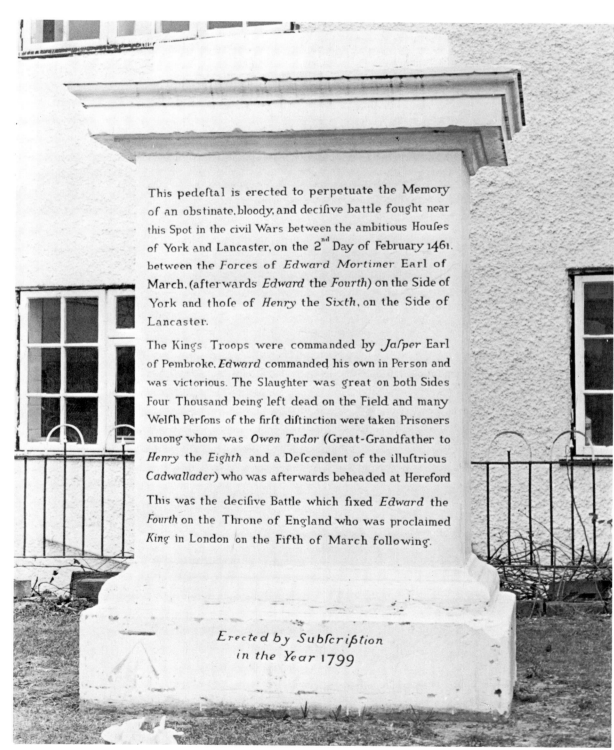

Right: The monument, erected in 1799, which commemorates the Battle of Mortimer's Cross, fought in 1461. Note the error in the inscription, giving Edward, then Earl of March, the surname of Mortimer.

This pedeſtal is erected to perpetuate the Memory of an obstinate, bloody, and deciſive battle fought near this Spot in the civil Wars between the ambitious Houſes of York and Lancaster, on the 2ⁿᵈ Day of February 1461, between the *Forces* of *Edward Mortimer* Earl of March, (afterwards *Edward* the *Fourth*) on the Side of York and thoſe of *Henry* the Sixth, on the Side of Lancaster.

The Kings Troops were commanded by *Jaſper* Earl of Pembroke. *Edward* commanded his own in Person and was victorious. The Slaughter was great on both Sides Four Thousand being left dead on the Field and many Welſh Perſons of the firſt diſtinction were taken Prisoners among whom was *Owen Tudor* (Great-Grandfather to *Henry* the *Eighth* and a Deſcendent of the illuſtrious *Cadwallader*) who was afterwards beheaded at Hereford

This was the deciſive Battle which fixed *Edward* the *Fourth* on the Throne of England who was proclaimed *King* in London on the Fifth of March following.

*Erected by Subſcription
in the Year* 1799

flank, Sir Richard Croft, acting as Edward's military adviser, allowing them to advance to the attack. The Yorkist right wing was in fact driven from the field in the direction of Croft, but the net result was to deprive the Tudor forces of a third of their army, and by the time they returned the battle was lost and three thousand of Tudor's 'motley crew' lay dead. Jasper Tudor and the Earl of Wiltshire stole away in disguise, and old Owen Tudor was captured.

Owen Tudor, the chronicler tells us, never believed that he would be executed by his captors. Perhaps he counted on being ransomed. The step-father of King Henry, after all, though militarily past his best, could command a pretty price. But this was a civil war, and much had changed even since the gentlemanly days of St Albans, and the heads of Edward's father and brother were rotting on the spikes of the gates of York. It was not until he saw the axe and the block, and felt the headsman rip away the collar of his fine red doublet that the grandfather of the future king accepted the inevitable. His last words were, 'That head shall lie on the block that was wont to lie on Queen Catherine's lap.' His severed head was displayed in the market-place at Hereford, where, a chronicler relates, a mad woman combed his hair and washed away the blood from his face, then surrounded the ghastly trophy with a hundred burning candles.

The Welsh bards lamented the loss of the sire of the Tudors. Robin Ddu refers to his death, and speaks of Jasper Tudor, Earl of Pembroke, as their great hope for the future. In a curious passage he compares the 'white' of the Yorkists and the 'red' of the Welsh dragon: 'Draig wen ddibarch yn gwarchae, A draig goch a dyr y cae.' (The dishonourable white dragon has triumphed, but the red dragon will yet win the field.)

It is interesting to note the contrast of the red and white, particularly in view of the traditional allusion of York and Lancaster. One addition was in fact made to the Yorkist heraldry not long after the battle, when Edward combined the white rose of York with the badge of the sun in splendour, producing the beautiful effect of the 'white rose en soleil' on the standard of Richard III. Was it perhaps a direct reminder of the 'Glorious Sun of York' which had smiled on them threefold that morning?

ST ALBANS

Meanwhile, Edward's cousin waited at St Albans behind the weird array of field defences which he had erected. There were guns to fire balls and arrows, and various sorts of net with nails thrust through the interstices so that when laid down they would present a carpet of spikes. 'Also they had pavises . . . with shutting windows to shoot out of, they standing behind the pavis, and the pavis as full of threepenny nails as they might stand. And when their shot was spent and done they cast the pavis before them: then there might no man come over the pavis at them for the nails that stood upright, but if he would mischief himself.' Warwick also had a plentiful supply of caltraps, devices consisting of four spikes arranged in a solid tetrahedron, so that however it fell one spike was sticking straight upwards. To supplement his firepower he also had under arms a small contingent of Burgundian handgunners, firing primitive arquebuses, some of which may have been operated by a matchlock action.

Thus prepared, Warwick awaited the army that would arrive first, his cousin's, or the Queen's, but as in so many battles so far described in this Chapter, a traitor in Warwick's ranks defected to Margaret and disclosed the precise layout of Warwick's defences. Such treachery is

perhaps not surprising. What is remarkable is the sophisticated way in which the Lancastrian leaders made use of the information. Her army had already veered to the west from the direct route to London. Now it was to turn back towards the east, to attempt a surprise attack on Warwick's right flank, avoiding the spiked defence line. The northern army therefore headed for Dunstable, taking a Yorkist detachment completely by surprise and either killing or taking prisoner their entire number. Consequently none got back with any news for Warwick, and that night, 16/17 February, the Lancastrian leaders achieved a remarkable feat. They somehow organized their loosely disciplined army in a night march which fell upon the unsuspecting Warwick shortly before dawn.

The untidy and bloody battle which followed was a Lancastrian victory, but an incomplete one. It was a victory in terms of the numbers slain across Warwick's wide front, though a Yorkist-biased chronicler noted with some satisfaction that Sir Andrew Trollope suffered a caltrap in his foot. The Burgundian handgunners do not seem to have have come into the story at all. Warwick himself escaped with a small band, to link up with Edward at Chipping Norton.

Whichever of the Lancastrian leaders deserved the credit for the flank attack, it is clear that Warwick was totally outmanoeuvred. It is interesting to speculate about

the part played by the Queen herself. Her presence, and commitment to the cause of her son, certainly inspired morale. Did she in fact lead in a military sense as well?

TOWTON – THE DAY OF RECKONING

From the moment of reunion between Edward and Warwick fortune seemed to favour them. They returned to London, finding to their delight that it had not fallen to the Lancastrians, and Edward of York was proclaimed King Edward IV. Realizing the precarious nature of the reign he had just initiated, Edward stayed in the capital only long enough to complete the formalities of kingship, then was off campaigning again. Frustrated at her failure to take London, and with her army idle in the south, Queen Margaret began an orderly withdrawal. By 22 March Edward had followed them as far as Nottingham, where reports reached him that the Lancastrian army had halted north of the River Aire, where they were holding the bridge at Ferrybridge, near Pontefract. A few days later, on 28 March, the Yorkist vanguard under the Duke of Suffolk encountered the Lancastrian guards, and under orders from Edward, who arrived with the main body, began a fierce fight for the bridge. As soon as the Yorkists looked like winning, the Lancastrians destroyed it and withdrew to the northern bank. King Edward, calmly assessing the situation, sent a force, presumably acquainted with the local area to find a crossing-point up river, which they achieved four miles away at Castleford. The high water of the late winter must have made the crossing difficult, for at least one chronicler asserts that a raft was used instead of merely fording, but the crossing was made. The crossing of the Aire was a major military achievement by Edward IV. A defended natural obstacle had been overcome, and some revenge gained, for in the fighting Lord Clifford was killed by an arrow. The river crossing was probably helped by a strange reluctance on the part of the huge Lancastrian army a few miles to the north to come to their comrades' assistance when they were needed. Memories of Blore Heath may have been awakened in certain hearts.

The next major obstacle on the Great North Road was the next River, the Wharfe, crossed by a bridge at Tadcaster some twenty miles to the north, but between Edward and Tadcaster lay the army he had been pursuing, deployed on a gentle ridge near the village of Towton. For the first time in the Wars of the Roses two major armies confronted each other, with the certainty of a battle, and the likelihood of treason was remote. It is hardly surprising in view of the local geography, the furious battling of the previous months, and the enmity built up since the deaths and executions at Wakefield and Mortimer's Cross, that the Battle of Towton should prove to be the

Below: The battlefield of Towton in summer, looking down the slope on the right of the Lancastrian lines to Bloody Meadow, and bordering it the sinuous River Cock, death-trap for many a Lancastrian soldier.

biggest, bloodiest and most decisive battle of the Wars of the Roses, bringing this particular phase of events to a dramatic close. It is unfortunate that we have so few contemporary accounts of it. The numbers involved are known, the positions are clear, but there is little else. Perhaps the remoteness of the location, and the sheer horror at so many lives being lost conspired to reduce the commentaries we have available. It is possible, however, to compensate this lack of source material by visiting the site itself, which is remarkably unchanged from that fateful Palm Sunday in 1461. The Yorkist army would have been strung along the southern end of the ridge, its flank resting on a small wood. The Lancastrians lined up to the north, straddling the two roads which join at Towton for Tadcaster. They must all have spent an uncomfortable night, bivouacked on the exposed ground, with a threat of snow.

On Palm Sunday morning, as villagers in nearby Saxton went to mass, a sharp, cold south wind began to blow. No advance was made by York, as Edward was awaiting the arrival of John Howard, Duke of Norfolk, who was to take the right flank. Warwick was in the centre, and his uncle, Lord Fauconberg on the left. At about eleven o'clock it began to snow. Taking advantage of this Lord Fauconberg ordered his archers to fire one arrow each, and then fall back out of range. The wind carried the arrows farther than normal into the Lancastrian lines, now almost invisible in the snow. But the taunt had the desired effect. Volley after volley of arrows were returned, falling short of the gleeful Yorkists who ran to retrieve them. It was a tremendous barrage, but little damage was done, as the Lancastrians were to discover when they advanced across the snowy ground to be met by hard-hitting salvos of arrows from the Yorkists. But the line came on, and on both sides archers were replaced by swordsmen and billmen who began to hack furiously at one another. As the men in the front line died or became exhausted fresh reserves from behind took their place. It may be that the opposing commanders organized some form of constant reinforcement, for it is known that the slaughter was so

great that a wall of dead built up between the opposing men-at-arms. One major Lancastrian leader, Lord Dacres, was killed during a break in the fighting. Withdrawing from the line he had sat down to refresh himself, removed his helmet, and was struck in the neck by a crossbow bolt which killed him instantly.

When Norfolk's troops arrived at last on the right flank, the battle began to turn in favour of the Yorkists, but the tide was was a long time on the ebb. Eventually the Lancastrians began to fall back, and at this point the lie of the land started to tell against them. The flat ridge on which the battle was fought slopes gently down on its eastern side, where the Duke of Norfolk was beginning to apply increased pressure. But on the western side the slope is steep, a fact that is not appreciable from the centre of the field. At the foot of this steep slope flows the little River Cock, about ten foot in width and in summer not more than two feet deep. In March 1461 it was in spate, and its banks are steep. The retreating Lancastrians were funnelled back along 'Bloody Meadow' towards the

only reliable crossing-point, a wooden bridge, itself at the bottom of a deep slope, which carried the then Great North Road. Once the possibility of safe retreat became unlikely, panic swept through the ranks and was exploited by the pursuers. The Cock claimed many who tried to force their way across it. The little bridge is said to have collapsed under the weight of armoured men, to be replaced by a ghastly dam of human corpses, packed so solidly that the luckier escapers could scramble across it. On and on they came, slithering down the snowy, muddy, and bloody slopes leading to the river, until as darkness began to fall probably 30,000 Lancastrians lay dead, a casualty list larger in percentage terms than that of the Battle of the Somme. In fact Towton claimed more lives than any other battle in England, at any time.

Being in such totally undeveloped countryside, Towton is able to exert a strange effect upon the imagination. Even in the height of summer, wandering by the lazy Cock, it is possible to conjure up images of those thousands. In winter, to leave the path beside the monu-

Below: The battlefield of Towton under snow, similar, but less severe conditions to those experienced by the opposing armies on Palm Sunday, 1461. This view is from beside the swollen River Cock, looking up towards the rear of the Lancastrian right flank. This area, known as Bloody Meadow, was the scene of the fiercest fighting in the largest pitched battle of the Wars of the Roses.

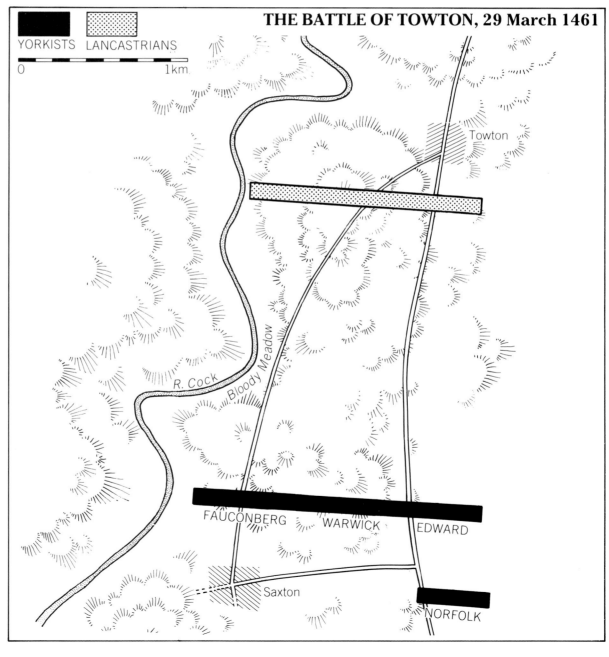

THE BATTLE OF TOWTON, 29 March 1461

YORKISTS   LANCASTRIANS

0   1km

Towton

Bloody Meadow

R. Cock

FAUCONBERG   WARWICK   EDWARD

Saxton

NORFOLK

ment, and walk down the slope to 'Bloody Meadow', slithering as the snow whips one's face, is to become one with the victims of that awful Palm Sunday, 1461, where Edward IV bloodily confirmed his throne.

Most of the slain found anonymous graves in huge pits dug nearby; the nobles had grander resting-places. Lord Dacres was buried with his horse in the churchyard at nearby Saxton. Henry Percy, third Earl of Northumberland and grandson of Henry Hotspur, was buried in York; one Lionel, Lord Welles, had his body secretly conveyed to the church at Methley, where his first wife's body already lay. His effigy now crowns the tomb, resplendent in armour, but denied a representation in alabaster of the Lancastrian collar, formed by the letter 'S'. The memory of the total defeat was too strong to risk that.

THE WAR IN THE NORTH

The Battle of Towton was a victory, decisive and final for thousands of individuals, as well as for the Lancastrian cause. It established the Yorkist dynasty, and effectively neutralized large-scale opposition for the next twenty years. Opposition, if it can be so called, continued, but minimally, at the extremities of Edward's new kingdom. We will study it in some detail, because the way Edward and his powerful cousin, the Kingmaker, dealt with such

opposition illustrates just how well the English knights were adapting to changed situations.

In Wales, resistance to the Yorkists was quickly dealt with. The Herberts, who had joined Edward before Mortimer's Cross, used their Welsh connections and military skills to wrest Pembroke Castle from Jasper Tudor. Along with the castle they captured Jasper's nephew, Henry Tudor. The Herberts were merciful victors and took the little boy into their care, where he prospered. Lancastrian resistance was much stronger on the Scottish border. Despite the deaths of the Second Earl of Northumberland at St Albans, and the Third Earl at Towton, the Percys remained stout Lancastrians. As Warwick the Kingmaker was mainly concerned with fighting Margaret and her allies, the period added a new dimension to the long Neville/Percy rivalry for control of the Marches. Throughout these years, however, there was no York/Neville rivalry. Warwick served his cousin well, in the harsh, unglamorous business of border warfare. In fact, Warwick's harrying of the Lancastrians in the north was very much a family affair. His second in command was his brother, John Neville, Lord Montague, and he was also assisted by his uncle, William Neville, Lord Fauconberg, one of the few remaining veterans of the French wars, and Edward's companion in arms at Towton.

Left: Monumental effigy of Lionel, Lord Welles, a Lancastrian knight who was killed at the Battle of Towton in 1461. His body was conveyed in secret to this tomb in Methley, West Yorkshire. The sculpture is very striking, showing clearly the fashionable hairstyle of the period, and is very detailed in its representation of a contemporary style of armour.
Below: The Battle of Towton. The artist who produced this dramatic reconstruction has placed the viewer in a similar position to that depicted on page 152. The Lancastrians have been driven down the slope in the driving snow, and the swollen River Cock begins to claim its dead.

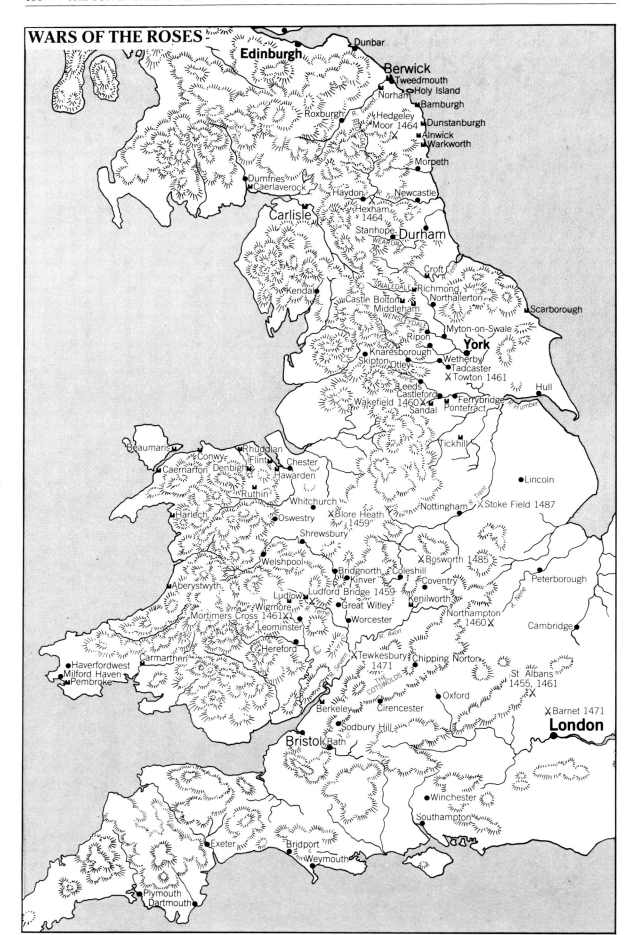

WARS OF THE ROSES

Dunbar
Edinburgh
Berwick
Tweedmouth
Holy Island
Norham
Bamburgh
Roxburgh
R. Tweed
Hedgeley
Moor 1464
Dunstanburgh
Alnwick
Warkworth
Morpeth
Dumfries
Caerlaverock
Haydon
R. Tyne
Newcastle
Carlisle
Hexham
1464
Stanhope
WEARDALE
Durham
Croft
R. Tees
Kendal
SWALEDALE
Richmond
Northallerton
Scarborough
Castle Bolton
Middleham
WENSLEYDALE
Myton-on-Swale
R. URE
Ripon
York
Knaresborough
Skipton
Otley
Wetherby
Tadcaster
Towton 1461
R. Aire
Leeds
Hull
Castleford
Wakefield 1460
Ferrybridge
R. Humber
Sandal
Pontefract
Tickhill
Beaumaris
Rhuddlan
Conwy
Flint
Chester
Caernarfon
Denbigh
Hawarden
Lincoln
Ruthin
Whitchurch
Nottingham
R. Trent
Stoke Field 1487
Harlech
Oswestry
Blore Heath
1459
Shrewsbury
Bosworth 1485
Peterborough
Welshpool
Bridgnorth
Coleshill
Kinver
Coventry
Aberystwyth
Ludlow
Ludford Bridge 1459
Kenilworth
R. Nene
Wigmore
Great Witley
Mortimers Cross 1461
R. Teme
Worcester
Northampton
1460
Cambridge
Leominster
R. Avon
Hereford
Tewkesbury
Chipping Norton
Carmarthen
1471
St Albans
1455, 1461
Haverfordwest
R. Severn
THE
COTSWOLDS
Milford Haven
Pembroke
Berkeley
Cirencester
Oxford
Barnet 1471
Sodbury Hill
London
Bristol Bath
Winchester
Southampton
Exeter
Bridport
Weymouth
Plymouth
Dartmouth

Opposite page: Within the recess of one of the crossbow loops in the Grey Mare's Tail Tower at Warkworth Castle is this crude carving of a crucifix. Perhaps it was carved by a prisoner, or by a sentry bored with his duties during the castle's long and eventful history.

CASTLES AND SIEGES

Gaining castles, only to lose them again, was to become a feature of this phase of the Wars of the Roses. The sense of urgency which had characterized the earlier, battle-seeking times of St Albans and Towton, seems to have been replaced by a more desperate retrenchment, motivated by the same concern over uncertainty of supplies, and doubtful loyalty of troops. In May 1461 Queen Margaret led a siege of Carlisle by a Scottish army, to which the Neville brothers responded by taking the Lancastrian Percy castles of Alnwick and Dunstanburgh, only to lose them again in the winter.

Of course, only places which had fortifications, or could have them readily built, were liable to siege; few places had any fortifications at all. The great Northumbrian castles were extremely formidable, as was Kenilworth with its vast artificial lake. London had imposing walls and the Tower, which Queen Margaret had been unable to vanquish in 1461, but of the hundred or so English towns which still had walls in the fifteenth century, many had fallen into disrepair. The reader will recall that neither at Northampton nor Ludlow were existing town walls used for defensive purposes, artificial palisades being erected elsewhere.

Control of castles, nevertheless, was important. They provided a base with storage facilities, and the heraldic symbols on the flags flying from the battlements were an uncompromising statement of ownership and presence. The actions of the Yorkist leaders after their victory at Northampton is very revealing of their attitude to castles. While Edward and Warwick had been crushing the fortified camp of the Lancastrians at Northampton, Warwick's father, Salisbury, had been attempting to capture the Tower of London, a 'real' castle, if ever there was one! It was bitterly defended by Lord Scales, whose men 'cast wild fire into the city, and shot in small guns, and burnt and hurt women and children . . .' Salisbury eventually forced a negotiated surrender, having met fire with fire by using 'great bombards', but if the Battle of Northampton had had a different result Scales might well have held out longer, preventing any Yorkist supremacy. As it turned out, the siege of the Tower provided a timely reminder of the importance of a strategic, well-defended base, so Yorkist attention turned rapidly towards the Welsh castles. In August 1460, the Constables of Beaumaris, Conwy, Flint, Holt, Ruthin and Hawarden received official orders to keep the castles secure, lest any should be appropriated by the Lancastrians and used as a base for future operations. In the following year, Queen Margaret realized the importance of castles when she failed to take London after the Battle of St Albans, a reverse which rendered her victory a Pyrrhic one. Perhaps minor towns and castles were hurriedly turned into fortresses as her rapacious army headed back northwards for its eventual defeat at Towton.

But after Towton, castles were all the Lancastrians had. What they needed in addition were allies, which Margaret sought in her native France. Louis XI's terms were strict (he demanded a mortgage on Calais) but with Margaret's readiness to agree to practically anything if it would ensure her son's succession, a small French expedition, under Margaret and her friend, Piers de Breze, collected King Henry from Scotland and landed at Bamburgh Castle in Northumberland on 25 October 1462. Dunstanburgh was already theirs, and Alnwick soon fell. An elated Queen led her army south, in much the same

spirit as she had advanced on St Albans the previous year, but this time the impetus quickly died. So few men joined her that the expedition was hurriedly abandoned, and 400 French soldiers were left on Holy Island, where they were killed or captured by Warwick, who had recommenced the sieges of Bamburgh, Dunstanburgh and Alnwick. As was so common during the Wars of the Roses, none had been garrisoned or victualled for a long siege – there just had not been the time, so Lancastrian hopes rested on the arrival of a Scottish relieving force. Seven thousand Yorkist troops took part in the three sieges, controlled by Warwick from nearby Warkworth Castle. Supplies for the besiegers were organized from Newcastle, where the Duke of Norfolk acted as quartermaster, ferrying grain, cannon-balls, arrows and spare armour to his comrade 'at the front'. As well as supplying reserves, Warkworth was a useful base from which to launch an attack on any Scots attempting to relieve the besieged. It was tedious work, and one of the towers of Warkworth bears possible evidence of the boredom experienced by a lonely sentry with an artistic flair.

The Scots army arrived on 5 January 1463, by which time Bamburgh and Dunstanburgh held respectively by a Percy and a Beaufort, had surrendered. Had the Scottish leaders acted more decisively they could have changed the whole course of the Wars of the Roses, for Warwick

reacted to their appearance as if in total surprise, and withdrew his men from outside Alnwick in a hasty retreat. The Scots, however, did not take full advantage of the situation, and like Queen Margaret at St Albans, failed to ensure that Warwick's indecision was the end of him. Instead the garrison of Alnwick abandoned the castle and joined the Scottish army. Next day Warwick occupied the property – with vacant possession.

Being short of volunteers for the lonely life of garrisoning a Northumbrian castle, Bamburgh and Dunstanburgh were returned to the safe-keeping of Sir Ralph Percy, who now proclaimed staunch pro-Yorkist sympathies. A few months later an army of Scots, French and Lancastrians reappeared in Northumberland, whereupon Sir Ralph Percy promptly surrendered them back to the House of Lancaster. Nothing daunted, the Neville brothers returned and caught Queen Margaret who was besieging Norham. Eventually all the fortresses were recaptured except for mighty Banburgh, and most importantly of all, negotiations began between King Edward and the Scots, in the hope of neutralizing Lancastrian support from across the Border.

From the end of 1463 Lancastrian hopes centred on the massive, gloomy fortress of Bamburgh, blasted by the east wind whipping over the sand-dunes of its lonely beach. Here, in the one-time capital of the ancient

Right: The unsettled conditions of the Anglo-Scottish border made it necessary for even religious institutions to have some form of defence against raids. This is the 'Vicar's Pele' in Corbridge, Northumberland, where a fortified pele tower doubled as the vicarage for the church.

Right: The Lion Tower at Warkworth Castle, which was built in the latter half of the fourteenth century as the grand entrance to the Great hall.

Right: These two boulders on the site of the Battle of Hedgeley Moor (1464) are known as Percy's leap, and tradition has it that Sir Ralph Percy, mortally wounded, jumped his horse the distance that the stones represent. They probably predate the battle considerably, but remain a curious monument to this little-known struggle which added another chapter to the long rivalry between the Percy and the Neville families for control of the Border country.

Opposite page, top: The site of the Yorkist right wing at the Battle of Barnet, where Richard Duke of Gloucester, later King Richard III, was in command.

Opposite page, centre left: According to legend there lived one Arthal, Earl of Warwick, whose name meant 'bear'. A later legendary Earl, Morvidus, slew a giant with a young ash tree torn up by the roots. Combining these two symbols the historical Earls of Warwick arrived at their crest of the bear and ragged staff, seen here beautifully depicted on the wall of Lord Leicester's Hospital, Warwick.

Opposite page, centre right: The abbey of Tewkesbury, as seen from the field formerly known as the Gastons, which was the site of the Lancastrian left flank during the Battle of Tewkesbury in 1471.

Opposite page, bottom: Bloody Meadow, Tewkesbury. Like its namesake at Towton, Bloody Meadow saw the fiercest fighting of the battle which finally sealed the fate of the Lancastrian dynasty.

Kingdom of Northumbria, the pathetic King Henry held solitary state. Early in 1464 he was cheered by the arrival of Henry Beaufort, Third Duke of Somerset, to join him in his exile. This young man, son of the duke who died beside the Castle Inn at St Albans, had been pardoned by Edward after the siege of Dunstanburgh, and was actively courted by him on behalf of the Yorkist cause. But he was a Beaufort, and that was enough eventually to make him quit the pleasures of Edward's lively and fashionable Court for the life of a guerrilla in the Scottish Marches.

A raid in 1464 broke the tedium of endless, unfruitful besieging. Warwick's brother, John Neville, Lord Montague, was on his way to Norham Castle, where he was to meet Scottish ambassadors and escort them safely to York for negotiations with Edward. Realizing that this conference could finally settle any Lancastrian hopes of a Scottish alliance, Henry Beaufort of Somerset attempted to ambush him near Newcastle. Lord Montagu had only a small force, 'fourscore spears and bows too', but managed to evade capture and proceeded on his way, only to be met near Morpeth by another Lancastrian force, under the command of Sir Ralph Percy, the former keeper of Bamburgh, and younger brother of the late Earl killed at Towton. The resulting Battle of Hedgeley Moor, on 25 April 1464, though a footnote to the main conflict, is interesting as a purely Neville/Percy affair, from which the Neville side emerged victorious, leaving Sir Ralph Percy lying dead. His last words are supposed to have been, 'I have saved the bird in my bosom,' presumably referring to the Percys' long-standing loyalty to Henry VI, of which Sir Ralph represented the last model. His nephew, another Henry Percy, was imprisoned by Edward IV, and only later restored to his rightful title when Edward needed a Percy as a counterbalance to Neville domination of the north. It was this Percy that was fated to die at Barnet fighting the Nevilles, both families having changed sides

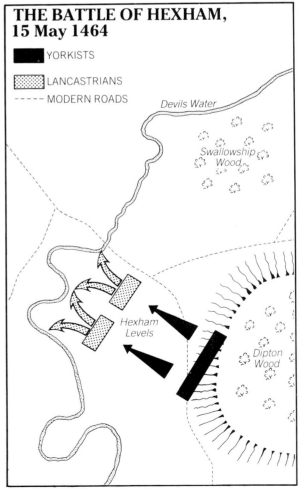

THE BATTLE OF HEXHAM, 15 May 1464

■ YORKISTS

▨ LANCASTRIANS

---- MODERN ROADS

Devils Water

Swallowship Wood

Hexham Levels

Dipton Wood

THE BLOODY MEADOW
THE SCENE OF ONE OF THE FIERCEST
COMBATS OF THE BATTLE of TEWKESBURY
4th MAY 1471

since Hedgeley Moor – so much for the notion of York and Lancaster!

If Neville honour had been satisfied against the Percys at Hedgeley Moor, it was soon to be additionally satisfied against the Beauforts. Lord Montagu escorted the Scots ambassadors safely to York, then hurried back north. Early in the morning of 15 May he smashed into the camp of Beaufort's raiding-party beside the Devilswater, south of Hexham. Henry Beaufort, Third Duke of Somerset, was captured, together with Lords Hungerford and Roos, and was beheaded shortly afterwards.

Two weeks later, as a gift from a grateful king, John Neville, Lord Montague, was created Earl of Northumberland, the title having been vacant since Towton. For the old Neville/Percy rivalry, it was the Nevilles' high-water mark. Filled with renewed vigour, the Neville brothers flung their energies into reducing the Northumbrian castles once and for all. The Scottish negotiations, which John had laboured so hard to bring about, had been successful, leaving the three castles ill-prepared and garrisoned by demoralized survivors of Hedgeley Moor and Hexham. Alnwick and Dunstanburgh quickly surrendered before the new Earl of Northumberland. Only mighty Bamburgh held out under the keeping of Sir Ralph Grey, and Warwick was determined to have it this time, 'Even if the siege should take seven years,' as his messenger grimly reported to Grey. To the defiant message was added a curious rider, that for every shot by the besiegers that damaged Bamburgh, a Lancastrian head would fall. Apparently Edward wanted Bamburgh intact, but it was unusual that such an intention should have been conveyed to the defending lord, particularly one who had already been refused a pardon! Nevertheless, Warwick, in the belief that anything that could be damaged could as readily be repaired, opened up on

Bamburgh with the fiercest artillery bombardment England had ever known. From positions among the sand-dunes and from inland the King's 'great guns', laboriously transported north for the business, blasted away at the fortress. The guns, each with a nickname, such as 'Newcastle', 'London' and 'Edward', rained shot of iron and stone on the defenders. Chunks of the stone ramparts splintered off and were sent flying into the sea. One gun, called 'Dijon' was particularly successful in precision work. Once the gunners had got the range they were able to fire repeatedly on Sir Ralph Grey's personal apartments, which one presumes were in the splendid Norman keep, and succeeded in loosening masonry which fell on his head and concussed him, so that he was for a while given up for dead. To the accompaniment of gunfire and a constant barrage of arrows at the ramparts to keep the defenders heads down, the castle was assaulted, but the guns had already won the day. Before the attack could be fully pressed home the garrison negotiated a surrender. Grey was dragged unconscious from where the gun 'Dijon' had felled him, and was later beheaded at Doncaster.

Bamburgh thus became the first castle in English history to succumb to gunfire, and the battle was a dramatic illustration of how the Yorkist monarchy, particularly in the person of Warwick the Kingmaker, was at the very forefront of military technology. Warwick appreciated totally the contribution which artillery could make to the winning of battles, by their saving of time, and consequently lives, in a war where, as we have seen, time was of the essence. He was also able to overcome the psychological barrier, the stubborn chivalric streak which still saw the employment of cannon as somehow 'not playing the game'. Warwick's object was to win, and win as quickly and efficiently as possible.

Left: The Devilswater, near Hexham in Northumberland, the site of the Battle of Hexham in 1464 where Henry Beaufort, Third Duke of Somerset, was surprised in camp by John Neville, Lord Montagu, and killed.

THE TRIUMPH OF THE CANNON

The name of the gun, 'Dijon' which felled Sir Ralph Grey, indicates its origin in the Burgundian capital, a centre of excellence in artillery. 'Dijon', we are told, was a 'brasin' gun, which probably means that it was bronze and cast in one piece. The iron guns mentioned above were probably of hoop and stave construction like a barrel.

These heavy-calibre guns would have been bombards, and all may have come from Burgundy. One well-known specimen from this source is the famous 'Mons Meg' in Edinburgh Castle, which once projected proudly from the ramparts, but is now displayed in a cellar where it bears a garish coat of paint: a surprise to the modern eye, which is used to seeing old guns with a patina of rust, but authentic, as rust had to be avoided at all costs and Medieval man liked bright colours. Meg herself is more than thirteen feet long, weighs five tons and fired a stone ball weighing 549 pounds. A large gaping hole in the wall of Norham castle is testimony to her destructive power, tested by the King of Scots in 1497.

The situation of Bamburgh may have aided the gunners in their control of the mighty pieces. The recoil, absorbed to some extent by a block of lead against timber, and the resulting sideways movement, threw the guns out of alignment each time they fired. Perhaps the capacity of the sand-dunes around Bamburgh to absorb recoil was exploited? It may well account for the accuracy of the shooting. It is more than likely that Edward's expenses for the siege ran to the employing of gunners to operate their own pieces. Good artillerymen were the most expensive mercenaries to hire, but if a good job had to be done with the least destruction it would be a worthwhile investment.

Before continuing our discussion of cannon, there is one more siege to consider. This one is interesting because it became, after the fall of Bamburgh, the last prop in the Lancastrian policy of holding castles, and the siege gave rise to the famous song, *Men of Harlech*. We last heard of Harlech during the rebellion of Glyndwr. During the War of the Roses it was held for the Lancastrians by Dafydd ap Ievan ap Einion, whose local influence had counteracted Yorkist domination in north Wales. 'King Edward', wrote the chronicler Warkworth,

'was possessed of all England (*sic*), except a castle in north Wales called Harlech.' Gregory wrote that it was 'so strong that men said it was impossible to get it'. In the autumn of 1464 Sir William Herbert, Earl of Pembroke since the taking of that formidable castle from the Tudors, was granted its constableship and began a long siege. Despite a grant of £2,000 from King Edward towards the costs of besieging, and the supply of various guns, Harlech held out for four years. Notwithstanding the fact that the defenders used firearms, Edward must have concentrated as much effort on Harlech as he had on Bamburgh, and their topographical situations were not dissimilar. The new weapon technology could be devastating, but it was not infallible.

In fact it was only in the sieges of the Wars of the Roses that cannon played a serious part in the war. However, there is ample evidence that they featured high in the preparations for war. As early as 1456, a royal warrant was issued appointing a certain John Judde, merchant of London, as Master of the King's Ordnance. The warrant plainly admitted that 'we be not yet sufficiently furnished of guns, gunpowder and other habiliments of war'. Judde was required to make field guns. Within a year he had supplied 26 serpentines, which were field guns mounted on mobile carriages, with a calibre of between two and six inches, and between three and seven feet long. He had also made one culverin, a type of gun smaller than a serpentine. These were transported to Kenilworth, whence they probably arrived for the Battle of Northampton, Judde's careful work brought to no effect by the mud and rain.

Occasionally, field guns, no matter how mobile, were a hindrance. At St Albans the Queen's flank attack so surprised the Yorkist gunners that they succeeded in shooting themselves. We know from Waurin's Chronicle that Edward took guns with him on the march north which ended at Towton but, as in the Northampton campaign, the weather was against their use, and the destruction of the bridge over the Aire prevented any heavy pieces being moved further than Pontefract. As for weapons of smaller calibre, we noted earlier the use of handguns by the Burgundian mercenaries at St Albans, but such weapons

Right: A sleeping crossbowman, from a Polish bas-relief. The figure is of the late fifteenth century, and is well armed with a sallet-style helmet.
Overleaf: Pontefract Castle. A painting attributed to Alexander Keirinex, who produced it for King Charles I some time between 1625 and 1630. It is the best extant illustration of this once formidable castle, and hangs in Pontefract Museum. The painting is reproduced by kind permission of Wakefield Art Gallery and Museums Service.

were not confined to foreigners. One of the Paston letters contains a vivid eyewitness record of defenders making a hole in the wall 'at knee height' to shoot their handguns.

CROSSBOWS AND ARMOUR

Artillery may have been the most visible development in military technology during the Wars of the Roses, but it was by no means the only one. Other tried and tested weapons were improved and expanded in their use, often from developments on the mainland of Europe. The commanders of the Wars of the Roses, far from being parochial and unimaginative, were eager to acquire any new technology and put it to use.

To begin with the crossbow. To the English a much despised weapon, it was given a whole new lease of life in the mid fifteenth century by the invention, in Europe, of the steel crossbow. Not surprisingly it packed a tremendous punch, doubling the range of the composite wooden crossbow's 200 yards to perhaps 450 yards, if modern tests are an accurate reflection of fifteenth-century practice. Steel crossbows probably started arriving in England in the late 1450s or 1460s. The more expensive variety were cocked by a rack and pinion activated by a crank. The speedy operation of this 'crannequin', as it was called, enabled a trained man to fire three times a minute, a considerable improvement on earlier practice.

With the universality of plate armour, a new type of crossbow bolt was introduced. Its head was of square cross-section, the blunt force of its impact being sufficient to unhorse a man, particularly if it caught in his armour. At short range, and the crossbow had always been a short-range weapon, they could crack armour plate if delivered almost at right-angles to the surface – an effect similar to hitting the armour with a powerful hammer blow. Like new artillery, however, cost was the factor that kept such deadly weapons in short supply, and most knights in the Wars of the Roses were reasonably safe from the old-style composite bow with its bolts designed for mail.

The English longbow remained the force it had always been, though mitigated considerably by the difficulty of deploying it tactically, because both sides used many archers. We have already seen how the Yorkist supremacy in archery at Towton was due to the good sense of Lord Fauconberg in exploiting a natural advantage, rather than any superiority of the archers themselves.

NEVILLE VERSUS YORK

It is perhaps no more than stubborn tradition that uses the term 'The Wars of the Roses' for the events subsequent to 1464. Words like treachery and turncoat become meaningless when taken out of context. The knightly families of the fifteenth century put their own survival above all other considerations. Thus the two remaining battles of the Wars of the Roses, Barnet and Tewkesbury, are well worth studying from points of view other than merely military history. Barnet is particularly fascinating in that it was an engagement fought between two commanders who had hitherto fought side by side: King Edward IV and his cousin, Warwick the Kingmaker. The background to this strange reversal of loyalties, whereby the 'proud putter up and puller down of kings', as Shakespeare calls him, met his death at the hands of his King, is a very complicated one. Briefly, Edward's impulsive marriage to Elizabeth Woodville, which ruined all the plans Warwick had for him, greatly curtailed Warwick's position in the country, so much so that Warwick was forced to use his

immense but declining influence to depose Edward and put the wretched King Henry back on the throne. At the Battle of Edgecote in 1469 Warwick defeated Edward's allies, the Herberts and the Woodvilles, and to a background of local rebellions, the most serious of which was the Lincolnshire Rising of 1471, Edward's power declined decisively enough to cause him to flee to Burgundy.

Edward returned to England in March 1471, landing at Ravenspur on the Humber. Bluffing his way through Yorkshire by claiming that he had come back merely to claim his Dukedom of York, and that he was a loyal subject of King Henry, he managed to evade three separate Lancastrian armies and entered London in safety. Warwick pursued him southwards, reaching St Albans, which must have recalled strange memories, on Good Friday, 12 April 1471. Edward, taking with him King Henry, who had previous experience of being forcibly taken to battles, advanced from London to meet him. On the Saturday, Warwick continued his advance almost to Barnet, halting on the cross ridge just north of Barnet at Hadley Green. Both commanders knew the lie of the land well. It was the main road out of London to the north, the

ridge being the highest point before York. There was some skirmishing as the two advance forces met, and as night fell both pulled back to their respective main bodies and battle lines were formed. As both sides drew up their forces in the dark it is not surprising that the opposing lines did not coincide, and the right of one overlapped the left of the other. That night the artillery-minded Earl of Warwick kept up a barrage from field guns hoping, as the chronicler puts it, to 'annoy the King'. Edward, however, though he possessed guns, did not return fire, for (shades of Towton!) he observed that his cousin's army had assumed that he was further from their lines than was the case, and the balls were passing harmlessly overhead.

Dawn on Easter morning of 1471 revealed a dense mist that clung to the ground, muffling the sounds from the opposing armies. Suddenly arrows began descending in random showers through the white blanket as Edward launched his attack. Guns fired, arrows and quarrels flew, as the two lines, at first grey and indistinct, plodded forward with eyes straining through helmet slits to catch a glimpse of the enemy. Suddenly the mysterious grey shapes became a splash of brilliant colour as the battle

ranks materialized. Screaming warcries the two armies flung themselves at each other. It was a mêlée of Towton proportions, but unlike Towton, where the narrowness of front channelled the opponents together, the extreme right on each side marched forward to encounter – nothing! The enemy were not there! In the dark the opposing troops had been drawn up out of line. On Warwick's right was the Earl of Oxford, an experienced soldier who immediately saw the possibility for a flank attack, wherever the flank might be.

Meanwhile the centre companies were furiously engaged. Edward and his brother George, Duke of Clarence, were hacking furiously at the Neville lines, where the centre was commanded by Warwick's brother John, Lord Montagu, whom Edward had deprived of his hard-won title of Earl of Northumberland at the time of Warwick's rebellion. On the Yorkist right Edward's other brother, Richard, Duke of Gloucester, was making good progress against Warwick's own division. The young man, who had accompanied his brother in exile, was only eighteen, younger than Edward had been at Northampton, and was serving in his first major military command. Perhaps Richard's inexperience prevented him from duplicating

Below: Harlech Castle, which is built on a naturally strong postion, managed to hold out for four years against the sophisticated techniques of siege warfare conducted by Edward IV. This brave resistance, led by one Dafydd ap Ievan ap Einion on behalf of the Lancastrian cause, forms the factual basis behind the song *Men of Harlech*.

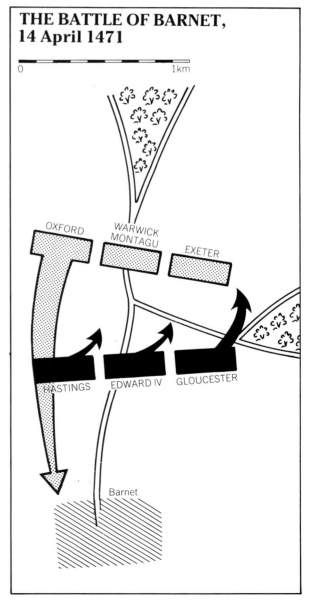

THE BATTLE OF BARNET, 14 April 1471

0   1km

OXFORD

WARWICK MONTAGU

EXETER

HASTINGS   EDWARD IV   GLOUCESTER

Barnet

Top right: The standard of Edward, Duke of York, later Edward IV, showing the badge of the falcon and fetterlock, and the white roses, on Edward's livery colours of azure (blue) and murrey (mulberry).

Centre right: The standard of Richard III, bearing the white boar, Richard's personal badge, and the white rose of York.

Bottom right: Standard of Henry Tudor, Earl of Richmond, later to become Henry VII. This is the standard which Henry would have displayed at Bosworth.

Opposite page, top left: The gilt-bronze effigy of Sir Richard Beauchamp, Earl of Warwick, in the Beauchamp Chapel, St Mary's Church, Warwick. Sir Richard Beauchamp was a loyal servant of the English cause in France particularly during the minority of Henry VI.

Opposite page, top right: The Battlefield of Bosworth, now carefully preserved and open to the public, where a reproduction of the Standard of Richard III again flies.

Opposite page, bottom: The much ruined Great Hall of Kenilworth castle, built by John of Gaunt. Kenilworth was an important royal fortress during the Middle Ages.

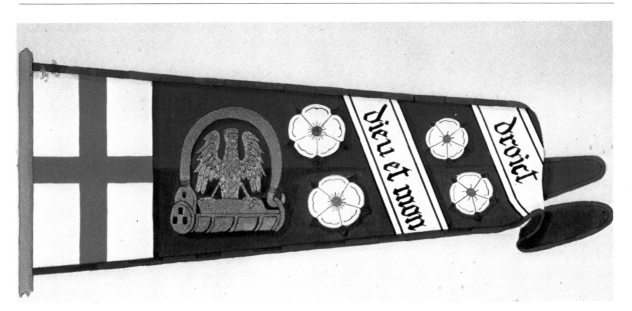

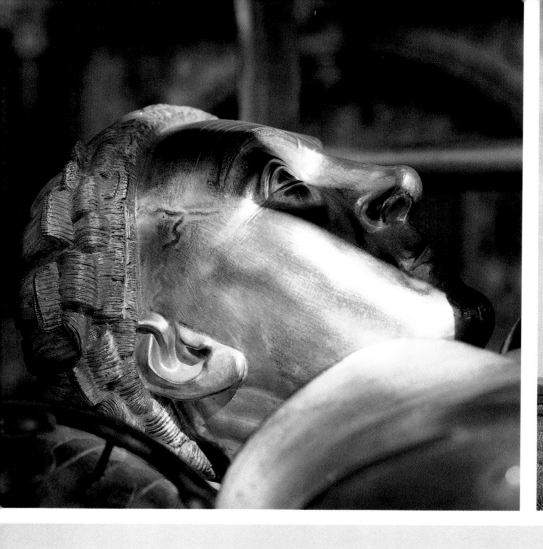

on his wing the bold, thrusting flank attack which Oxford was delivering against the Yorkist left, three-quarters of a mile away through the mist. In view of what was to happen next Edward must have thanked God for Richard's caution. Oxford's enthusiastic column hit the flank of Lord Hasting's division and knocked them sideways. Sensing victory Oxford's men pursued them through Barnet and out towards London, where many, assuming the battle was won, or not caring in the anonymity of the fog, began looting the neighbourhood. With great difficulty Oxford rallied his troops to lead them back. It would have been far better for the fortunes of Lancaster if he had let them continue looting. Instead he carefully, but hurriedly, retraced his steps with the remnants of his excited army.

The temporary absence of the Earl of Oxford's division had allowed Montagu's centre company to spread out to the right in an attempted envelopment of the Yorkists. Suddenly what should they see but a flying column of troops bearing down upon them slightly to their right. The first thing that caught their eye was the livery badge sewn on to the front and back of every tunic. It was the white star of Oxford, but in the thick mist, and to excited troops on their guard for an attack out of nowhere, it appeared to be the Yorkist 'white rose en-soleil', the memorial of Mortimer's Cross, and the emblem at which they had hacked and beaten for the past hour. Arrows and bolts were discharged at the newcomers, who, under no doubt as to the identity of their attackers, drew the obvious conclusion: Montagu's men had turned traitor. The cry of treason went up, sending a chill through Warwick's army that even his presence could not allay. From that moment the day was lost. Edward brought up his reserves and Warwick's army broke.

The above account, of the misidentification of Oxford's livery, is well-known, but it has become distorted down the years. The above is the original version in Warkworth's Chronicle. Note that Oxford's men did not actually attack Montagu's by mistake, though it may well have seemed like it as the battle lines had probably wheeled through 90 degrees because of the turning motion of the flank attacks.

A lesser rivalry was also settled at Barnet. Fighting for Edward was Henry Percy; the Fourth Earl of Northumberland, whose younger brother was killed. No chronicler mentions that he actually came to grips with John Neville, who had once taken his title, and who was killed during the battle, but it is possible that one sought out the other in the concealing fog. And the Kingmaker? Killed by an unknown hand as he tried to reach his horse, left at the rear as was the custom of the English knights.

TEWKESBURY – THE SECOND TOWTON

On the very day that Warwick the Kingmaker died in the name of the House of Lancaster, the heir of that House, accompanied by his formidable mother, landed at Weymouth. Among the deals which Warwick had struck with Queen Margaret was the marriage of the Prince of Wales to Warwick's daughter – what a weapon marriage was in the Middle Ages! But his son-in-law was too late to save him. The Royal party received the news of Warwick's death the next day and were inclined to return to France. But the two Lancastrian lords who had met them at Weymouth persuaded them to stay. One of the pair was Thomas Courtenay, the Earl of Devon. The other was the latest of a long line of Beauforts to serve the House of Lancaster. Edmund Beaufort, Fourth Duke of Somerset, bore the same name as his father, who had been killed in the first engagement of the war. His younger brother John accompanied him.

Margaret's strategic problem was as follows: not as many west country troops had joined her ranks as had been expected. As the victorious Edward was no doubt advancing to meet her it was vital that she reach Wales, where the ever-loyal Jasper Tudor was enthusiastically raising an army. She first sent scouts towards the east, to make Edward think she was moving on London, and then, pausing briefly at Bristol to collect supplies and a badly needed, but slow-moving, artillery train, rushed her army towards the lowest bridge on the River Severn, at the city of Gloucester.

While the Queen was still in Bath and intending to make for Bristol, Edward was at Cirencester, soon to cut across her path. Somehow he had to be fooled into changing the direction of his advance. If Edward could be made to think that the Queen intended to stand and fight, as a good general he would choose the nearest natural strong-point possible – which was Sodbury Hill, on the southern spur of the Cotswolds. Taking the initiative, and a great gamble, Queen Margaret sent her vanguard to Sodbury Hill, and followed with the rest of her army. Edward's scouts observed the move, and the scouts of both sides met by chance at Sodbury. In the ensuing skirmish some Yorkists were captured. This convinced the King that battle was imminent, so he cautiously slowed his advance, giving the entire Lancastrian army time to get clear of the vicinity. All that afternoon (2 May) and throughout the night, King Edward sat on Sodbury Hill, while his baffled scouts tried in vain to find the army that had seemed so ready for a decisive encounter.

That army had trudged wearily into Berkeley the same night, having gained a lead of twelve miles in the race for the river-crossing and the comparative safety of Wales. There were only fourteen miles to go, and very early next morning the Lancastrians hurried on their way. By the time the news reached Edward only one thing could prevent them crossing the Severn: if the walled city of Gloucester refused the Queen admittance. In that case she would have to march upstream to the next crossing-point – a ferry just south of Tewkesbury. That city was undefended and had no wall, but a ferry crossing would take much longer than a bridge, and time was the major factor in this campaign.

If it was to be Tewkesbury there would be a battle. Edward was sure of that, so he deployed his army in three divisions. It would not move so quickly, but a fast-moving detachment had already gone ahead to Gloucester. It was a race they won, and after hurried consultations with the Governor, another Richard Beauchamp, the gates of the city were slammed in the Queen's face. After two hours of demands, pleas, and threats of assault which the Governor knew well she had no time to carry out, Margaret gave the reluctant order to move on to Tewkesbury. They arrived at the ferry at four o'clock in the afternoon, tired out after a 24-mile march in fifteen hours. The slow ferry crossing could not be risked – Edward would be upon them while half their army was on the far bank. Nor did they dare withdraw across the Avon into Tewkesbury; it would have been a better defensive position, but they would have lost the ferry to Edward. No, here they had to stay.

The Yorkist army were as tired as their enemies. That night both hosts rested within sight of the beautiful Tewkesbury Abbey, and waited for morning. Queen Margaret had achieved so much, but just too late. The Tewkesbury campaign was a remarkable strategic operation from which she emerges with much credit. It reminds one of Margaret's advance to St Albans, ten years earlier, when her army's daring moves made a fool of Warwick. Yet the Lancastrian commanders of 1461 were nearly all dead by 1471. Could the following events be the proof that the brain behind the Lancastrian war of movement was the Queen herself? In the Tewkesbury campaign though not the subsequent battle, she certainly managed to outwit King Edward IV.

The morning of 4 May 1471 found the two armies about 400 yards apart, and between them 'foul lanes, and deep ditches and many hedges . . . a right evil place to approach'. The battle opened with a barrage of arrows and artillery. Then Edmund Beaufort, Fourth Duke of Somerset, showed himself a worthy inheritor of his family's fighting tradition. He observed that the Yorkist left wing, under Edward's talented brother, Richard of Gloucester, came to an end some 500 yards short of a round, densely wooded hill. It should be possible, Beaufort reckoned, to sweep his right wing out and advance unseen to attack the enemy's flank from the advantage of the hill. But this was not to be an isolated move. At the appropriate moment Lord Wenlock and the Prince of Wales would advance and engage the centre, catching the Yorkist left and centre from opposite sides; The Earl of Devon would take care of the Yorkist right, which was slightly detached from the rest of the army.

It was a plan that deserved to succeed, and it would have done had not the good generalship of King Edward forseen the very danger which Beaufort planned to exploit. Not wishing to risk his brother's division by stretching it too thinly towards the hill, he had detached a band of 200 spearmen who were now lying in wait. As the chronicler quaintly puts it: '. . . charging them to keep a close watch on that part of the wood, and to do what was necessary if the need should arise, and if they saw no such need . . . to employ themselves in the best way they could . . . ' – sensible delegation of responsibility by a commander who knew what he was doing.

So the spearmen waited, and along came Beaufort's division. Waiting until the bulk of the Lancastrians had passed them by, the small force hit them in the flank. It was a complete surprise, but need not have been a disaster if the centre attack had been carried out. But there were no signs of movement from Wenlock and the Prince. Perhaps, not knowing of the ambush, they were confused by the absence of consternation among the Yorkists. Had the attack in flank not taken place? Angry at what he saw was an almost treasonable lack of support by Wenlock (who incidentally, had fought for the Yorkists at Towton) Beaufort spurred his horse back and remonstrated with the inactive Wenlock. He called him coward, and traitor, and was obviously convinced that the latter accusation was the correct one. Before Wenlock could protest innocence or admit guilt Beaufort lifted his battleaxe and smashed it down on Wenlock's bare head.

Northampton had been lost by the act of treason. Barnet had been lost by the suspicion of treason. Now Tewkesbury was to be lost by the presumption of treason. Beaufort's furious murder of his ally split the Lancastrian army in two, and the Yorkists rapidly took advantage of the situation. Hundreds of Lancastrian knights were driven back to the low-lying field by the river called 'Bloody Meadow'. Many were drowned trying to cross the Severn where it is joined by the Avon at Abbey Mill. Many others scrambled across the Avon, or ran over the bridge to seek sanctuary in the Abbey. But sanctuary meant little to Edward IV. His younger brother had almost gained

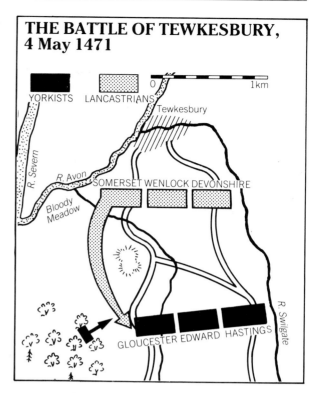

THE BATTLE OF TEWKESBURY, 4 May 1471

sanctuary after Wakefield in the little chapel on the bridge – there was to be no hiding-place for Edward's enemies: '. . . a priest . . . at his Mass and the Sacrament in his hands, when King Edward came with his sword into the church required him by the virtue of the Sacrament that he should pardon all whose names here follow . . . '

The chronicler, Warkworth, provides a list of those taken from the Abbey and beheaded. Edmund Beaufort, Duke of Somerset, who had already acted as executioner himself that day, heads the list. His brother John already lay dead somewhere in 'Bloody Meadow'.

Different battlefields have their special atmospheres under different conditions. Towton on a cold winter's day with a wind blowing and snow falling has its own ghosts. Barnet's ghosts linger in the morning mist on Hadley Green, beside the hedge which sheltered the Earl of Oxford before his fateful flank attack. Tewkesbury's ghosts are the products of a contrast, brought about on a sunny day. They come alive when one leaves the bright sunlight for the chill of the ancient Abbey, desecrated by King Edward's revengeful presence on that distant May morning.

His noblest victim lies beneath the choir: Edward, Prince of Wales, son of Queen Margaret and Henry VI, or, if Yorkist propaganda is to be believed, Edmund Beaufort the Elder, father of the other Edmund who had been torn from sanctuary to meet his fate. But exactly what was the fate of the Prince of Wales? In all probability he died fighting in the thick of the battle, a worthy descendant of his grandfather, Henry V. The four earliest chronicles all state that this is how he met his death. A later, Tudor account has the Prince taken alive and brought before Edward by Sir Richard Croft, the veteran of Mortimer's Cross, where he speaks defiantly to the King and receives a slap in the face from the King's gauntlet. At this point he is set upon by the Yorkists standing by and speedily done to death. As I noted, it is a Tudor chronicle (by Edward Hall), and has the almost inevitable note that one of the Yorkist murderers was Richard of Gloucester . . . well, it would, wouldn't it?

Right: The ruins of the Castle of Saint-Aubin du Cormier are the silent witnesses of the site of the battle in 1488, which led to the end of the independence of the Dukedom of Brittany, and its absorption by the French crown.
Far right: The Château de Bonaguil, built towards the end of the fifteenth century and therefore one of the latest examples of French feudal architecture.
(Photograph by Daphne Clark)

12. The Fall of Great Houses

T HE TWENTY YEARS between 1470 and 1490 witnessed the eclipse of three of the greatest names to appear in this narrative. In England the House of York, in Brittany the Montfort Dukes, and in eastern France the Valois Dukes of Burgundy all came to an end on the battlefield.

CHARLES THE BOLD

Charles the Bold, Duke of Burgundy, succeeded his father Philip the Good in 1467, at a time when the three-way relations between England, France and Burgundy were at their most active and controversial. Negotiations had been going on for some time regarding a royal marriage between Duke Charles (or Count of Charolais as he was before his father died), and Edward's sister, Margaret of York, and speculation was rife. In May 1467, John Paston actually made a bet with a London mercer that he would pay 80 shillings for a horse he was buying if the marriage went ahead within two years, and forty shillings if it did not! Charles' accession speeded the process considerably, notwithstanding the fact that Warwick was currently negotiating an Anglo-French alliance. Naturally enough the French did all in their power to persuade against the marriage taking place. But on 17 May 1468 the English Parliament was able to announce the forthcoming marriage of the King's sister to 'one of the mightiest Princes of the world that beareth no crown', and a royal scheme for an invasion of France to recover Gascony and Normandy, no doubt with the support of Edward's new in-laws. The marriage took place on 3 July 1468, accompanied by large-scale feasting and tournaments, an aspect of the knightly life at which the Valois dukes excelled. The friendship between England and Burgundy was further cemented by the rulers exchanging membership of their orders of chivalry – Edward IV becoming a Knight of the Golden Fleece in 1468, and Charles receiving a Garter in 1469.

Relations between Burgundy and France were, by comparison, rather cool. Louis XI sought support from the Duke of Brittany, Francis II, using Charles's acceptance of the Garter as evidence that he was 'the mortal and long-standing enemy of the realm'. The King's persuasion soon turned to threat. Either Brittany would help him against Burgundy or be attacked itself. Burgundy's response was to renew an alliance with Brittany against France.

Such manoeuvrings were soon overshadowed by the revolt of Warwick the Kingmaker against Edward, the action that was ultimately to lead to the Battle of Barnet. At the beginning of Warwick's rebellion, Duke Charles of Burgundy, who had extensive possessions in the Low Countries, assisted Edward by harrying Warwick's fleet in the Channel, and attempting unsuccessfully, to confine the Earl to Calais. In January 1471 Edward IV was a royal refugee at Charles's court. The Duke gave him £20,000 for his expenses, which Edward spent wisely on hiring transport for the army which was to bring him victory at Barnet and Tewkesbury.

Charles the Bold's support of Edward, which was utterly decisive in re-establishing the Yorkist dynasty, demanded a response. Thus it was that in 1472, when Charles attacked France, Edward promised warships and archers for the Burgundian army. It is doubtful if they ever arrived, a typical act, according to one Burgundian writer, by 'those wicked islanders, who are born with tails'. The English, who were 'like angels in the morning and devils after dinner, and who spent all their time eating', had cheated the Duke of Burgundy out of his money.

This comment is a little unfair. In the early years of his reign the English were among Charles the Bold's most valued foreign troops, although they tended to be present in only small numbers. Some had taken part in his campaign againt Liège in 1467, and in the 1472 war against France there are recorded eleven knights, 27 mounted archers, and sixteen archers on foot. They were, no doubt, mercenaries, and therefore a law unto themselves, but Edward was supposed to have sent 2,000 himself, and it must be their absence that is the source of the comment quoted above.

Edward made up for this omission the following year, when English troops distinguished themselves at the siege of Nijmegen in July, capturing the Nieuwstad gate and raising their banners upon it. In 1474 Edward sent a further thirteen knights and 1,000 archers, who, together with mercenaries, served at the siege of Neuss that winter. They must have acquitted themsleves well, because a letter from one of the Duke's captains states: 'The English have been more watched and admired in our army and better esteemed than were our robes of cloth of gold and costly adornments at the last feast of the Golden Fleece.' He records elsewhere, in a telling simile, that 'shot from hackbuts and culverins flies at us thicker than arrows in an English battle'. Following Neuss a company was retained as a permanent part of Charles's army, under the command of Sir John Middleton.

The 'Company of Ordinance' of Sir John Middleton was one of the many companies which made up Charles the Bold's armies. The Duke's forte was military organization, and between the years 1468 and 1476 he issued a number of documents, his 'Ordinances', concerned with the organization and discipline of his armies, including the creation of permanent companies, compulsory drill and manoeuvres, and the establishment of *corps d'élite*. Regulations for troops had been prepared before, but Charles's were presented in such detail, down to uniform colours and weaponry, that they became the model for every army in the sixteenth century. Charles the Bold was an enthusiast. He is mentioned at the siege of Neuss as

sleeping in his armour, constantly writing reports and checking details.

It is unfortunate that Charles the Bold's enthusiasm and skill at organization did not extend to the actual winning of battles. Neuss is a good example. The siege was well-resisted, and dragged on until 1475, giving his enemies ample opportunity to attack his territories elsewhere, and dream up fantastic alliances against him. One such plan, put forward by Albert, the Elector of Brandenburg, envisaged France and Switzerland engaged against Burgundy, while England was neutralized by joint invasions from Scotland and Denmark. Crazy as these schemes may have been (one included the Turks in its calculations) they prompted Charles the Bold to do some planning of his own, and one result was an undertaking by Edward IV to ally himself with the Duke of Brittany and effectively restart the Hundred Years War. Perhaps the strangest aspect of this plan was that it was actually carried out.

EDWARD'S INVASION OF FRANCE

The series of treaties signed between England and Burgundy in connection with a new French war, promised much to both sides. Charles agreed to help his brother-in-law recover Gascony and Normandy, and be crowned King of France at Reims. Most of eastern and north-eastern France were to be given to Burgundy, and Edward promised to invade with 10,000 men by 1 July 1475. The Scottish frontier was made more secure by the betrothal of Edward's youngest daughter, aged five, to Prince James of Scotland, aged two, and among letters to various European potentates Edward wrote to King Louis

demanding the return of Normandy and Gascony. The King of France replied by sending Edward the gift of a fine horse, followed shortly by a further gift of a wolf, a boar and a donkey. The wolf, apparently represented Edward, the boar (wild?) Charles the Bold, and the donkey, Francis of Brittany.

Edward's preparations for war bring echoes of earlier times. All bowyers were to make their existing bowstaves into bows. The 11,000-strong army, the largest and best-equipped ever to leave England, included 9,143 archers, plus an additional 2,000 who were sent to Brittany. Command, under the King was shared between his two brothers, George Duke of Clarence, and Richard of Gloucester.

The English army was transported to Calais during the month of June, and Edward joined his troops on 6 July, to find that the grandiose scheme was on the point of being totally abandoned. He had not followed Charles the Bold's advice to land in Normandy, where the Breton troops could more easily link up with him for an advance on Paris, and now Charles himself had wasted his initial advantages by unnecessarily prolonging the siege of Neuss. His treasure was spent, and his own army in so dilapidated a condition that he was ashamed to let the English king see it.

The sensible thing would have been to go home there and then, but Edward, his handsome head full of stories of Henry V, set off for Lorraine to join up with the Burgundians. There was some skirmishing near Saint-Quentin, and then it was reported to Edward that King Louis was waiting on the other side of the Somme to dispute the crossing of the river. As King Louis's large

army had taken advantage of Edward's delay at Calais to devastate the region through which the English had just marched, the threat had to be taken very seriously indeed. The days of the devastating English chevauchée, let alone Agincourt, seemed to be over, but the French king was willing to talk terms.

The two monarchs met on the bridge at Picquiny. Memories of the bridge at Montereau, where Charles's grandfather, John the Fearless, had been assassinated, producing an unprecedented security problem. But all was well, and an agreement was reached whereby the English would immediately leave France, a truce of seven years would be established, and a 'league of perfect amity' arranged between the two kings, covered by payment of an annual pension to Edward. All this was to be sealed by a marriage between Edward's eldest daughter, Elizabeth of York, and the Dauphin Charles, as soon as the parties concerned were of age. An unwritten stipulation provided for the liberation of ex-Queen Margaret of Anjou, for which consideration Edward exacted a further payment. She returned to France, and a pension, in November.

As a measure of how things had changed since the days of Agincourt and Castillon, we see that throughout the documents Edward is called 'King of France'. This apparently gave Louis little concern; his sole aim was to get rid of the English as quickly as possible. It is none the less strange that Edward should have turned back from a purpose in which he had invested so much time and money. He had the pension from Louis, but even that looks like a sop to annoyance rather than a response to a military threat. We know that Edward was disappointed in his allies. The Burgundians had suffered badly at Neuss, and the Duke of Brittany was so dilatory that he failed to produce his own troops, and hesitated before accepting the English archers he had been sent. Not that relations between England and Brittany were all that cordial anyway. Brittany was the refuge of Henry Tudor, the last hope of the Lancastrian line, and at times Duke Francis came close to agreeing to his extradition. One strange coincidence concerning Henry Tudor's exile in Brittany was that he bore the title, inherited from his father, of Earl of Richmond, which had been given to Edmund Tudor by Henry VI, the same title which for centuries had been borne by the Dukes of Brittany.

Even without the help of England and Brittany, Charles the Bold continued on his path to military immortality. By the end of November 1475 the Burgundian 'kingdom' was beginning to look like a reality. Charles could now march across his domains from Holland to Lyons. It was at this point that he finally overreached himself. After a few weeks rest at Nancy he crossed the Jura for a winter campaign in Switzerland, accompanied by a number of English soldiers who had elected to stay in action rather than return home with Edward. In fact, 2,000 had stayed after the Treaty of Picquiny, at which Charles, who had observed the Wars of the Roses at close quarters, had remarked drily that they might as well stay with him and fight the French than go home and massacre one another.

THE DESTRUCTION OF BURGUNDY

Throughout this book reference has been made to the two major roles of the lower-class foot soldiers: to fire missiles, and to produce a 'living fence' of pike or spear, both intended to break up the charge of the mounted knight. The Scottish schiltrons are among the earliest examples of the use of the latter technique, which was to achieve its near perfection in the tactics of the Swiss. In the early fourteenth century the main Swiss weapon had been the halberd, eight feet long and with a blade as well as a spike, with which the Austrians had been defeated at Morgarten. The Battle of Laupen in 1339 confirmed their potency when they defeated a cavalry army in the open. At about this time they began changing to the 18-foot long pike, and for the next two centuries suffered no major defeat. At Sempach in 1386 they won another great victory, this time over dismounted knights.

During the fifteenth century the Swiss perfected their offensive tactic of a densely-packed phalanx, presenting a body like a moving porcupine. As the political structure of the Swiss Cantons prevented them from uniting successfully the Swiss had gone on to become Europe's finest mercenary soldiers. They were first seen in France in 1465, and their conduct led to many more 'bookings'. By this time they had further elaborated their techniques by combining pikemen, crossbowmen and handgunners in units of three, so that each man might help his comrades. In 1474 Louis XI recruited Swiss mercenaries to help him against Charles the Bold, the first of several arrangements which led to Swiss troops becoming a

Right: Charles the Bold, last of the Valois Dukes of Burgundy, hacked to death at the Battle of Nancy in 1477. From a portrait by an unknown artist. (Van Pompe archive, Leyden)

Left: An illustration from a manuscript depicting the Battle of Sempach in 1386, when the Swiss won a victory over the Austrian knights.

regular feature in French armies during the sixteenth century.

The war which Charles the Bold was planning to conduct against the Swiss was of course not against bands of mercenaries, who fought, literally, for money and nothing else, but against the nation from which these hardy men were drawn. His campaign began with the taking of the castle of Grandson, on the Lake of Neufchâtel, which surrendered to him on 28 February 1476. Swiss sources state that Grandson surrendered to Charles when he promised to spare their lives. In fact a horrible massacre ensued, the entire garrison being either hanged from the walnut trees which surrounded the lake, or drowned within its waters. This atrocity, and it was not Charles's first, set the scene for a savage war in which no prisoners were taken.

The Swiss came to the rescue of Grandson in March. Charles deployed his army in a line hoping to encircle the phalanx, but all attacks against the Swiss were repulsed. Eventually the Burgundians fled, leaving surprisingly few casualties but an enormous quantity of booty. The regulations regarding the sharing of spoil, which had

been so carefully formulated to guide the ever-victorious Swiss, were instantly forgotten in the scramble for the diamonds, plate, jewels, tapestries, coins and other treasure found among the baggage. Much of it was dismantled or torn apart and stuffed into bags and pouches, and that which survived for the official share-out was to occupy the legal minds of the Swiss federation for the remainder of the century.

In an earlier chapter we referred to booty as being a time-honoured practice of war, condoned by chivalry. Grandson was the high-water mark of plunder, but these Swiss Wars also marked the virtual disappearance of one other chivalric tradition which had been limping along through the fifteenth century – the ransom of prisoners. The reader will recall the refusal to ransom the Captal de Buch a century before, and the savagery that seemed to conclude any capture during the Wars of the Roses. The Swiss, to whom the taking and ransoming of prisoners was an encumbrance to their movement and the acquisition of loot, smashed their way into the castle of Grandson and took the members of the Burgundian garrison, whom they immediately flung to their deaths

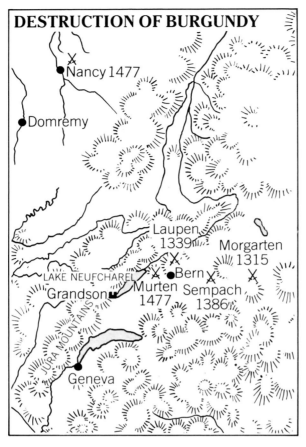

DESTRUCTION OF BURGUNDY

from the battlements. From this time onwards nobles were butchered together with the common soldiers, who had usually suffered that fate anyway, and an undertaking to employ Swiss troops carried with it the unspoken warning to an enemy that this was war to the death.

Charles's next encounter was at Murten where the Swiss battle order, which laid down that no prisoners were to be taken was followed to the letter. Charles had with him a number of English, under Earl Rivers, and was again defeated, with less loss of booty, but considerably greater loss of life. In spite of all his careful planning, his Ordinances and his recruitment, Charles had been defeated twice by an army of townsmen. But worse was to come. While still plotting revenge against 'these boorish Swiss', as one of his Italian captains called them, trouble sprang up in Lorraine, which he had conquered in 1475. Charles directed his energies towards recapturing Nancy, whose inhabitants, not at all unreasonably, feared the fate of Grandson and resisted fiercely. Little is known of the details of the long siege, though it is said that one Burgundian soldier was so fed up with the privations that he suggested that Charles be put into a bombard and fired into the city. He was hanged for his impudence.

The army of perhaps 20,000 men that came to the relief of Nancy included about 6,000 Swiss. The resulting battle was fought in the snow, and like Grandson and Murten, Charles's enemies took him completely by surprise. It took two days of meticulous searching through the thousands of frozen bodies littering the battlefield before the corpse of the impetuous Duke was found. His horse had fallen at a stream during the rout, and he had been killed by a blow to the head. Beside him lay thousands of Burgundian soldiers and their mercenary comrades. The remnants of Charles's large English contingent (originally 1,000 men) straggled home within the next two months.

One captain, a certain John Turnbull, returned home with 34 men. He had taken 96 with him to Burgundy.

With Duke Charles died the Valois Duchy of Burgundy. He left a daughter, Mary, by his first wife, who had long been waiting in the marriage market. While negotiations went on the King of France began to absorb what was left of the Empire of his greatest enemy.

A CRISIS FOR YORK

In a strange way the death of Charles the Bold helped precipitate a serious crisis in the English House of York. Edward's brother, George, Duke of Clarence, had recently lost his wife, and was inclined towards Mary of Burgundy as a replacement. His sister, Mary's stepmother, was in favour, but Edward could not countenance his unreliable brother becoming a European ruler and thus involving England in the fortunes of France and Burgundy for years to come, and the match was forbidden.

Clarence had sided against Edward at the time of Warwick's rebellion. By contrast, his other brother, Richard, always acted with exemplary loyalty towards the House of York and the person of his brother the King. Richard had acquired quite a reputation as a soldier, serving at Barnet and Tewkesbury, after which he was rewarded by being made effectively Viceroy of the North, exercising a devolved government of northern Britain from his favourite castle of Middleham in Wensleydale. He was in charge of the operations of the latest Percy, Earl of Northumberland, who had fought beside him at Barnet, and in the absence of the Nevilles a peace descended upon the Border Marches which stood in marked contrast to the years of disorder which had preceded it.

The military exploits of Richard of Gloucester have always been overshadowed by other matters concerning his accession to the throne. Prior to becoming King Richard III he had taken part in Edward's invasion of France, and was apparently the commander most in favour of pressing on from Calais, but his most notable successes were against the Scots.

Relations with Scotland had been cordial since 1464 as a result of Edward's peaceful diplomacy designed to neutralize Lancastrian support from that direction. The Battles of Hedgeley Moor and Hexham had both arisen from those diplomatic manoeuvres. Now that the Lancastrian threat was past, apart from the problem of the fugitive in Brittany, Edward was able to seize the initiative and attempt to recapture Berwick, which had been surrendered to the Scots when Henry VI fled across the Border after Towton. Richard of Gloucester was appointed Commander-in-Chief on 12 May 1480, and by the month of June the Scots had obligingly responded to the English build-up by raiding across the Border as far as Bamburgh. Richard chased them back, and hostilities were suspended until 1482, when Parliament voted a considerable sum for war against the Scots. The Scottish government was in turmoil, and threatened with an imminent incursion of an English army consisting of between 6,000 and 10,000 men, under Richard, and led in the vanguard by the Percy, Earl of Northumberland, and Lord Scrope of Bolton, two families of immense experience in Border warfare.

Berwick was the first objective, and the town soon fell. Leaving a detachment to continue the siege of the castle, Gloucester continued through Berwickshire on a virtual chevauchée, while one wing of his army burned Roxburghshire as far as Jedburgh. Richard may have reached the outskirts of Edinburgh when the Scots came to treat. In any event, the two armies entered Edinburgh together

Right: Sir Ralph Fitzherbert, from his tomb in Norbury Church, Derbyshire. His collar bears a pendant of a white boar, granted by Richard III. Fitzherbert died in 1483.

the following day, an armistice having been agreed. Berwick surrendered as Richard marched south again, and the six-week long campaign came to a triumphant end.

RICHARD III

The events concerned with the untimely death of Edward IV, the accession of his 12-year-old son, Edward V, and the sudden assumption of power by Richard III, are sufficiently well-known in their outline to require no repetition here. As to the conduct of Richard with regard to the mysterious disappearance of his nephews, Edward V and Richard, Duke of York, it is now the unorthodox view to suggest that Richard had some part in their murder. The prospect of a boy King, with the likelihood of friction between the late King's family on one side and Queen Elizabeth's on the other, boded ill for the future of the Yorkist dynasty, while Henry Tudor was waiting in Brittany and providing a focus for all renegade or dispossessed Lancastrians. It was, therefore, in the best interests of the House for Richard, an excellent administrator and accomplished soldier, to become king. But were the boys murdered, and if so on whose orders? We will never know.

Whatever the fate of the Princes, the greatest threat to the House of York lay in Brittany. Henry Tudor, Earl of Richmond, had been captured at the fall of Pembroke castle in 1461, and had stayed an exile in Brittany since 1471, since when both Yorkist kings had attempted to have him returned. He had been absent from England for fifteen years, a period of time which moulded his view of himself and also of the country whose throne he claimed. Henry's later view, that it was he who united the warring factions, and restored peace to the realm, is often put down to Tudor propaganda, and his own consummate statecraft, yet this view of himself as a king in exile coming to bring a new era is probably an accurate reflection of the opinion he had of himself. On Christmas Day, 1483, Duke Francis II of Brittany proclaimed Henry King of England at Rennes Cathedral. At the same time, Henry pledged himself to marry Elizabeth of York, the late Edward's daughter whom that monarch had always intended for the Dauphin. He, of course, was by now King Charles VIII and married to someone else. Henry clearly saw his union with Elizabeth as a symbolic act, over and above the purely political result of neutralizing any future opposition. Even more symbolic was the naming of their first-born son, Arthur. This was a break with a tradition of two centuries that had produced a succession of Edwards, Henrys and Richards. But what a choice! It was in fact a return to an even greater tradition, to Geoffrey of Monmouth's tales of the legendary Arthur, King of the Britons. Is this how Henry saw himself and his successors, as a divinely ordained Prince returning from exile? We do know that Henry believed firmly in his descent from Cadwallader, the last of the British kings, and lost no opportunity to proclaim it. It was a conviction strengthened by his early years in Wales under the care of the indestructible Uncle Jasper, and reinforced by thirteen years in Brittany, where the independent Celtic spirit of the Bretons cherished the legends of Arthur. In 1484 Richard's attempts to secure Henry's extradition finally failed when he slipped across the border into France, to enjoy a final year of exile at the French court. The new king welcomed him there, and did all in his power to strengthen Henry's belief that he was to overcome the apparent readiness with which their cousins across the Channel deposed their kings, in contrast to the civilised state of things in France. We may assume that Henry did not ask too many searching questions about Burgundy.

When Henry Tudor landed at Milford Haven in August 1485 he shared an identical concern with the reigning sovereign. Neither knew exactly on whose support they could rely. Both sides had their passionate loyalists, but beyond them there was a grey area of doubt. For example, the Tudors were traditionally strong in Wales. Richard III's representative there was Sir Walter Herbert, of the Yorkist family of Earls of Pembroke. He had been sounded out by the Tudor faction, but had apparently not committed himself. The two brothers of the Stanley family of Cheshire (of whom the elder, Lord Thomas Stanley, was Henry Tudor's stepfather), had supposedly committed themselves to the Tudor cause. So had Gilbert Talbot – son of the glorious Lancastrian Talbot, whose actions had crushed the first flames of Yorkist revolt in 1451. The Percy family, of whom the Earl of Northumberland had marched with Richard to Scotland, were expected to follow the King, but the Percys could be unreliable.

Both rivals followed a predictable course once the landing had taken place. Henry Tudor proceeded to raise support, and Richard began to raise troops. The latter may have experienced some relief in the thought that the hour had come, for he was a born soldier, and in his element with the arrangements now to be made. His plan was to collect his northern supporters, the Percys, and, he hoped, the Stanleys at Nottingham, and then march south to join the southern contingent at Leicester. These would include the forces of John Howard, the Duke of Norfolk, who had been knighted by Edward IV on the field of Towton where he led the right wing, and who had crossed over to Calais with Richard as one of Edward's expeditionary force in 1475.

Henry Percy took a long time to reach Nottingham, and it was with some haste that Richard took him to Leicester on the evening of 20 August, where they joined the Duke of Norfolk. The following morning the army left Leicester to take up its position at Bosworth. At sunrise on the morning of 22 August one factor which had puzzled Richard, the absence of Stanley, was immediately solved. To the north lay the forces of Lord Stanley, with their white buck's head badges on red coats. They did not appear inclined towards either army, but Richard took the sensible precaution of assuming they were hostile, and arranged his forces accordingly. He placed the likewise doubtful Earl of Northumberland in his rear. Henry's army moved up to the attack in battle formation – Talbot on the right wing, Oxford in the centre, and Henry Tudor himself on the left. To reach Richard's army they had to wheel round a large marshy area to their right, leaving their left flank exposed to a possible attack from the Stanleys, who had advanced towards the centre of the action. Richard ordered an advance downhill at the Tudor army, who were still dressing their ranks, and the assault was led by the Duke of Norfolk. It was a sensible move – to have hesitated would have exposed Richard's vanguard to the French and Burgundian gunners whom Henry had brought with him. But Oxford's men held firm, and packed them more tightly together to resist Norfolk's attack, whose advance was being slowly split in two. At this point the Duke himself was killed.

By now there was something of a stalemate, and the decision which the Stanleys must soon be forced to take would decide the battle. Henry took the initiative and, with banners flying, rode over towards the Stanleys to beg

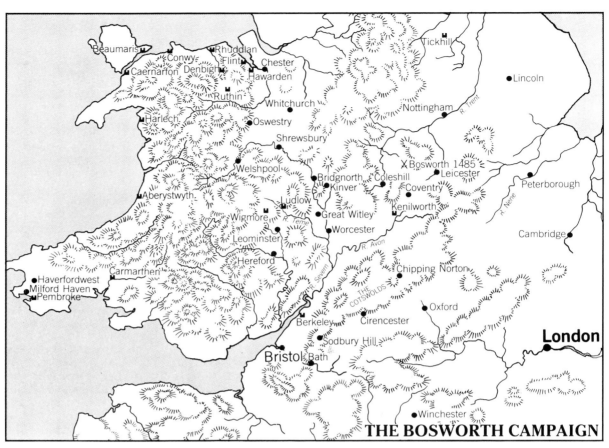

THE BOSWORTH CAMPAIGN

Right: Henry VII, victor of the Battle of Bosworth and founder of the Tudor dynasty. This impressive sculpture by Pietro Torrigiano (1472–1528) is of painted and gilded terracotta. (Victoria and Albert Museum, Crown Copyright)

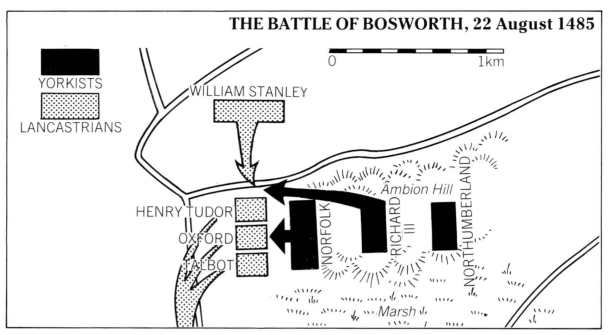

THE BATTLE OF BOSWORTH, 22 August 1485

YORKISTS

LANCASTRIANS

0   1km

WILLIAM STANLEY

Ambion Hill

HENRY TUDOR

OXFORD

TALBOT

NORFOLK

RICHARD III

NORTHUMBERLAND

Marsh

Right: The Battle of Bosworth, as depicted in the beautifully detailed battlefield model on display in the battlefield centre at Bosworth. (Photograph by courtesy of Leicestershire County Council)

their assistance. From Richard's vantage-point he could see their every move, and as they showed their flanks to him he knew the moment was ripe for a cavalry charge. All his experience, of Barnet and Tewkesbury, of the lessons he had been taught of Agincourt and Formigny, showed him that here was the perfect target for a knight's move.

Of what would such a move consist? To charge, certainly, but with what? The hitting power of the armoured knight depended upon penetration as well as speed, and the penetrating object was the lance. This weapon, clumsy and heavy, had to be lowered to the horizontal and held there while the horse worked up to the gallop. A century earlier it had been held beneath the right arm, with the attendant danger of breaking that arm when the impact took place. Suits of armour were now fitted with a strong lance rest on the right breast, and we may imagine, at Bosworth, 1,000 heavy lances descending from the vertical to brace against the rest, as the force gained speed downhill. The knight was now a form of human projectile. There appeared to be no foot soldiers in his way, and if any were they were ridden down, their arrows bouncing harmlessly off his armour, as the knights recaptured their chivalric traditions.

Right: John Howard, Duke of Norfolk, who was knighted by Edward IV on the field of Towton in 1461, took part in Edward's short-lived invasion of France in 1475 and was killed at Bosworth in 1485.
Below: 'King Dick's Well', on the battlefield of Bosworth, where Richard III is said to have refreshed himself prior to the battle which ended his brief reign. (Photograph by courtesy of Leicestershire County Council, who maintain the battlefield)

Thus the last Yorkist King of England, whose family had done so much to keep England at the forefront of military development, led what was to prove the last charge by mounted knights in English history. In some ways it was an anachronism, in others a foretaste of things to come, for the heavily armoured knight was being used at the peak of his perfection, encased in armour, and impervious to hand weapons, the consummation of Crécy, Otterburn and The Battle of the Thirty.

Such was the force of the charge at Bosworth that King Richard's lance was rammed clean through the body of Henry Tudor's standard bearer, William Brandon. Drawing his sword, Richard began to fight his way towards his rival. At that point Stanley decided – for Tudor, and the red-coated men-at-arms fell upon Richard's flank. Henry Percy, Earl of Northumberland, watching the latest move from high at the rear, summed up the situation and began to withdraw his troops, who had taken no part in the fighting. With the actions of Stanley and Percy we witness the most dramatic illustration of the meaningless nature of the phrase 'The Wars of the Roses'. We have seen allies fight then change sides, or change sides during a battle. Now two armies wait until the very last moment before deciding – and one decides not to fight at all! Richard fell somewhere in the field, the small coronet he wore on his helmet being hacked off by an axe. An anonymous soldier, with an eye for the chivalric prize of booty, stuck it into a hawthorn bush, hoping to retrieve it later. It was found there by Sir Reginald Bray, who brought it to Lord Stanley. Henry Tudor, Earl of Richmond, the returned exile, ever one for symbolism, accepted the coronet as a crown.

Bosworth was not, in fact, the last battle of the Wars of the Roses. That honour goes to the Battle of Stoke in 1487. Here Henry VII crushed the Simnel conspiracy by defeating a strong army that included 2,000 German mercenaries in an engagement that lasted longer than Bosworth. But Bosworth had seen the death of a king – and in that respect was utterly decisive.

THE END OF BRITTANY

Francis II, Duke of Brittany, last of the de Montfort line, had sheltered Henry Tudor during his years of exile. The relationship between the de Montfort Dukes of Brittany and the French King had always been questionable, as we have seen repeatedly in these pages. With the new confidence which came with the destruction of Burgundy, and the final settlement of the English dynastic problem, Charles VIII of France was able to end the matter by force. A powerful French army, including a strong artillery train and a large number of Swiss, moved into Brittany. As on so many occasions the taking of Fougères provided the curtain-raiser. The final battle took place at St Aubin-du-Cormier, where the Ducal army was heavily defeated. Shattered mentally by the defeat, the Duke died a few days later, leaving a daughter, Anne.

THE TRIUMPH OF THE KNIGHT

The death of the Duke of Brittany marked the beginning of the greatness of France as a military nation. Freed from the curse of English invasion, and benefitting at last from the years of development in artillery and fortification, Charles VIII began his Italian Wars in 1494. The use of mercenaries, a trend we have noted throughout the fifteenth century, was now well-established, enabling the French King to choose the troops he wanted, at a price he could afford. Yet we note that in the resulting army, half the troops consisted of heavily armoured, mounted

Left: Sir Reginald Bray, who is traditionally credited with having found Richard III's crown in a hawthorn bush after the Battle of Bosworth. Bray took it to Lord Stanley, who placed it upon the head of Henry Tudor.

Below: The frontier fortress of Fougères in Brittany was taken on behalf of the English in March 1449 by Aragonese mercenary called François de Surenne.

knights. As we come to the close of the High Middle Ages it is pertinent to ask why it was that an arm which seemed to be obsolescent in 1298 could have triumphed so thoroughly in what was the best-regarded army in Europe at the time?

The answer lies in the thread we have followed throughout this book. Just as the samurai survived as a class in Japan because they were ready to adapt to changing conditions of social and military life, so did the medieval knight survive because of the adaptations we have followed here. The armour worn by Charles VIII's knights was an example of perfection in the art of armour-making. Weight and protection were now combined in the best proportions that would ever be possible. The lance rest, as noted above, turned the knight into a deadly projectile. But the most important lesson of all was how the knights could be used. The secret was what it had always been, that success lay in a combination of arms, so that when knights were used appropriately, and protected adequately against missiles, they could still be devastating two hundred years after Bannockburn.

I made the point earlier in the book that I have tried to avoid the traditional English chauvinism which sees the High Middle Ages as one long series of brilliant victories by English archers against incompetently-led foreigners. By the end of the fifteenth century English knights, as well as archers, were regularly to be found in European armies. They took with them their experience of the savage days of the Wars of the Roses, so let us end with a Spanish chronicler's comments upon one such mercenary band, led by Richard, the Third and last Earl Rivers. He was a man of his time, a veteran of Bosworth, and his father and brother had both suffered execution at the hands of King or Kingmaker. In 1486 he took with him to Spain a band of 100 knights and 100 archers. They joined their fellows in a Crusade, probably the last time the word was used for a military campaign, which had as its purpose the expulsion of the Moors from Granada. The chronicler notes with approval Rivers's prowess with the battleaxe, and goes on to describe his army, the inheritors of a tradition that spanned Halidon Hill, Crécy and Bosworth: 'This knight . . . brought with him . . . men who had been hardened in certain civil wars which had raged in their country. They were huge feeders, and deep carousers . . . often unruly and noisy in their wassail. Though from a remote and somewhat barbarous island, they yet believed themselves to be the most perfect men on earth.'

Right: The tomb of Sir Edward Redman, who died in 1510, shows in excellent detail the style of armour common at the end of the period covered by this book. Plate armour is now complete, and well made.

References

The interested reader is referred to the following selective list of references:

Allmand, C. T. 'War and Profit in the Later Middle Ages', *History Today*, 1965

Anderson, W. F. *Castles of Europe*. London, 1970

Barnie, J. *War in Medieval Society – Social Values and the Hundred Years War*. London, 1971

Bean, J. M. W. 'The Percys and their Estates', *Archaeologia Aeliana*, 4th Series, 35 (1957)

Bean, J. M. W. Henry IV and the Percys. *History*, 44 (1959)

Bellamy, J. G. 'Northern Rebellions', Bulletin of the John Rylands Library, 47 (1965)

Broome, D. M. 'The Battle of Poitiers', *English Historical Review*, 53 (1928)

Broome, D. M. 'The Ransom of John II, King of France', *Camden Miscellany*, 14 (1926)

Burne, Alfred H. 'John of Gaunt's Chevauchée', *History Today* (February 1959)

Burne, Alfred H. *Crécy War*: A Military History of the Hundred Years War from 1337 to the Peace of Bretigny, 1360. Greenwood Press, London, 1977

Burne, Alfred H. *Agincourt War*: A Military History of the latter part of the Hundred Years War from 1369–1453. Greenwood Press, London, 1976

Contamine, P. *Guerre, État et Société à la fin du Moyen Age*. Paris, 1972

Cuvelier, Jean. *Chronique de Bertrand du Guesclin*, ed. E. Charriere. (Collection de documents inédits sur l'histoire de France) Paris, 1839

de Molandon, B. *L'Armée Anglaise Vaincue par Jeanne d'Arc*. Paris, 1892

Dillon, H. A. 'Letter on a trial for armour', *Archaeologia*, 51

Dillon, H. A. 'Armour', *Archaeological Journal*, 1895 and 1903

Evans, H. T. *Wales in The Wars of the Roses*. London, 1955

Galbraith, V. H. 'The Battle of Poitiers', *English Historical Review*, 54 (1939)

Gollancz, I. *IchDien*. London, 1921

Hatto, A. T. 'Archery and Chivalry', *Modern Languages Review*, 35 (1940)

Hewitt, H. J. *The Black Prince's Expedition of 1355–57*. London, 1955

Hewitt, H. J. *The Organization of War under Edward III*. Manchester University Press, 1966

La Borderie, G. *Histoire de Bretagne*, vols. 2 and 4, Rennes, 1902

Luce, Simeon. *Histoire de Bertrand du Guesclin*. Paris, 1876

Molinier, A. *Les Sources de l'histoire de France*, 6 vols., Paris, 1901–6

Morris, J. E. 'Mounted Infantry', *Transactions of the Royal Historical Society*, 3rd Series, 8 (1914)

Nicholson, R. *Edward III and the Scots*. Edinburgh, 1971

Page, John. 'The Siege of Rouen', *Historical Collections of a London Citizen*, Camden Series, 1876

Perroy, E. *The Hundred Years War*. London, 1951

Phillpotts, C. 'The French Plan of Battle during the Agincourt Campaign', *English Historical Review*, January, 1984

Puiseux, M. *Siège et Prise de Rouen*. Paris, 1867

Puiseux, M. *Siège et Prise de Caen*. Paris, 1858

Ramsay, J. M. 'The Strength of English Armies in the Middle Ages', *English Historical Review*, 29 (1914)

Redstone, V. B. 'Mercenaries, 1327–1330', *Transactions of the Royal Historical Society*, 3rd Series, 7 (1913)

Rowe, J. H. 'A Contemporary Account of the Hundred Years War', *English Historical Review*, 12 (1926)

Rowse, A. L. 'Sir Henry de Bodrugan', *History* (1944)

Savage, H. 'Sir Gawain and the Order of the Garter', *English Literary History*, 5 (1938)

Sharp, M. 'The Jodrell Deed and Seals of the Black Prince', Bulletin of the John Rylands Library, 7 (1922)

Simpson, M. A. 'The Verneuil Campaign', *English Historical Review*, 1934

Steel, A. 'The Financial Background of the Wars of the Roses', *History*, 40, (1955)

Tout, T. F. 'Medieval and Modern Warfare', Bulletin of the John Rylands Library, 5 (1919)

Tout, T. F. 'Some neglected fights between Crécy and Poitiers', *English Historical Review*, 20 (1905)

Turnbull, S. R. *The Book of the Samurai*. London, 1981

Turnbull, S. R. *The Samurai – A Military History*. London, 1977

Wrottesley, G. *Crécy and Calais*. London, 1898

Wylie, J. H. 'The Battlefield of Shrewsbury'. *Transactions of the Shropshire Archaeological and Natural History Society* (1903)

Index